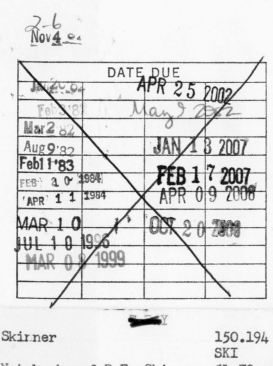

Notebooks
B. F. Skinner

Other books by B. F. Skinner:

The Behavior of Organisms: An Experimental Analysis
Walden Two
Science and Human Behavior
Verbal Behavior
Schedules of Reinforcement (with C. B. Ferster)
Cumulative Record: A Selection of Papers, Third Edition
The Analysis of Behavior: A Program for Self-Instruction
    (with J. G. Holland)
The Technology of Teaching
Contingencies of Reinforcement: A Theoretical Analysis
Beyond Freedom and Dignity
About Behaviorism
Particulars of My Life
Reflections on Behaviorism and Society
The Shaping of a Behaviorist: Part Two of an Autobiography

Notebooks

B. F. Skinner

Edited, and with an Introduction by
Robert Epstein

PRENTICE-HALL, INC., Englewood Cliffs, New Jersey

The author wishes to express thanks for permission to quote from the works listed below:

Selections from October 11, 1973, and November 27, 1966, Magazine. © 1966/1973 by The New York Times Company. Reprinted by permission. Quote by Sam Newlund, *Minneapolis Tribune*, March 23, 1967. Reprinted with permission from the *Minneapolis Tribune*. Review by N.C. Chaudhuri, The Times Literary Supplement, February 3, 1978. Times Newspapers Limited, London. Excerpt © *San Francisco Chronicle*, 1972. Reprinted by permission. Excerpt from UPI article. Reprinted by permission of United Press International. Excerpt from "Wraparound: Improving the Nick of Time," by Gwyneth Cravens. Copyright © 1973 by Harper's Magazine. All rights reserved. Excerpted from the January 1974 issue by special permission. Excerpt from Letter to the editor, *The Sciences*, Jan./Feb. 1976. Excerpts from essays by various authors appearing in *The New York Review of Books* dated 5-22-76 and 3-3-77. Reprinted with permission from *The New York Review of Books*. Copyright © Nyrev, Inc. Excerpt from *London Diary*, by Maurice Richardson, in the *New Statesman*, March 8, 1958. Brief quotation from "Books" by Marcus G. Raskin (*Strategy and Conscience* by Anatol Rapoport), from August 1964 edition of *Scientific American*. Permission from W.H. Freeman and Company. Excerpt from *Ambassador's Journal* by J.K. Galbraith. Reprinted with permission from author.

Designer, Linda Huber
Art Director, Hal Siegel

Notebooks, B. F. Skinner
Edited, and with an Introduction by Robert Epstein
Copyright © 1980 by B. F. Skinner

10 9 8 7 6 5 4 3 2 1

Library of Congress Cataloging in Publication Data

Skinner, Burrhus Frederic, date
Notebooks.
Includes index.
1. Psychology. 2. Behaviorism. I. Epstein, Robert. II. Title. [DNLM: 1. Psychology—Essays. BF21 S628n] BF121.S538   150.19′434   80-20094
ISBN 0-13-624106-9

To Lou and Ken Mulligan

Contents

Introduction

I first met B. F. Skinner about the time I began graduate work in psychology, in the fall of 1976. When he asked me, shortly after, to spend a few weeks editing some notebooks, I readily agreed. He had already collected and organized several hundred pages into two binders, and, as far as I knew, there weren't many others. I expected, consequently, that the task could be completed in a short time.

It proved to be Sisyphian. Every time I finished editing a stack of notes, Skinner discovered another untapped shelf or file drawer. And he has continually retarded my efforts by writing *new* notes. Even with this volume complete, I am still far from the top of the hill (though unlike Sisyphus, I'm not complaining).

The editing was very much a collaborative project. Skinner would give me a pile of notes, and I would catalogue them. I would file some and return others with suggested changes. He would meanwhile have unearthed or written more and finished revising some I had given him; thus the cycle would repeat itself. In the process, a single note might be passed back and forth six or seven times. We exchanged small stacks several times a week for about two years in assembling this collection.

I have been asked many times what these notebooks are about. I have replied, somewhat extravagantly, "Everything."

That is shorthand for philosophy, education, sex, politics, religion, language, economics, history, art, literature, music, people, wit, and items in the news. Not to mention Rumpelstiltskin, chess, and Pig Latin. Perhaps I should have said, "Everything of interest to B. F. Skinner" —which is a great deal indeed.

Because of the wide range of material and the many circumstances under which the notes were written, this is as much a book about Skinner as it is by him. Indeed, many of the notes concern Skinner himself—his verbal slips, his mistakes in perception, his style of dress, and even a dream. The notes give us a glimpse of what it means to be a behaviorist in private as well as in public. Skinner the behaviorist emerges through the notebooks as the be- havioristic man—and behaviorism, as a way of life.

Skinner has been an avid note writer since his college days, when he planned a career in writing. He began his first formal notebook during the year he spent in Scranton after graduating from college. In 1928 he abandoned a writing career and entered Harvard to do graduate work in psychology. There his writing skills served him well. He published more than 25 papers and a lengthy book within the next ten years, making him one of the most prolific psychologists in the country. He continued to keep note- books during this period, recording designs for experi- ments and equipment, the results of his research, and his plans and progress as a psychologist. He also collected extensive notes for a second book, which he planned to call *Sketch for an Epistemology*. Skinner used the notes of this period, most of which still survive, in reconstructing his early days for *The Shaping of a Behaviorist* (1979).

In the spring of 1955 Skinner was on sabbatical leave in Putney, Vermont, where he wrote one of his best-known papers, "A Case History in Scientific Method" (1956), and brought *Verbal Behavior* (1957) into its final stages. (The manuscript of *Schedules of Reinforcement* [1957] was in abeyance, awaiting his return to Cambridge in June.) In Putney, he began writing short essays in a 7- by 8-inch ruled spiral notebook. Unlike earlier notes, these were dated and titled, and most could stand alone. He has since filled more than one hundred of the spiral notebooks with them and dictated many more for transcription. The notes in this collection were culled from more than 2,000 typed pages of such material.

Skinner has written notes for many reasons, one of which has been to provide material for use in papers and books. "Freedom and the Control of Men" (1955) and "The Phylogeny and Ontogeny of Behavior" (1966) were composed largely of notes. Much of *About Behaviorism* (1974) had also existed as notes, and 33 notes were appended as such to the chapters of *Contingencies of Reinforcement* (1969). Two manuscript-length collections of notes remain unedited, to be used in books Skinner plans to write when he finishes his autobiography. One of these deals with the techniques used to "discover what you have to say"; one such technique is note writing.

Skinner writes notes to promote novel behavior—to "tap his creativity." Good ideas come and go. Jotting them down or recording them on a tape recorder preserves them for use at a convenient time. Skinner has arranged conditions under which fresh ideas are seldom lost: He has carried a cassette recorder in his briefcase, has kept notebook materials close at hand during leisurely moments by the pool or on vacations, and has kept a tape recorder by his bed. Some of his best material is based on recordings made in the middle of the night.

Note writing is also a kind of exercise for Skinner. He subscribes to the writer's dictum, *"Nulla dies sine linea"*— no day without a line. A notebook has made this possible, even on the remotest beach. The notebooks have further served as repositories for material which, though worthwhile, would not normally justify major works. They have made it convenient to analyze topical issues and to continue writing in fields in which he has already published extensively. Many of the notes in this collection are, for example, elaborations of *Verbal Behavior*. Finally, the notebooks have been the starting points of many new projects. The following pages contain a great many suggestions for new analyses and experiments.

I have loosely described the notes in terms of "ideas" and "creativity." Skinner would characterize them differ-

ently. Note writing is behavior. Many would call it the
expression of mental events—the record of thoughts. The
behaviorist counters: Thought, too, is behavior, and it is
not the cause of note writing. Skinner has surely said things
to himself or otherwise behaved covertly before writing
notes. But covert behavior does not *cause* overt behavior.
Rather, both Skinner's "thinking" and writing are products of other factors: his genetic endowment (difficult at
this point to characterize), his environmental history (both
novel behavior and writing have been richly rewarded), and
the current circumstances (he is, say, alone by the pool
where little behavior occurs to compete with "reflection"
and writing; a pen and notebook are at hand).

A behavioristic analysis is relevant to the notes in
another way: Behaving organisms are not the *agents* of their
actions; they simply behave. Thus Skinner does not origi-
nate his verbal behavior, covert or overt; it originates *in him*,
or, in other words, it simply occurs. We capture this
outlook in the vernacular when we say, "It occurred to me
. . ." The notes, loosely speaking, are some things that
occurred to B. F. Skinner. Collected in this volume is a
sampling of Skinner's verbal occurrences (subsequently
edited), distinctive in that they were not controlled by
particular audiences or tasks. (For a more detailed discussion of these issues, see Skinner's *Verbal Behavior* and
Science and Human Behavior [1953].)

Skinner's notebooks are not mere repositories for new
ideas; they are, rather, a workplace for these ideas. Hence
the notes have been constantly revised and updated over the
years. Many were again revised for this collection, as I have
noted above. Nearly all have undergone minor stylistic
changes, and perhaps 20 percent have been retitled. What
little shorthand there was has been eliminated. Factual
errors have been eliminated as far as possible, longer notes
have been condensed, and in a few cases related notes have
been combined. In some cases names have been updated; in
"Cross-Sections" (see Index), for example, *Beyond Freedom
and Dignity* was called "Freedom and Dignity," the title

Skinner had in mind until shortly before the book went to press. In a few cases, Skinner recast an entire entry.

Because of the revisions, the historical value of many of the notes is doubtful. They should stand here as the best possible versions—from Skinner's current perspective—of items he wrote over a period of 25 years. (The dates upon which notes were originally written may still be of interest in some cases and have therefore been included in the index.)

Here is an example of a note revised for this collection: "The Fireman's Hat" was originally written on December 16, 1962, and entitled "The Red Fireman's Hat." The title was changed because the referent of the word "red" was ambiguous. A short newspaper clipping ("Pre-Christmas Fast Relaxed by Pope") is pasted on the original notebook page, followed by:

cf. the bishop presiding at a banquet: "Those who must smoke may."

What does it mean to be "unable to meet the obligation of abstinence and fasting on Christmas Eve"? One simply *must* eat? Why?

Isn't this rather like Benchley's unwillingness to wear out the magical powers of the red fireman's hat which helped win Harvard games against Yale? He put it away when the cause was hopeless, as the Church wisely refrains from imposing obligations which will not be observed. Better to grant a dispensation than to create a host of little sinners who may move on to bigger sins to destroy the magical controlling power of the Church.

The revised version, included in this collection, begins with a quotation from the newspaper clipping, followed by:

What does it mean to be "unable to meet the obligation of abstinence and fasting on Christmas Eve"? One can abstain from eating anywhere at any time.

This is rather like Robert Benchley's unwillingness to wear out the magical powers of the fireman's hat which he wore to help Harvard win against Yale. He put the hat away when the cause was hopeless, as the Church wisely refrains from imposing obligations which will not be observed. Better to grant a dispensation than to create a host of little sinners, who may move on to bigger sins.

In the revised version, the first paragraph and last phrase were omitted, and the note was made more readable throughout. Some notes, on the other hand, such as "Contralateral" (see Index), written in 1960, are virtually unchanged.

Omitted in the editing process were notes that overlapped other material Skinner has published or is planning to publish, that were suitable for too few readers, or that were redundant in the collection. Personal notes and many that would have required extensive rewriting were also excluded. My inclination was to publish as many as possible that seemed to make some positive contribution—in elaborating or clarifying Skinner's work, in exploring new territory, or in shedding light on Skinner himself. In spite of his occasional ("unconscious"?) attempts to misplace a few of the more sensitive notes, Skinner shared this aim. (A publisher had once suggested to him that the notes be published posthumously. He wasn't at all excited by the prospect.)

Because of the multiple revisions of many entries, it would have been difficult, or, at the very least, misleading, to place them in a chronological order. We have, instead, ordered them in a way that we hope will make interesting reading.

A full table of contents would have been unwieldy in a collection of this size. A comprehensive index should better assist the reader in locating particular notes. The single index includes the full title and page number of every notebook entry, in addition to proper names and subject headings. My goal was to make it detailed enough to allow readers to find notes quickly that they could remember only vaguely. The index should also be useful for locating groups of related notes. (See the note at the beginning of the index for further information.)

A number of notes refer to members of Skinner's family by first name only: Eve (his wife), Julie (his elder child), Deborah (his younger child, also called "Debs"), and Lisa (Julie's elder child and his first grandchild, now called "Kris"). There are also several references to Natural Sciences 114, a course given at Harvard during the 1950's and early 1960's. This was Skinner's first "Skinnerian" course, for which he wrote *Science and Human Behavior* and in which he pioneered the use of teaching machines. For definitions of technical terms, the reader should consult the Brief Glossary, as well as *Science and Human Behavior* and *Verbal Behavior*, or current texts on learning or operant conditioning.

The following people have given much appreciated help in the preparation of this book: Jean Kirwan Fargo, Sharon Greene, Rose Guarino, Suzanne Harmon, Carol Kirshnit, Eve Skinner, Nell Stoddard, and Therese Statz Vezeridis. I am also grateful to my wife, Sandra; even with major new responsibilities (6 lb. 14 oz.), she devoted many hours to the book and many more to me.

Enough technicalities. Enjoy the notes—and through them, Fred Skinner.

Robert Epstein
Cambridge, Massachusetts
July 1980

Notebooks
B. F. Skinner

How to Give Orders to a Baby

Lisa, just a year old, picks up blocks, shells, and so on and puts them in any convenient receptacle. I took advantage of this when some friends came for cocktails. She tried to pull herself up on a small side table and spilled a dish of cocktail tidbits on the floor. I put the dish on the ground and said, "You must pick them all up and put them in the dish." Which of course she did, as I knew she would. Had I not then explained, our visitors would have believed that this one-year-old was obeying a rather complex order. Even so, will the case turn up in a textbook?

Educating Harvard Professors

In the early sixties, a meeting of the Harvard faculty was devoted to the selection of students. Someone referred to the tendency of teachers to build in their own image. Is it the goal of the University to select and educate future members of its faculty? The question was found amusing. No one raised the question of where future faculties were to come from. Four of the ten speakers were, from their accents, clearly not educated in America. Will America ever again get a similar windfall? A similar issue arose more than 300 years ago, captured in the inscription on the gate of Harvard Yard: "After God had carried us safe to New England and we had builded our houses . . . one of the next things we longed for and looked after was to advance learning and perpetuate it to posterity, dreading to leave an illiterate ministry to the churches when our present ministers shall lie in the dust."

Zeitgeist

About a year ago I had an idea for a *New Yorker* cartoon. A Christmas volunteer with a bell and a pot-and-tripod holds a sign reading "Help the needy," and, nearby, a bum holds a cup and sign reading "Give direct." I told this to several people and thought of sending it to a friend, Charlie Martin, the *New Yorker*'s CEM. This week's issue has the cartoon exactly as I imagined it, except that the bum's sign reads "Eliminate the middle man." I doubt that the idea got from here to there. Similar variables produce similar behavior in different skins.

Rumpelstiltskin

A Freudian analyst might reveal the latent content in the story of Rumpelstiltskin in this way:

A miller (one who deals in seed!) boasts of his beautiful

daughter and of the beautiful children she could have. A young king, childless (seedless) by an earlier marriage or by mistresses, is intrigued, marries her, and charges her to "spin straw into gold" by bearing him children. She is unable to do so, and one night when she is in tears, a man who resembles the king offers to make her pregnant. She must, however, promise to give him the first child. In desperation, she agrees. She bears a child, the king is overjoyed, and everyone is happy. Remembering her bargain, she sends spies to find the man who impregnated her, and when his name is discovered ("Rumpelstiltskin!"), she has him murdered.

Easily spun straw.

Crazy Mary

A writer in an issue of *Holiday* describes the Harvard scene of 25 years ago, and mentions Crazy Mary. I remember her well. She roamed Harvard Square in a long, faded coat reaching to her heels and filled out, one guessed, by many layers of dresses and petticoats underneath. She carried two large black oilcloth market bags which gave her the swaying balance of a horse with heavy saddle packs. Her voice was soft, her speech a heavy brogue, her manner a little tense and pleading. She used to ask for "carfare to get home to Dorchester"—a dime. She would walk about the Square for hours, evidently unconcerned that those who had given would see her asking others. Had she a good memory, or was she sensitive enough to the expressions of those she approached to spot recent victims? Or did she not care?

How did she start? Had she at one time really needed carfare to get home? How, over the years, were her behavior, her costume, her manner shaped by her successes? The bigger the bags and the more tattered her clothes, the more effective the appeal? But differential reinforcement had gone too far. She was not the perfect picture of someone in need. There was a touch of the complaining aggressiveness of the experienced panhandler.

Comma

Last evening a man, calling from Oregon, asked me if my name was really Edgar Pierce. He had read my name and title on the cover of *Walden Two*—"B. F. Skinner is Edgar Pierce Professor of Psychology"—with a comma after "Pierce."

Fictions in the News

A student at the University in Austin took a rifle into a tower and fired at people in the streets. He killed 13 and wounded 30. There have been a rash of explanations. The boy's father spoke of tensions and "snapping." The "breaking point" had been reached. The university psychiatrist spoke of frustrated achievements and aspirations. Doctors found a small tumor near the brainstem.

The boy's father unwittingly got closer to real causes. He described himself as a gun addict—always hunting—brought up his boys to shoot. The boy was in the Marines—taught to shoot again. Killing from a tower reminds one of the assassination of President Kennedy, also in Texas.

But the environmental history gets little notice. The mental and physiological fictions prevail. Whatever effect, if any, the tumor had, it did not *cause* the behavior of taking an arsenal of guns and ammunition to a tower, barricading the doors, and shooting innocent people. It could not even have interfered with "cortical inhibition normally suppressing such behavior," or if it did, we still have to explain the behavior.

The Uxorial Manner

Rehearsing a play, David Gates and I were going through a scene on stage. Our wives were talking to each other about their parts. An entrance came due. Thinking it was Eve who was missing her cue, I called out, "Helen enters!" Then I realized that Claire Gates was playing Helen and immediately regretted the manner in which I had spoken. It was impolite to anyone but my wife! Everyone else was acting in the same way—exhibiting a special spouse-repertoire.

Children also suffer from a special parent-to-child repertoire. It is almost impossible to treat a child—especially your own—as you treat an adult.

Beyond "Beyond"

Beyond Freedom and Dignity was a misleading title. It suggested that I was against freedom and personal worth. I did not advocate imposing control; control existed and should be corrected. Only the complete anarchist refuses to recognize that the individual must be restrained for the good of the group and, as we now see, the species. But restraint is a threat to freedom only if it is aversive. If acting for the good of the group is positively reinforced, people will feel as free and worthy as possible. I am in favor of that. It is the best way to promote government by the people for the people.

Physician, Heal Thyself

Peggy Lamson has done a series of articles about the Boston Red Sox. The other day I suggested that she discuss with the manager a plausible technique of breaking up a batting slump. My guess is that a player is told what he is doing wrong or shown movies or videotapes of himself as he strikes out or grounds out easily. I suggested that, instead, he be shown a short film of himself hitting home runs. A videotape device in the back of the dugout could have short cassettes for each player. He is to look at his film a few minutes before batting.

Why do I think it will work? It could be a kind of imitation, but a more likely effect should be eliminating some of the current aversive effects of the slump. The player would say that he "feels better about himself" as a batter. Slight tensions in posture and movement might follow.

Later it occurred to me that it might work for shortstops and others who have been making errors. Let them see themselves playing brilliantly.

And just now I saw the significance in my own case. After reading some of my own published writing (it almost always seems good to me because I have kept at it until it *is* good according to my standards), I write freely and energetically for some time.

"Get Well or Else!"

Electric shock therapy seems to have begun as pure aversive control. The patient recovered to avoid further treatment. Jones (*The Life and Work of Sigmund Freud*, vol. III, 22) discusses Freud's memo on it with respect to war neuroses thus:

"The therapy that had been evolved to meet this situation, first of all in the German Army, was to apply electrical treatment in such doses as to be even more disagreeable than the thought of returning to the front." (Why "the thought of returning to the front" rather than "returning to the front"?)

When the treatment began to fail, the current was

increased. "The fact has never been denied that in German hospitals there were cases of death during the treatment and suicides as the result of it."

A psychiatrist told me once that he had used "operant therapy" in a U.S. Army hospital in Vietnam. He had called the patients together and told them that if they did not go to work they would get electric shock therapy! That, he said, is the kind of therapy that people understand.

Misreading I

I have frequently read bits of texts in ways which show a very loose control by the stimulus. Here are some examples:

Just after listening to a news announcement on TV about preparations for a 22-orbit flight, I looked at a box labeled SPACKLE and read it as SPACE. I was surprised to find the word there. I immediately checked to confirm the presence of the five letters in the right order.

A picture in *The New York Times* for November 15, 1967, showed pickets, one carrying a sign reading STOP THE SLAUGHTER OF THE COAL INDUSTRY. Of the last word, only INDUST could be seen. I read it as NUDIST. Note that it is an anagram. (Possibly there is more prompting or probing in the game of anagrams than I argue for in *Verbal Behavior.*)

In a passage about a bird sanctuary on a lake, the first sentence in a paragraph began, *The drake was sitting. . . .* I read it as *The duck was sitting on the lake.* An earlier passage had described a duck moving about on the water. *Drake* was uncommon and unexpected. *Drake* and *lake* overlap. The expression *was sitting* (meaning on the nest) was rare in my verbal experience.

Mix-Ups

A few days ago the English papers carried the story of a government office in Africa which sent two letters to different governments in the wrong envelopes, with unhappy diplomatic results. Freud suggested that mixing envelopes could be an unconscious act, as in solving the problem of simultaneous love affairs. (Sinclair Lewis's *Arrowsmith* did something like it by deliberately inviting both women to the same luncheon.) Was the secretary who was responsible unconsciously getting his boss into trouble, or was he the spy of a third government, or did he have political aspirations into which the resulting mess fitted? But is not a simple mistake still the most plausible explanation?

I can certainly plead not guilty in another mix-up. I sent some friends a copy of *Walden Two*. Somehow the package came open in the mails, and the label was reattached to some books propagating the Catholic faith. Fortunately my friends were skeptical enough to write to check on it.

Old Acquaintance

He smiled when I opened the door, told me his name, said he had known me as a member of Jay Connaway's discussion groups years ago. I had gone to one meeting at Jay's so I said "Oh, yes." He expected to be asked in, came in, said, "Do you want to see some watercolors?" I expected him to go outside, retrieve a sample case hidden in the shrubbery, but he pulled a gadget from his pocket. By peeking in a hole and operating a lever you could see ten different, pleasant paintings. He said he was not an artist but an art director. What company? None, at the moment. Still looking for the right spot. He asked me if I were still at Rutgers (where I have never been). Said he had all three boys with him, and I said to remember me to them. He said the last time he was here, we were living in the other house (we have always lived in this one). He suddenly had to go. I had never seen him before and I'm sure he could have said the same of me before he left.

Liberalizing Sex

Reading Sumner's *Folkways*, I am impressed by the liberalizing of sexual mores that was already in progress when Freud began to publish. I suspect Freud has been given altogether too much credit for the change. In fact he may have been a conservative or even reactionary force, because he offset the growing relativism of comparative anthropology by claiming to demonstrate the ubiquity of *one* sexual system. The current liberalization is scarcely Freudian at all. In fact many psychoanalysts are prudes.

Westward Ho

That is the name of my motel. The office and adjacent space are disguised as a series of saloons, supply stores, and so on. Wagon wheels lean against the wall. The chair I am sitting in has wagon wheel sides. The telephone is a wall model with an anachronistic dial and a hand phone hanging in place of the receiver. (I have just realized that I did not try to talk into the wall mouthpiece.) A sign on the phone reads, "Howdy Pardner." The desk lamp is a wooden stirrup. The bedspread has a saddle and two shoes embroidered on it, surrounded by a square of ranch brands. A large colored photograph of a lake in the Rockies and a painting of an Indian and his squaw adorn the walls. Branding irons are screwed to the wooden ceiling.

The plumbing is ultramodern.

Courtroom with a View

In *A Treasury of Laughter* Louis Untermeyer quotes from *Abraham Lincoln, The Prairie Years* by Sandburg. Lincoln is fined by a judge for making people giggle in court, but the fine is remitted when the judge hears the joke, which "had to do with 'taking up a subscription to buy Jim Wheeler a new pair of pants.'"

There was more to the story as I heard it from a friend (of a friend?) of the judge. I sent it to Sandburg, whom I had met at Bread Loaf, Vermont, and who I knew was writing about Lincoln. Lincoln and several others were sitting around a table in court. Lincoln had his feet up, and a hole could be seen in the seat of his pants. One of the men passed a paper around the table: "The undersigned subscribe the sums set opposite their names to buy Abe Lincoln a new pair of pants." When all had signed, the paper was passed to Lincoln, who added, "Abe Lincoln subscribes the following sum to cover the end in view."

Poetic Illogic

> *Yonder a maid and her wight*
> *Come whispering by;*
> *Wars' annals will fade into night*
> *Ere their story die.*

Consoling for those, like myself, who prefer love to hate, but not convincing. Surely Hardy did not mean that the story of that particular maid and her wight would last longer than the story of Waterloo. It was love that would last. But it is unfair to pit the general against the specific.

> *Above us the missile*
> *Goes whooshingly by*
> *Love's annals will fade into night*
> *Ere that story die.*

That is just as good an argument for the greater endurance of hate.

I love poetry and am moved by it, but it is basically a kind of fraud. It is truth for the moment, to match or support a feeling, and like music is justified accordingly. I do not want to destroy it. But it must not be taken seriously. Or permitted to interfere in serious matters.

Accepting a Coincidence

Last night I dreamt that the phone rang. I picked it up and said, "Hello."

"Fred?" A touch of a drawl.

"Yes."

"This is . . . " and a friend spoke her name. A very quiet, sad voice.

"Oh, hello," I said. But there was no answer. The line was dead.

I woke up.

Suppose, now, there is news this morning that my friend is dead. Or her husband. Or that one of her children or grandchildren is dead. Or that one of them has been hurt in an accident. Could I keep from taking the thing seriously? Could I completely dismiss it as a coincidence? I'm not sure.

Distorted Tact

A witty remark, long out-of-date, is to the effect that a lady differs from a diplomat in the following way. When a lady says *No*, she means *Maybe*; when she says *Maybe*, she means *Yes*; but if she says *Yes*, she is no lady. When a diplomat says *Yes*, he means *Maybe*; when he says *Maybe*, he means *No*; but if he says *No*, he is no diplomat. In both definitions a remark is moved along a continuum of *Yes, Maybe, No*—away from a presumably punishing consequence at one end. The lady's usage moves to the right, away from the punished *Yes*, and the diplomat's to the left, away from the punished *No*. Why not go all the way? Why should the lady not say *No* and the diplomat *Yes* in every case? There are presumably negative consequences which keep the responses within bounds. The diplomat will be called to account, the lady will get no more invitations.

Geographical Music

Listening to the radio, I heard at most one bar of music before an announcer, speaking above the music, began: "Music for the Irish Sea—." I was startled, but when he went on, "... and for the ear to hear," I saw at once that he had said: "Music for the eye to see." And I also saw at once why I had misheard him. The music was Mendelssohn's *Fingal's Cave*. One bar's worth had put me in the Hebrides.

When Does Helping Help?

Watching myself with Lisa, I have been more impressed by this point. In my concern for helping a child I destroy the contingencies which would teach her to behave. I save her from annoyances and destroy the contingencies which would teach her to save herself. For example, I push branches aside which are getting against her face and deprive her of the chance to learn how to avoid branches. I pull on a sock and deprive her of the chance to learn to do it herself.

George Eliot

Miscellaneous notes: Some of her conversation is real speech and, like Trollope's, it conveys character, mannerisms, moods, states. But much is no more natural speech than Shakespeare's iambic pentameters. In *Daniel Deronda* we overlook the fact that Mirah, a 19-year-old girl, would not tell her story in rounded, cadenced sentences, or that the 22-year-old Gwendolen would not pack her sentences with calculated wit. They have composed little essays which they now read. All the by-products of the work of composition have gone into George Eliot's wastebasket.

By "feeling," Eliot seems to mean several different things—emotional reflexes, dispositions, inclinations. To say that one "feels inclined" to say "No" may mean no more than that one *is* inclined, but if one says "No," it is not because one is inclined to do so in the sense of having a feeling. The thing is confused by the fact that many of Eliot's characters are self-searching. They know they are inclined, and they see the consequences and may not like them. The point to be made is that these forms of self-knowledge are not causes of action. Eliot talks about feelings very often as a way of talking about probabilities of action. She is looking for the causes of action but finds it necessary to settle for the apparent causes of feelings.

Good Luck

A car stopped beside me at a red light. On the dash were a plastic statue of the Virgin and a similar but larger statue of St. Christopher. Hanging from a sun visor were two white rabbit's feet.

Hearing Something as Something Else

I was sitting in the garden listening to music through earphones. A few drops of rain began to fall, and I could see circles forming on the pool at my side. A slight defect in the phonograph record made a click in one ear. I heard it as a drop of water striking the phone on that ear. When the rain stopped falling, I found myself turning to look at the pool to see if it had started again whenever I heard a slight click. Rather ominous clouds no doubt helped me hear the clicks as rain.

Evolution of a Culture

In *The Changeling*, by Thomas Middleton and William Rowley, a play reflecting the culture of early seventeenth-century England, there are two topics of equal importance: murder and a bride's virginity.

We have made *some* progress.

Slips of the Tongue

A radio announcer referred to the *moon-er landing*, and corrected himself immediately to *moon landing*. A pretty obvious blend of *moon* and *lunar*.

Nixon made many verbal slips in the 1960 campaign for President. Speaking on farm surpluses he said, *We can get rid of the farmer—the surpluses by* . . . Speaking about the future he said, *We must think of our children and our grandfath—grandchildren*. Speaking of his running mate he said, *Henry Cabot Liar-Lodge—and I are* . . . His enemies argued that he might have been referring to his wife when he said, *America can't stand pat.* . . .

A psychiatrist talking about a patient: *Analysis was her last help—hope*. Had he given up hope? Or was he sure it would help?

Zen and the Art of Piano Reminiscence

I have never been able to memorize music. In 1933 or 1934 I spent all of Thanksgiving Day memorizing the first C-Major Prelude in *The Well-Tempered Clavichord*. I forgot most of it almost immediately, and I can now play no more than four or five bars.

I have also never been able to sing a tune or pick one out on the piano note by note. Nor play one on the saxophone or recorder.

But recently I discovered that I could extemporize at the piano in a pleasant way. I began with a chord in both hands, played a note or two with the right, found another chord, and so on. Much of it seemed beautiful.

The curious thing was that I needed a special moderate state of attention. I could not simply play without thinking. Everything went wrong if I did that. But if I thought too hard, I went for recognizable chords, sequences of tones, and so on. When I was in just the right state, I was "exalted." I was positively directed but not concentrating.

Alas, there was not much variety. I found myself always in the key of E-flat major. The effort to start and stay in a different key spoiled the state of attention. I have abandoned the whole enterprise.

The Control of Men

Geoffrey Gorer, in an article in *The New York Times Magazine* (November 27, 1966: "[de Sade] reported, in fictional form, the pleasures to be derived from the unfettered exercise of power over one's fellow men and women. De Sade linked these pleasures with the pleasures of sex; this was the only metaphor which contemporary science made available to him and it was congenial to his temperament."

Was the sadism merely *control?* If so, de Sade was no innovator. The master of every slave was a sadist. Every ruler. Every priest. Every successful teacher. Surely it was *punitive* control that fascinated de Sade.

The same misunderstanding may explain the remark of a psychiatrist in a dispute about operant conditioning in a Minnesota hospital: "Allowing sadists to cower behind the apron of operant conditioning . . ." (Minneapolis *Tribune,* March 23, 1967, p. 19).

But operant conditioning has rescued thousands of patients from punitive control. It is the *traditional* form of institutional care that would appeal to de Sade.

Faculties

I looked for a noncommittal synonym of "intelligence" to fill the blank in "Why do we not show as much ——— in human affairs as in, say, physics?" I found nothing I liked. Then I tried adjectives. "Why are we not as ———?" "Intelligent?" No, not quite right.

Then I realized that I was trying to refer to things *in* us rather than to our behavior. I really wanted a synonym for *successful.* "Why are we not as successful in dealing with, analyzing, understanding . . .?" "Why are we not as effective . . .?" "Why have we not constructed as powerful a science . . . of human affairs . . .?"

Deliberation

A school program contained this item: "10:00 to 10:30 Unscheduled."

Is this any more absurd than setting aside time for doing nothing? The deliberate cessation of activity—like the "thought stopping" of the psychotherapist—is not relaxation. It is a definite, possibly compulsive, action.

A very different design is a way of life in which one does not always *have* to do something, as in following a schedule. It is a feasible design, but much more difficult to arrange. It could be the goal of a planned culture such as a Walden Two.

Mental Metaphor

It is said that both Bach and Wagner "could penetrate to the essence of a poetic idea and translate it into musical terms."

But what did they really do?

1. They read a poem that appealed to them.
2. They wrote music to which it might be sung.

They were successful if the music had the same effect on the listener as the poem. The effect was not an essence, and it was not translated.

Did Bach and Wagner know how to "say the same thing in different modes"? Yes, if saying the same thing means having the same effect.

Gesture? Expression? Response?

A girl in the front row started to ask a question. "Yes, Judy," said the Headmaster. "Stand up when you ask your question." The girl then acted in a way that was familiar but hard to describe—in part a wince, a twisting; in part a shrug, the verbal accompaniment of which might have been "Oh, all right!"; and in part a protest: "Why do you have to say that?" The girl was hurt. She had been caught doing the wrong thing, and she was going to have to stand and be seen just after being verbally punished. (She may have remained sitting in the first place because standing and being seen were aversive, and now they were worse.)

The behavior is typical enough in a classroom or in responding to a person in authority. It is characteristic of adolescence. But we have no word for it. In fiction, the gesture would have to be represented by a soliloquy, a third-person paraphrase of what the girl was thinking or of how she would describe the situation, or, if possible, a reference to a character in literature noted for similar behavior.

Linguistic Games

Leonard Bernstein, in his first Norton Lecture, had fun improvising the infant's first word MA from M-M-M and the vocalization A-A-A which follows when the infant "opens its mouth for the nipple." He then considered what happens when you add an L. MAL—bad, but *also* small. Bad because small. (I should have supposed that big things were more likely to be bad for babies.)

He could have gone further. Obviously the overriding neurosis of our time is concealed in the word *mammal*. We are all mammals. *Ma-mal* is clearly a complaint: A small breast is bad. A symbol of the starvation we all face à la *Mal*thus.

Malheur à Mahler.

Telephone Conversation with Captain Field, Port Clyde, Maine

Is this Captain Field?

Yup.

This is Fred Skinner.

Yup.

We'd like to go out to the Island with you tomorrow morning.

Yup.
What time does the boat leave?
Ten thutty.
Ten thirty?
Yup.
Well, we'll be glad to see you.
Yup.
See you at 10:30, then.
Yup.
(I have known him for 35 years and had not seen him or talked with him for five.)

Analyzing Character

Yesterday in lecturing on religion in Natural Sciences 114, I noticed a recurrence of a mannerism in which I turn again and again to point toward the blackboard though nothing very appropriate is written on it. This appears to be a kind of escape; I am turning away from my audience. Evidently, I was afraid of the reaction to my remarks on this subject. Literally, I found it hard to *face* my class—to face up to their probable reactions.

Should we call it an unconscious activity? Yes, if I had missed its aversive character. The existence of something on the blackboard was relevant. I should not have turned to an empty board. (I do turn to a recently erased board.) I thus *rationalize* turning away by doing so as if I were turning toward something—where "as if" means either (1) the two behaviors have the same form, or (2) they are controlled by the same variable.

The Heavens Declare . . .

A year ago we returned from a dinner party at about 10:20. I went out beside the pool and dropped into a chair. I looked straight up and immediately saw a satellite, directly overhead, very bright, moving WNW to ESE. It took ten or more minutes to drop into the trees to the east.

I have seen four other satellites but only by looking for them. I have often wondered when I should notice one unscheduled, and now it has happened.

Incidentally, I can't explain why I saw it so quickly unless I know the night sky better than I think. I have never learned to look at stars. I can find the Big Dipper and, from it, the North Star, and that is about all. Yet upon looking straight up on this clear night I immediately noticed a stranger. It was moving so slowly that I doubt whether I could have detected its motion within five seconds (unless it was very close to a bright star, which it was not). Yet I fixed my sights on it in much less time. There was a slight emotional reaction to the possibility that it might be a satellite before I was sure.

It would be a mistake to say I saw an unscheduled satellite "without having to look very long," because since this happened, I have scanned the night sky whenever possible, like the person who has the *bad* luck to win a large stake when first gambling. A bit of a variable-interval schedule with a *long* mean interval.

A few nights ago I told this story to a friend in our garden, and he said he had never seen a satellite. I looked up. "There is one now," I said. And it was true; there was. I was reminded of the story about Thoreau, who, when walking with a new acquaintance, was asked, "Where can you find Indian arrowheads?" And he replied, "Here," and stooped down and picked one up.

Ramuntcho on a Motorcycle

He stood waiting for her astride a light motorcycle. He was just as Pierre Loti might have described him—dark, of medium height, perfectly in command. She came out and mounted behind him—her arms around his waist, her skirt caught up between her legs, trusting, submissive. He stepped smartly on the starter, turned the motorcycle to one side as if it were a horse, urged it forward a step, straightened it, and they shot forward and down a narrow street of Ascain. The relation between them was—not epitomized, not symbolized, but merely *clarified* by the motorcycle. Ramuntcho the leader, his girl the happy follower, whose only function was to cling tightly and lean to right or left as the course dictated by Ramuntcho required.

In a few minutes he came back alone. He had evidently picked her up where she worked and driven her home. That may have been the course *she* dictated.

Neglect of Duty

I sat beside a priest on a flight from Boston to Chicago. He began to work on a manuscript before takeoff and paid no attention as we accelerated down the runway and were lifted into the air. As we came in, out of a several-layer stack, he was reading a cheap detective story and paid no attention as we touched down. I was aware of a certain resentment. Did I feel cheated because I had wanted to laugh at him when I saw signs of prayer? Or was I angry because he was neglecting to help us get the plane up and down again? If he believed in prayer, here was a chance to be of service.

Daylight

Somewhere I have saved a quotation from Benjamin Franklin about daylight-saving in Paris. The French still need advice. So do the Spanish. In Laredo children played in the streets at ten in the evening, and the last movie ended at 1:30 in the morning. All through France we have found it difficult to get our *petit déjeuner* before eight. In Ascain I waited until almost 8:30 *pour regler ma note.* No one was up except a scrub girl. A sign (seen too late) above the desk advised those leaving before 8:00 to *regler leur notes* the evening before. Here in Tarbes we were told we could have breakfast sent up by 8:00 but that 7:30 was a little too early.

Incidentally, innkeepers seem to be surprisingly trusting. In Laredo we worked hard to find someone to pay before leaving. In Montauban we were not asked to register, were given a beautiful apartment several blocks from the hotel, and again had to search for someone (he turned up in pajamas) to whom to pay our bill before leaving at 8:30. (A solitary waiter had given us *petit déjeuner.*)

Force of Coincidence

The strange effect of seeing a word just as one says it or hearing it as one is reading it may be responsible for some of the belief in clairvoyance, ESP, or psychokinesis.

In watching a baseball game one may anticipate a play ("He'll hit into a double play." "He'll hit a grand slam home run."), and occasionally the play follows. It has some of the effect of the simultaneous comment.

Caveat Meditator

"The basic aim of Hindu mystical life . . . is to convert all inward experience into physical states perceptible to the senses."

N. C. Chaudhuri
The Times Literary Supplement
February 3, 1978

My only quarrel is with the word "convert." Inward experience *was never* of anything but physical states. The procedures of the mystic may only classify, define, further the discrimination of private stimuli.

The Only Hope—Lost?

An article in *The Guardian* this morning comments on a cricket game between Britain and Pakistan in Karachi which had to be abandoned because of rioting. It marks, the writer said, the decline and fall of the British invention of fair play.

One has that feeling about much of what is happening in the world today. In a way it is not unlike the Nazi's reversal of social progress. And both can be traced either to the abandonment of certain kinds of social control or to the emergence of new forms. Violent police and military action is not far from the violence of sit-ins and mob action (even though the latter are often offered as protests against the former). What have gone out are the more subtle forms of control, still aversive *au fond*, but moderate. The aversive control of mild social sanctions was at least an improvement, and it may be a necessary step on the way to positive control.

Paradox

How does one arrive at incompatible statements, both of which are true? The statements may not really be incompatible if a word in common has different meanings. Antonyms may have different referents: one can say *sorrowful, yet always rejoicing*, or *unknown, and yet well known*, or *having nothing, and yet possessing all things* (*Second Corinthians* 6:9–10) because a person may be sorrowful and rejoicing about different things, unknown by some yet well known by others, and without money yet rich in friends. But why are such responses strong? Is speaking in paradoxes a way of ringing intraverbal changes, opposites having strong "associative value"? Is the reader intrigued by discovering that conflicting statements can be made, the uneasiness about contradiction or illogicality thus dismissed? Or is the effect like that of practicing the opposite: acting bravely when afraid, doing something you don't want to do, praising an enemy?

Search?

Notes made in recalling *W. K. Clifford:*

> *Compton*
> *Crawford*
> *Court*
> *Pearson, Pomfret* (confused with K. Pearson, roughly a

contemporary in a related field?)

> *Pearson, Person*
> *Cr*
> *Cl*
> *M*
> *Clear*
> *Newsome*
> *-Person !!!*

(feeling of commonplace name)

> *Comfort*
> *-ford*
> *Chalice*

(2 initials – one M)

> *Gilbert*
> *A C*
> *Pof*
> *Pearson* (again)
> *C—*
> *Clifford !!!*
> *W. C.?*
> *W. K.*

(How would a cognitive psychologist describe this—as a walk through the storehouse of memory, order blank in hand, looking for a designated object on a shelf? But what was on the order blank?)

Epiphenomenon

An interviewer asked: Would I call feelings and mental states epiphenomena? I said no. *Webster's Third New International* defines an epiphenomenon as "a secondary phenomenon accompanying another . . . and thought of as caused by it." For most people, that would make behavior the epiphenomenon. I may seem to imply that feelings are epiphenomenal when I call them "by-products" of behavior. A better expression is "collateral products." The feelings and the behavior are both caused by genetic and environmental histories together with the present situation.

Hallucinatory Behavior in Animals

Certain drugs induce animals to behave "as if they were seeing things, hearing things, feeling things, etc." I think that is the right way to put it, rather than to say that they have visual, auditory, or tactual images. They are indeed behaving *as if*—in other words, as they behave when certain stimuli are present.

Suppose we try to get a pigeon "to tell us it is seeing afterimages" or, to put it correctly, to behave after seeing certain stimuli as it behaves when stimuli of complementary properties are present. We first reinforce pecking a reddish spot moving about on a screen and allow pecking spots of other colors to go unreinforced. A small but intense blue-green light is then flashed in the pigeon's eyes. If it begins to peck the screen, it is behaving as it behaved when the reddish spot was there. A human subject who had acquired self-descriptive behavior would report that he or she sees a red afterimage.

Consider, now, the case in which a drug is said to induce a cat to "play with a nonexistent mouse." We reinforce some such response as pressing a lever when a mouse is present in an adjacent enclosure but not when any one of a number of other objects or animals is present. We then give the drug. If the cat "sees a mouse," it should press the lever, since that is behavior also controlled by a mouse as a stimulus. If the drug has different effects on phylogenic and ontogenic behavior, that is a fact worth knowing.

Uh—

At the faculty meeting yesterday several speakers said *uh* a great deal—one or two as often as every four or five words. With one it appeared to be premature vocalizing, before shaping began. It was not needed to hold the floor, but it may have been reinforced by the avoidance of silence. The damage was severe.

A friend who uses long *uh*'s when excited and at a loss for words also uses autoclitic floor-holders like *Let me just say* or *I would note* to the point of amusing his listeners.

State and Individual

Hobbes's use of "war" to represent interpersonal relations makes clear the ubiquity of aversive control in daily life. But is not the undeniable ubiquity of war in international relations possibly the product of war among persons? Idealists have insisted that each is of a different nature, but seldom the same idealist in both cases.

Fault

If students do not learn, is it their fault? No, their teachers have not arranged effective instructional contingencies. Is it then the teachers' fault? No, the culture has not arranged effective contingencies for them.

Is it then the fault of the culture? By the time we reach this question, the notion of fault is at fault. How shall we punish a culture? In moving from student to teacher to culture, we move steadily away from the feasibility of punitive measures—from the cane for the student, to dismissal for the teacher, to—what for the culture?

A culture could be said to be punished if it does not survive (this is the ultimate selective consequence), but we change it, if at all, through other means. We look for alternative measures. Similarly, we can look for other ways of improving the behavior of teachers and students—as by designing contingencies under which productive behaviors are reinforced.

Humane?

In talking to a group of young law professors, I brought up the question of depriving prisoners (or psychotics, retardates, or children) of goods and services which "they have a right to expect" in order to use them as reinforcers. Isn't this inhumane?

Why have they a right to expect them? They have been given them, that is true, but why? To prevent riots? To appease? To enable them to live with dignity? Out of sympathy?

What does it mean to have the "care" of prisoners? To do nice things to them in return for their treating you nicely? But what is the effect of these noncontingent goods? When you simply give people things they have the time, skill, and energy to get by themselves, you allow their behavior to atrophy. You make it less easy for them to "kill time," and stultified boredom or escape from boredom to violence follows.

Of course, those who have enjoyed these "rights" will protest when they are taken away, as patients protest the doctor's order not to smoke, drink, or overeat. But should protest affect policy? If one's goal is to develop effective, active, productive, interested people, then one should make sure the goods they get are contingent upon their behavior.

Expectation

When we say that a musical theme "frustrates our expectations," can we describe the fact in another way?

Certain standard sequences heard again and again lead us to "anticipate" the next note in the theme in the sense of hearing it as a perceptual response, or singing or playing it on a familiar instrument. We see this when we are wrong, when the last note in a well-known song is deliberately flatted for humorous effect. Anticipation is, like reading along with the writer, a tendency to make a corresponding response. A new sequence is, as such, a new stimulus. It is not an expectation that has been frustrated but a well-defined response—like stepping off a curb one has seen as a flat surface. Standard behavior is ineffective, and the result may be punishing or, if not too serious, amusing.

The Unconscious as History

We know about our behavior but not about its causes. Hence we believe that *we* cause it. But we do not always *seem* to be causing it and hence the belief in an unconscious: We behave because of causes which we do not know about.

We do not learn about unconscious processes from our

feelings; we infer them from anomalous behavior such as slips, forgettings, and dreams, and from the products of free association. But these are simply ways of reviewing the past. The hard evidence is always in the past, and best of all in an authentic past, because the remembered past is not history but one of its products.

Recollection of an Early Event

I had asked Eve to put some castor oil on several skin patches on my back. I lay prone on the bed. As she paused to put the cap on the bottle of oil before blotting my back, I recalled the time my father was treating several bad boils on my buttocks with carbolic acid, touching each one first with acid, then with alcohol. When something spilled on the skin under one knee, instead of wiping it up at once or flooding it with alcohol, my father (and I, too, I suppose) waited to see whether it was acid or alcohol. It was acid, and a bad burn made me limp for weeks.

Similar elements contributing to the recollection: lying prone on a bed in order to be treated, a treatment consisting of a liquid daubed on small patches of skin, liquid coming from a small bottle held by the applicator. In addition, Eve had paused to cap the bottle to prevent *spilling* oil on the bedspread.

The Origin of a Verbal Response

A primitive verbal system might arise as follows: A mother learns to respond to sounds made by her first baby which are correlated with various strengths of the baby's behavior. Thus, if the baby makes a particular kind of sound when ready to suck, the mother will come to put the baby to her breast when she hears it. When she begins to respond quickly in this way, she effectively reinforces the baby's response, and the hungry baby then acquires a "mand" similar in topography to the original unconditioned response. The topography may shift, however, as the baby makes different sounds. The case is very different with a second baby. The mother has already been conditioned to respond to a phylogenic response and will more quickly shape a more distinctive pattern. The second child should learn more rapidly and acquire a rather standard topography.

Composing and Painting

Musical mimicry is common. The violinist can imitate a laugh, a catcall, a chattering old woman. Composers have attempted naturalistic reproductions of nature: the sounds of spring, the pomp and circumstance of a procession, a running brook. As a language of emotion, music soon exhausts onomatopoeia. Much of what remains are "traits"— calm, turbulence, tension, fulfillment, surprise, order, disorder. Composers seem to be more creative when what they write is not too closely controlled by corresponding stimuli.

Bruckner was a would-be lover frequently rejected as ridiculous. He could not *paint* the condition (the "sad tenderness") of his body at such times. But he could hit on phrases and harmonies which sustained or intensified such a condition—and generated more of the same.

Composers do not have extensive vocabularies of emotion, either of echoic responses in imitation or of tacts in description. They create stimuli having comparable effects.

(This shows both the advantages and disadvantages of a behavioral *interpretation*. Many music critics have, I am sure, said much the same thing, and what I have said may seem to them callow. But it is in a form which facilitates contact with the analysis of other subjects.)

Hearing Myself Think

Last night, visiting in Santa Barbara, I went to a play. I had the foresight to take my hearing aid and used it to good effect. A few moments ago I was trying to "put something into words on paper." I was clearly dictating to myself, but the words were not coming, at least clearly. I suddenly saw that I had moved to put on my hearing aid, which lay in sight on the dresser.

Critic

The word once meant a judge, but it soon came to mean a faultfinder, i.e., a punisher. Since "criticism" still tends to have the meaning of faultfinding, "appreciation" is used for other ways of responding to a work of literature, art, or music, and "book reviewers" are presumably less likely to find fault than critics.

How readily we turn to punishment. It is so much easier to say how writers have failed than how they have succeeded—as it is easier for the teacher to spot and punish failures than to commend successes.

Is it in part a question of credit? A mistake seems clearly due to the person who makes it, whereas a correct act or statement may simply be learned and hence attributable to outside sources. *Our* mistake lies in supposing that there are no reasons, except fallibility, for a mistake. But errors are as completely determined as successes.

The Negative Audience I

There are things we tend not to say because saying them has been punished. Here are a few examples:

The rat that the *Minnesota Daily* named Pliny the Elder got a marble from a rack by pulling a chain that hung down from the ceiling of the apparatus. In describing the demonstration, I always felt a bit uneasy about the expression *pulling the chain*, and my students reacted with some obvious nervous amusement, because in those days many toilets were still operated by pulling chains which hung from elevated tanks. *Pulling the chain* meant flushing a toilet. Many people today have operated such toilets but not as a standard practice, and *pulling the chain* seems to have lost all of its "negative strength."

I was making a list of things to add to the manuscript of *Beyond Freedom and Dignity*. I had put half a dozen substantial notes on one sheet and a lot of small ones on another. The second sheet filled up, and I started a new page and headed it *Small adds continued*. Before I finished *adds*, as an abbreviation of *additions*, I quickly crossed it out as a misspelling of *ads* (as in *advertisements*). Then I saw that the spelling was correct and wrote the word again, but I was uneasy about it. My professor of English Composition at Hamilton College deducted one letter grade for every misspelling on a paper.

I resisted writing *better ways of raising children* because I used to tell my classes of the economist who could not avoid the spoonerism *wazing rages*. I have had to fight to say it correctly as if it were a tongue twister. Evidently it has become aversive and therefore conflicts with *ways of raising*.

I frequently try to abbreviate *pigeon* as *pig*, as in *Proj. Pig.*, but my response to *pig* invariably intrudes, and I lengthen to *pigeon*. I have noticed the same tendency in avoiding *Ass* for *Association* (*Am. Ass. Adv. Sci.*), *Anal* for *Analysis*, and *cont* for *continued*. A friend tells me he uses *pro* and *contra* rather than *pro* and *con* because the French *con* bothers him. I was merely amused, however, by those animal psychologists who used to shorten *cul de sac* to *cul*.

Micturition

A three-year-old girl pressed her hand to her genitals to keep from urinating, a rather common response in young children. Was it in part a "metaphorical" extension (or generalization) of responses which actually stop leaks? Or an actual physical stoppage, as when a man sitting in a chair tightly crosses his legs? Or a counterirritant, lessening the painful stimulation of "micturition" (in the old sense of "wanting to urinate")? Or a response occasionally reinforced when it functions to induce someone to take the child to the toilet? Or all of the above?

Brothers

A lovely darning needle or dragonfly alighted on the chair beside me in our garden. Four lovely veined wings with dark spots at the ends of the leading edges. Eyes? I waved my hand and it was gone. The beautiful design, the far more beautiful microstructure of its nervous system if it could be seen—is all that a by-product, a casual throwaway of an evolutionary process? It is hard to believe. I can understand those who are skeptical of *accidental* mutations, but given how many millions of years . . . ? It is as hard to believe as the Grand Canyon—though the workings of wind, rain, and river are easier to *see*.

Slavery

An article in *The Times Literary Supplement* raises the question of whether ancient slavery was a necessary evil if a concept of *humanitas* was to evolve. Did people need the leisure produced by slaves to lead considered lives? Artistic lives? Poetic lives?

Much depends upon how much leisure was needed, and how bountiful the world. The dirt farmer struggling long hours to support his family was not going to spend much time in contemplation or creative leisure. Greece was almost a barren land, and slaves were needed for "culture." But what did the evil of slavery do to Greek thought about humankind?

Today, labor-saving devices give everyone free time. Ought they not to yield a different view of society in which there will be no trace of master-slave exchanges?

Myth

Someone at the London School of Economics asked me, "If mentalism is really so powerless, why has it held the field so long." I said that that was a question for the historian of ideas, and I mentioned Onians' *The Origins of European Thought* and Plato's "discovery" of nonphysical inner forces (I should also have mentioned Homer on μένος, ἄτε, etc.), and later physiologizing, such as the humors. I did not point to the difficulty in seeing the control exercised by the environment, especially selection by consequences, but I pointed to evolution. My questioner might have asked Darwin, "If natural selection is so powerful, why have people believed so long in the creation of species according to Genesis?" The myths that explain the origin of the universe and the existence of living things, especially man, have been extremely powerful and are not yet displaced by a scientific view. Mind is a myth, with all the power of myths.

Calculated Deception

The manipulation of behavior through trickery seems to have been very much in the air early in the nineteenth century. In Choderlos de Laclos's *Les Liaisons dangereuses*, le Vicomte, out to seduce la Presidente, discovers that he is being spied on by her servant—evidently to discover whether he is having an affair with someone else. He therefore stages a scene in which he plays the role of a compassionate benefactor. He learns that a family is to be dispossessed, arranges to come on the event "by accident," pays off the debt, and then, apparently overcome by the gratitude shown by members of the family, makes a further generous gift. He is pleased to note that all this is observed by *l'éspion*.

In Stendhal's *Lucien Leuwen*, Lucien is made to wait in an anteroom at his mistress's, who is out of town though he does not know it, and overhears the complete staging of a false *accouchement*, designed to give him the impression that his mistress has just had a baby. In Stendhal's *Lamiel*, the young girl kept against her will in the country simulates tuberculosis in order to be taken back to Paris where she can be attended by the doctors, and she does this by concealing a pad of cotton in her cheek, on which she has put a few drops of blood from a bird that has been killed. In a coughing spell she then spits blood. Someone has noted that Casanova has a good deal of this, and *Lui* in Diderot's *Le Neveu de Rameau* describes examples.

"Paternalism"

A writer to a London newspaper complains of the government's paternalism in demanding that a warning be printed on cigarette packages. He will continue to smoke in protest although he would prefer to stop. This is an example in miniature of the history of the struggle for freedom. Having escaped from violent, aversive control maintained for the good of the controller, one continues to escape from control for the good of the controllee.

A valid objection is that a *warning* is aversive. Can we dispense with all control under which people change their behavior to escape from aversive consequences? The "reasons" for stopping smoking (as for *stopping* almost any-thing) are punitive. A warning is a rule concerning aversive consequences; it clarifies the natural contingencies but does not add contrived punitive consequences, as would be done, for example, by making smoking illegal.

What are the positive consequences of not smoking?

1. Being free of a particular kind of control. Not suffering panic when one has forgotten one's cigarettes.

2. Better health now—no cough, say. Happier infer-ences about the condition of one's lungs now, rather than in a cancerous future.

3. Pleased friends. "Thank you for not smoking."

4. Money to spend for other things.

Why not a governmental campaign? "I bought my hi-fi with the money I saved during one year of not smoking."

Would anyone call that form of paternalism objec-tionable? The culture is simply transmitting to *everyone* the lessons some people have already learned.

Oratory

At Commencement last month, Ken Galbraith sat just behind me. During the Senior Oration he tapped me on the shoulder and said, "That sounds like *Beyond Freedom and Dignity*. They were better when they sounded like *The Affluent Society*."

I agreed.

The Sociologist in the Field

When we were in Russia (in May) fresh strawberries were in the market. The hotels served them, particularly at receptions or teas. Everyone in our party ate them except Bob Merton and me. Merton was professionally alert to the dangers of fresh fruit, and I remembered the farmer who used to clean cesspools and "backhouses" in Susquehanna, driving out of town with his horse-drawn odorous tank-cart and returning a few weeks later with the largest and most succulent strawberries we had ever seen.

At Tashkent we visited a collective farm. The manager took us to a room where we were seated around a long table for a discussion of the work of the collective. After a few minutes two men in colorful costumes entered carrying great plates of strawberries and dishes of finely ground sugar. The manager gleamed with pride as these were set before us. Merton and I looked at each other. He did not hesitate for an instant.

"We eat," he said quietly.

Local Powers

Gavin Maxwell (*Ring of Bright Water*) seems to accept the belief that the people in his area in northwest Scotland had second sight. Someone says that green water will flow over two young boys, and they grow up and are eventually drowned.

The local predilection was for recalling such remarks. Who would ordinarily remember? If there have apparently been examples, one looks for second meanings in all remarks and may remember some as omens.

It is the remembering that accounts for the numbers of cases, not the gift of second sight. A local culture builds up which makes further instances more and more likely to be noted.

The Artist's Influence

In "Creating the Creative Artist" I made the point that only Picasso can legitimately show the influence of earlier Picassos. We reject too strong a Picasso influence in another artist for many reasons, but especially because the Picassos he has seen are clear-cut external sources and hence reduce the extent to which his work is to be attributed to internal sources. But Picasso is the most likely of all to have been influenced by his earlier paintings. He has learned from them. He is very probably not above repeating his successes—not necessarily successes with the public but with himself—but that does not bother us. Earlier Picassos are *his*—the *expression* of the inner agent we strive so hard to defend—and hence no threat to his later worth as an artist. But we object to the artist who *merely* repeats his earlier triumphs.

Sunlight on Icicles

The sun is diffracted brilliantly through an icicle hanging down across our living room window. The icicle lets the sunlight through, bending the rays just enough to make it glitter, and in doing so avoids its own destruction. Not to glitter—to absorb the light and melt—would be to die.

A poet or a metaphorical prose-writer could make a lot of this. We are alive only to the extent that we affect others. We are dead as soon as we live for ourselves. "The only immortality," said Ernst Mach, "is the changes we work in the world." To live for oneself is to miss both immortality and a brief span of life here and now.

Sun-Phallus

A psychiatrist told me that one looks at the sun because the afterimage is shaped like a penis. I have tried looking, and it is. Does this explain what Jung attributed to a racial unconscious? According to *The New York Times*, a vision of an insane man was reported to him when, as it happened, he "was reading a book by a German philologist, Albrecht Dieterich, which dealt with a liturgy derived from a so-called magic papyrus in Greek. In the liturgy described in the papyrus, the initiate was asked to look at the sun, where he would see a tube hanging down—swinging to the right to produce the east wind, and then to the left to produce the west wind. The parallel between the vision of the insane man and the liturgy was striking because there was so little chance that the patient had ever had any acquaintance with the Greek papyrus."

Early Psychedelia

In Kalamata (in Greece) the church is rather beautiful. A mass was in progress when I entered. An almost suffocating odor of burning beeswax. The whole church filled with points of light—great chandeliers and hundreds of candles. (Some communicants brought their own candles—long beeswax tapers—and I had seen many with them in the street, but just inside the door an attendant in a booth was doing a big business.) Four saints, à la Mme. Toussaud, a great deal of silver work, including a large repoussé panel which newcomers kissed. A priest intoning a long passage from a book with gold covers, singing at two or three pitches with an occasional fall to a lower pitch, at which the people crossed themselves—right to left.

The priest stopped, closed the book, and marched toward the altar, and I left.

Sympathy

The Goncourts describe a scene: A young jay has been caught. Its wing is twisted to make it cry, while someone waits with gun cocked to shoot its mother when she answers its call of distress. The authors compare the human case of the beggar twisting his child's arm to make him cry to arouse the sympathy of passersby.

Was the old socialist principle of "increasing the misery" of the worker designed to get sympathetic action from the unmiserable, as well as aggressive action from the miserable?

The Appointed Rounds

During a heavy snow storm our postman, a man probably in his sixties, waded through the drifts in our front yard to deliver a few letters. Eve met him at the door and said, appreciatively, "Neither snow, nor rain, nor hail, nor gloom of night. . . . "

"Oh," he said, "is that the prediction?"

Man and Machine

Whether or not they succeed in making machines think like people, the computer specialists have already made people think like machines. We are all said to be *taking in* and *putting out information* and *processing* it as it passes through. Young thinkers are urged to think that way and are given machines to help them do so. Even so, the computerists are Johnnies-come-lately. It was the logicians who first discovered that by manipulating words and symbols as mechanical objects they could compose sentences and that by manipulating them in prescribed ways they could compose only true sentences. It was also the logicians, alas, who first insisted that sentences, true or false, were always composed that way.

Animism

Primitive man, rapidly whirling a rhomb, believed that its murmuring hum was the voice of a spirit. Why did he not think the noise he made by striking a stick against a tree or clapping stones together was a voice? Perhaps because the hum sounded like speech, sustained and resonant, but a more likely reason is that the cause of the sound was unknown. The uncaused is the product of an unseen creator, as apparently uncaused human behavior is attributed to an inner man.

Tim

(Tim, a boarding school student, has bummed a ride on a long-distance moving van and is not aware that he has been the object of an intensive three-day search. He turns up at his parents' apartment in New York and is on the phone with his parents at his school.)

Mother: Tim? Tim? How could you do this? Tim? Are you listening? How could you do this to me? Do you know what you have done? Tim? How could you do this? We thought you must have been killed or something. Tim—are you listening? Hold up the phone! How could you do this? We simply couldn't *believe* you could do this to us. Your aunt and sister are here. We couldn't believe it. . . Tim?

Father: Tim? Where are you now? Are you all right? Well, you stay in the apartment tonight. No, stay in the apartment. I'm all right. I want you to know how serious this all is, Tim. The police have been searching all over. It's been in the papers. You realize what you've done. It's been awfully hard on Mommy. Yes, she's all right. You can get in the apartment. Yes, take all the mail upstairs . . . Yes, yes . . . Do you want to say anything more to Mommy? (No.) You go upstairs and take a bath and get dressed and call me in half an hour. Will you do that? All right. I'll expect a call in half an hour.

The father pointing out the seriousness of what Tim has done. The mother *punishing* him with not a word of inquiry about his condition or any helpful advice. He has hurt Mommy and must suffer. And his mother is an internationally minded, public-spirited, ethically thoughtful person.

Historical Prediction

Though reputable historians (Trevelyan, E. H. Carr, and others) disclaim any special ability to predict the future from their knowledge of the past, and others, like Reinhold Niebuhr, make a virtue of unpredictability by claiming that it argues for human freedom, history is still taught as if it bore on the future, and political science bases many of its principles on historical analogies. Occasionally a historian is honored for his predictions—Keynes for the consequences of the Treaty of Versailles, for example. And two or three of these in a row endow a person with real authority. For many years I used the following parallel in lecturing to my Harvard undergraduates.

A man wishes to establish himself as an authority on the future (predicting the outcomes of horse races or elections, perhaps, or changes in the stock market). He chooses a given event susceptible to *yes* or *no* prediction (say, "The favorite will win the Kentucky Derby"). He sends postcards to 8,000 prospects, to half of whom he predicts *yes*, to the other half *no*. After the race has been run, he has 4,000 prospects to whom he has correctly predicted the outcome of one race. He divides them again, predicting *yes* to one half and *no* to the other half for another race. Further divisions yield 500 prospects to whom he has predicted four races correctly, with no failures. He then offers to predict any ten races for one hundred dollars (or any one race for, say, twenty-five dollars). If he divides his predictions among his customers, he will acquire a gradually reduced clientele, but one that will be willing to pay very large amounts for further predictions.

I then ask the class:

"How many historians are there?" and I never need to go further.

So far as I know I did not borrow this idea, although it has no doubt been considered by others. It is not far from the "tree" in my paper on "the repeated guessing of alternatives." Nevertheless, a television play on the theme appeared after I had given the lecture for several years, and a man was indicted for trying it in financial counseling. It is unlikely that I was responsible, but assuming that I was, should I have stopped giving the lecture? Not if, as another result, people are more skeptical of predictions of the future, even with the wisdom of history.

Possession

According to McNeill (*Rise of the West*), a Brahmin priest was expected to be able to recite at least one of the Vedas. The practice was, of course, essential during the several centuries when the Vedas had not yet been written down. It must have had a selective effect, since priests would have been recruited from those able or willing to memorize long passages. It must have helped in the dissemination of the work, since a memorized passage can be duplicated in many copies (the body is like a printing press, once the plates have been prepared).

But above all, the memorized Veda must have endowed the priest with the character of an oracle. The sacred word was *in* him. He spoke *for* the Author. Like a character in a play, he *was* for a time the Author.

Wit?

Driving home from Wellfleet on Cape Cod, we passed a shop coyly named "The Better Mousetrap." It was right on the sidewalk alongside the road, and I said, "There is no room for a path to the door."

Why did I say it? We tend to comment on unusual objects, and I may simply have cast about for something appropriate and found the intraverbal available. But I also presumably said it to amuse, and the intraverbal was useful for a different reason. My listeners were presumably inclined (no matter how faintly) to make the same remark, and that is an important condition in wit. (Now that I have examined it, of course, nothing remains to laugh at.)

(Sarah S. B. Yule gives this version: "If a man can write a better book, preach a better sermon, or make a better mouse trap than his neighbor, tho he build his house in the woods, the world will make a beaten path to his door." She ascribed it to Emerson but it is not found in his works.)

The Moonies

What is wrong with the religious cults which seem to appeal to so many young people? Why should we object to them?

They are said to induce people to feel exalted, dedicated, or committed. These are admirable feelings when they are the by-products of productive or creative work. When we approve such work, we indirectly strengthen the feelings, but it is the work we approve. To approve a religious cult because it generates similar feeling is to waste approval if we then strengthen only—

1. Complete inaction. Meditation and the empty mind.
2. Service to a no-good, like the Reverend Moon.
3. Trivial activities like selling flowers.

Bits of My Childhood

While working at my desk, completely absorbed, I saw bits of my childhood. I thought a recent letter asking me to write about my teacher, Mary Graves, might be the explanation. But then I noticed that Eve was moving about in the kitchen and was doing something that made a noise that reminded me of my father or mother starting the coal fire in our kitchen stove when I was a boy. Something about the pitch or timbre of the coal scuttle or shovel. A much more likely explanation.

The Themes of Music

I listen to Wagner while paying as little attention as possible to the words. I resent it when I understand the German. I am aware of the material. The whole ring-cycle is, as someone has put it, simply a cheap family quarrel. But I never read it in the music.

I have often felt that this was a defect in Wagner—that he could write such trash and take it seriously. There seemed something incongruous in the beauty of the music which he presumably wrote to express such themes.

Now I have another example that makes me feel better about Wagner: Berlioz's *Grande Messe des Morts*. I first heard it in the Ely Cathedral and shall never hear it, I suppose, without remembering that sublime background. But the words!

> *When the wicked are confounded,*
> *Doomed to flames of woe unbounded,*
> *Call me out of the deep pit.*
>
> *Deliver me from the lion's mouth,*
> *Lest hell swallow me,*
> *Lest I fall into darkness.*

Who would have guessed it, from the sublime music itself?

Civilizing Forces

Nashville is pretty far south. The secretaries at George Peabody College have strong southern accents. The town is "dry" but everybody drinks. The Gideon Bible in my room is in mint condition. We had a cocktail party in a room on the second floor in which the radiator was frilled by peeling paint. A concrete porch runs along the front of the hotel. In a row of stamped metal chairs the customers sit and watch and hear six lanes of traffic thrumming by. (No doubt I have not seen the attractive parts of town.)

I have just been trying to find a radio station on which the announcers do not speak in a heavy accent with folksy ungrammar. I found one but it was in Chicago. During the night I tried to find some music. All hillbilly songs. "You left me 'fore my ring had turned to green." One announcer said, "An' now let's have some more music. The best music in the worl'."

There is little danger that radio will have a leveling effect on the national character.

I Am

"I've got to. You see that, don't you? I'm just myself. I'm what I am. I can't help it."

Translation:

"I've got to . . . I'm just the product of my past history. The situation is what it is. I can't change it."

Shift from a responsible but driven I to the environment, and light appears: Maybe I can change the *situation*.

Prestige

In Massachusetts in the early seventeenth century, only certain people were allowed to be members of a church—or sometimes even to go to church. Those who belonged had excellent reasons for going. It was an honor. Going bestowed prestige, with many collateral advantages in trade and daily life. Even voting rights were reserved for church members until about 1690. But then unrestricted admission was advocated.

The same thing has happened in college education. At large state universities and even more so with open admission, as at CUNY, the distinction conferred by being a college student has almost vanished. Having a college education is nothing to study *for*.

Concealed Boasting

In accepting a resolution by Congress thanking him for his service as a military leader, Douglas MacArthur said essentially this: "I have received the highest award that can be conferred by the American government on one of its citizens. It was conferred by the most forward-looking lawmakers of the world, rendering an opinion of my services unswayed by emotion. These lawmakers spoke the voice of the people of America. I was a great general."

This version being objectionable, he spoke as follows: "I am grateful to receive this highest award conferred by the American government on one of its citizens. I am grateful to the American Congress; that body, famous as the most forward-looking lawmakers of the world, after a lapse of sufficient time to be swayed neither by sentiment nor emotion, has rendered an opinion of my services that I feel does me too much honor.

"I am grateful to the American men at arms who were my comrades in the vital exploits involved. A general is just as good or just as bad as the troops under his command make him. Mine were great! Something of the luster of this citation glows on each one's shoulders. . . .

"I am grateful to each member of the Congress who voted for this resolution, and thereby joined in its general purpose. This body wields the power of the nation, they speak the voice of the people. Accordingly my thanks are deeper than any words can convey."

Punitive Control of Verbal Behavior

Damaging statements about other people are punished legally as libel or slander. The Romans escaped by putting such statements in their wills, to be read after they were dead and hence out of reach.

The Emperor Augustus is said (Suetonius, *Lives of the Caesars*, Book II) to have vetoed a law designed to prevent this means of escape by suppressing freedom of speech in wills.

Books written to be published after one's death permit the writer to escape, but not the publisher. Letters to be sent after one's death are presumably successful.

Not a Product of Walden Two!

It does not take a good man to produce a good design. As Diderot pointed out in *Le Neveu de Rameau*, the noble plays of Racine were written by an ignoble man, and the same has been said of Wagner's *Tristan und Isolde*. Possibly Diderot was thinking of his contemporary, Rousseau, who could write a remarkable book about the education of an imaginary child, Emile, while committing his own children to an orphanage, or expound a social covenant while sponging on anyone who would put him up.

Euphemism

The bag in the pocket in front of me reads:

FOR MOTION DISCOMFORT

To be accurate it should read:

FOR VOMIT

Or at least:

FOR MOTION SICKNESS

Yet one can defend the euphemism. The bag and its label must be prominently displayed; otherwise the sick passenger will not find it. But the word *sick* will probably make a nauseated person sicker, and the word *vomit* almost certainly will.

Bottled Up

According to Ronald W. Clark, when Russell first saw Bernard Berenson in Florence, he did not get Berenson's feeling in the pit of the stomach when he looked at pictures. An "inner feeling for art and architecture" was to remain "still largely bottled up in Russell . . . for a decade and a half until Lady Ottoline Morrell released it." What was bottled up? And what did Ottoline *do?*

Clearly Russell was capable of enjoying art and architecture, as he proved by doing so, but the enjoyment came from his affair with Ottoline. With someone else it might have been music. When younger, it was mathematics.

No one is born with "inner feelings" for art and architecture (or for mathematics). Nothing "developed" except Russell's world.

Standards

"The trouble with the Boston Police," said my taxi driver, "is the standards are too low. They should raise salaries and raise standards. I took their exam in math a few years ago. A friend of mine wanted to be a cop. He was no good at math, and he didn't need it to be a cop, so he said to me, 'Why don't you take the exam, too? You can sit beside me and we'll work out signals.' It was multiple choice. If the first answer was right, I pulled my right ear. We had it all worked out. I went into it cold and I got 86. It was multiple choice—just a matter of common sense. My friend's on the force now. He don't need any math."

Promoting Recall

Driving with Deborah in Wales, I said that there was a Welsh town with a very long name. Then I tried to recall that very long word in Shakespeare. I went over related material. It was in Act 5, Scene 1 of *Love's Labours Lost;* E. Durning-Lawrence had "deciphered" it in his *Bacon Is Shakespeare;* and so on. But nothing much happened. Then I went over it again and got *-ous* as the probable ending but felt it was not right. Then I got *-atibus.* I started to say, "It ends with *-atibus,"* and instantly the whole word came in a rush—*honorificabilitudinatatibus.*

I heard an announcement on the radio that a radical piece of music by Prokofiev was to be played. The announcer mentioned Stravinsky, Diaghilev, and possibly one or two other people. The music was very strange. A few minutes later, as it was being played, I tried to recall *Prokofiev.* I kept getting *Petrouchka.* I started through the alphabet. With great force, letters would suggest Russian composers. My research centered on *p . . . r. . . . Respighi* invaded Russia momentarily, and *Raskolnikoff* became a composer. I kept thinking of an old book of Russian piano pieces, trying to visualize the pages of a polka by the man whose name I was looking for (but thinking of the Classical Symphony).

I turned on my radio and heard—*cycle, the* Moldau, *A Columbia recording.* I tried to recall the name of the composer. There was some delay in starting the music, and I had given up before it began, expecting to hear the name at the conclusion. But after a few bars, just as the main theme entered, I found myself saying quietly, easily, with no effort, *Smetana.*

On the train from New York to Philadelphia, I saw a tower with a crude electric bulb on the top. I took it to be a memorial to Edison. I remembered a place in New Jersey associated with him. I recalled it as *Nelo* but knew that was not right. I rejected *Tesla* as the name of another inventor. Then I saw a sign: *Menlo Park*. *Menlo* has all the letters of *Nelo*. It has only two of *Tesla* but the pattern is fairly similar.

Trying to recall the name of the Rubens Hotel, I got *Bruins*. Note that this is an anagram of *Rubins*, which is very close.

Interest

The young Stendhal was a compulsive evaluator of his effects on others, particularly women. At a party at his cousin's:

"When, six feet away from her, I made some trivial amusing comment to P. or to A., she would reply to it, *proof of sustained attention.*" (My italics.)

The distance is partly social. It would depend for its significance on how many were present, how big the room, how many were talking, etc. Yet Stendhal sees its significance in measuring the extent to which he interested his beautiful cousin.

Revolutionary

She came in to talk about my colloquium at Northeastern on the 20th. She had been in Washington for at least a week in various protest marches and had returned the day before to take part in the Boston Common demonstration. She had been gassed in Washington, when gas got into the ventilating system of the Georgetown University lounge. She had been chased to her room the night before by a tactical policeman with a dog. She knew Rennie Davis, and her (male-type) roommate was related to Abbie Hoffman.

We talked about pot smoking. The Boston Common evidently reeked of grass during the demonstration. She said she was *very* careful not to have any in her apartment or on her person.

"That is the first rule of the revolutionary," she said. "Don't get arrested for minor offenses."

Aversive Control

In England, because of the heavy fogs, most roads have "cat's eyes"—small metallic bosses down the middle of the road, in which there are reflectors which pick up and return the headlights of a car. These serve another useful function by generating an appreciably aversive rumble or bumping when a wheel passes over them. The result is an effective contingency under which a driver stays in a lane or gets in and out of a lane quickly. The effect is something like that of the rough-surfaced center lane once common on three-lane highways in America.

Tempo

In Venezuela I was to be picked up at 5:00 P.M. for my lecture. M——— and G——— arrived at 5:30, we got to the University just before 6, and the lecture started at 6:10. There were apologies. "Heavy traffic." The next day I was again to be picked up at 5. G——— arrived at 5:30. There had been rain; traffic was unusually heavy after a rain. We got to M———'s office at 6 but he was not there. I spoke with the translator, but no one knew where M——— was. At 6:15 he came in. I stood up but he gestured to me to sit down, and only a minute or two later did we leave for the auditorium. The elevator was going up rather than down but we got in. It was very slow. We got to the hall at 6:20 and I began at 6:30. The translator had been promised that she could leave precisely at 7:30 so I timed my lecture accordingly.

The next morning I was to speak to the Psychology Faculty. There were conflicting rumors. Was the meeting to be at 9 or 10? I was to be picked up at 8. M——— came at 8:30. We assembled in his office—but "assembled" is scarcely the word. The staff trickled in. There was a search for an empty classroom. We went to one, arranged a circle of chairs, which was repeatedly enlarged, with much scraping, as each new member came in. When we were nearly ready to start, M——— went out and was gone several minutes.

We were to be picked up at 5:30 for dinner that night. Six of us waited in the lobby for G———. He arrived punctually at 6 just as we were starting to leave without him. "Was I late? You did say six, didn't you? I was so proud of being right on time."

Apparently no one expects anything else. Hours are agreed upon very casually, and not carefully noted, and no plans are laid to allow for traffic problems. People sit and wait as if this were part of life.

As indeed it is, in Venezuela.

Do I really envy them? What is it like not to be controlled by clocks and calendars? I think I like my own tempo.

Against the Grain

I was playing with Lisa when she was about three, and when I held something she wanted away from her, she bit my hand. It was such a surprising deviation from her general warmth and gentleness that Eve was startled. "She bit you!" But I was not surprised; I had handled too many animals. Obviously there is still a modicum of "viciousness" in the human species.

Julie said yesterday that Lisa is at the moment very mean to Shane, her closest friend. Julie is doing the right thing, reinforcing being nice to Shane rather than punishing being mean. How else does one civil-ize a child?

Breakdown

It is said that crime increases when "the family breaks down." In Florida, blacks are said to commit more crimes than Cubans because the Cubans are more "family-oriented." The Chinese family on the West Coast is "breaking down" and hence more Chinese commit crimes.

What seems to break down in such cases is face-to-face control, which must then be replaced by the institutional control of a police force.

Letter Writing

In *Verbal Behavior* I assumed a delay of at least a day or two in the receipt of a letter, but this was not always the case. In eighteenth- and nineteenth-century London, messages were carried across the city rapidly. A man might write a long letter which would be read within the hour and answered as quickly. This must have meant a much more powerful reinforcement and a greater likelihood of writing letters.

"Culture Shock"

The expression suggests an environmental action, but the facts seem to be these: (1) A repertoire acquired in one culture is seriously inadequate in another. (2) The extinction which is then inevitable generates depression or aggression or both. "Shock" is not a very appropriate metaphor for either event. Like "selection pressure," it suggests an active, rather than a selective, cause. There are also expressions in medicine which seem to convert a process into a blow, as in a "heart attack" or a "stroke."

Sacrifice

The libation, the burnt offering, the sacrifice of the first-born—all have, evidently, a parallel in love. Aldous Huxley (*Antic Hay*, p. 269) has Mr. Mercaptan refer as follows to the Council of Carthage: "which, in 398, demanded of the faithful that they should be continent on their wedding night. It was the Lord's right—the *droit* of a heavenly Seigneur." *Jus primae noctis.*

What is the explanation? Appeasement of a possibly jealous God? Returning thanks in kind? Fear of enjoying a possibly punishable act? The happy man punishing himself in order to feel less guilty about his happiness? Is there a clue in the actual *Droit de Seigneur*, according to which a feudal Lord had the right to enjoy the bride of a serf before her husband—as the tribute paid by the serf in grain or cattle may explain a burnt offering?

Precognition

This morning, walking down Brattle Street, I passed the home of a friend who has installed a burglar alarm, and I wondered how often it went off by accident and what it sounded like. As I walked along, I began to hear what I thought was a police car, but as it got louder, I realized that it was a burglar alarm in a house across the street.

It would be easy to think that I had "precognized" it, but a much more plausible explanation is that I heard the alarm before I was aware of hearing it.

The Wrong Word Written I

Writing on *The Technology of Teaching* (while listening to a Chopin nocturne), I substituted *broadly determined* for *broadly interpreted*. The second syllable, *ter*, is accented in both, and there is also a great overlap in letters, including two groups (*in* and *ed*) in addition to *ter*. Moreover, *interpreted* spelled backwards gets as far as *deter* before breaking down as a palindrome.

In a letter to Deborah, I started to write *If the negative isn't lost*, but I wrote *legacy* instead of *negative*. Is *l* in *lost* relevant?

In a note, I wrote *teaching* instead of *cheating*. Some relevant facts: (1) Cheating is commonly punished, and the word may be aversive. (2) I have been writing *teaching* scores of times every day for many years. (3) One word is an anagram of the other.

Writing about Utopian visions based on physical technology, I wrote: *Technocracy. Waste new sources of power*. I meant *vast* not *waste*. I corrected it only as far as *vaste*. I may well have been calling it all a waste. In *Seven Types of Ambiguity* William Empson analyzes Shakespeare's *The dead waste and middle of the night*, noting that *waste* may be *waist* (as of an hourglass) or *vast*.

I was writing about ethics and listed four relevant words: *right, wrong, good,* and *bad*. But I wrote *wright*. Was it a blend of *right* and *wrong*? If so, the reasons were probably formal rather than thematic.

Immortality

At a seminar yesterday a Jesuit brought up the question of natural aversive events which would persist as a problem even if aversive control could be eliminated. What would I do about pain?

I went over techniques of teaching people to "take" aversive stimuli, mentioned the reality of painless childbirth, hypnotic analgesia, etc. He then got on to death and the loss of loved ones. I mentioned cultures in which death is accepted calmly, drew a comparison between a recent Irish Catholic funeral in my neighborhood and the meeting of the friends of Percy Bridgman, and said that, so far as I could see, the consolations of religion scarcely made up for the fear of death generated by "scaring hell out of people."

I had already brought up the matter of personal survival after death as foreshadowing the notion of survival as a value and had pointed out that the Jews got along without the idea of immortality. After class, the Jesuit told me that he could never understand the Jewish prophets. How could they have existed, as they appear to have done, without believing in an afterlife? He seemed genuinely puzzled.

Charity

The great examples of successful American businessmen were not generous. The Carnegie, Rockefeller, and Ford Foundations were simply solutions to the problem of what to do with a great deal of money when one must give up control. Carnegie confirmed the stereotype of the stingy Scot, Rockefeller was famous for giving dimes as tips, and Ford was openly against charity. Were they insensitive to gratitude or contemptuous of it as a means of getting favors? Or did they see that the contingencies in charity are faulty? If "to each according to his need" is defective, why not "to none according his need"?

Verbal Puzzle

In writing *fearing*, I wrote *feal* and immediately thought of the movie I saw yesterday (*The Sand Pebbles*) in which a young Chinese had trouble saying *r*, coming up with *l*. Had the movie confused *me*, or was the slip quite unrelated until I made it, whereupon it reminded me of the episode in the movie?

Cultural Design

Sometimes a five-year-old will have more trouble learning a discrimination than a pigeon. I have half-facetiously put it this way: Children have learned one thing—what they want to do (tend to do) is probably wrong. Therefore, under favorable contingencies, they regard what they tend to do as dangerous and do something else instead.

Tired Verbal Behavior

When I am verbally fatigued, I not only get wrong words or gross malaprops, I get distortions. Just now, while talking to myself covertly, I said *poining down* and struggled for a moment to get it straight as *pointing out*, where the *d* in *down* seems to have picked up the *t* omitted from *pointing*.

A typographical error?

The Rewards of Barbering

La Flamme's barber shop is trying to outlast the current era of long and unkempt hair. It is almost always empty and only two, or at most three, barbers stand by its eight chairs. My barber of 23 years, Freddie, is still there. His family is barely surviving the bad times.

This morning there was no customer in the shop. I told Freddie I wanted just a trim, because I was to be on Dick Cavett's television show next week. His manner changed completely. Instead of the usual perfunctory job, he began to act like an artist. He would stand off to judge an effect, move in to snip a small lock, stand back again. This was life. There was some point to his job. Someone would notice.

Preprandial Principle

A principle of self-control: In looking at a menu, ask not what will taste good but what will feel good an hour or so from now. (Vary the time to suit the case.)

I Told You So

A plane is announced by number.

Wife: "Is that our plane?"

Husband: "I don't know. It may be."

Wife: "I *asked* you to find out what number it was."

They were glaring at each other in what seemed like habitual bad temper.

Why is that kind of remark punishing? Because it establishes intellectual superiority? "If you had only listened to me."

Poltergeist

A skeptic might make a convincing point in this way: In giving a lecture on animistic beliefs, openly contemptuous of psychic phenomena, he could say, "Only a fool would believe that there are disembodied spirits in this room— poltergeists which blow down your neck, knock things about—" Whereupon a small slide projector standing some distance away on the lecture table flips over on its side. He stands for a long time silent, evidently stunned and embarrassed.

He then puts the projector back in place and shows how he can tip it over at will by operating a radio switch in his pocket. He asks members of the audience to note whether they had been disturbed by the possibility of an unseen force, whether they would have agreed that a poltergeist had acted, or whether they had immediately suspected a trick.

Blame

To blame one may seem to be to assign a fault to someone as a trait or to assign responsibility as a possession. The word *blame* comes originally from "blaspheme," which was to utter impious words—that is, to say something opposed to religion. It was in constant use and was reduced to *blame*, and it came to mean "to find fault with," as if the fault were in the person, but it also meant "to censure," in the sense of the opposite of praise, or to reprove or chide or scold. These were all verbal punishments or negative reinforcers from which people could escape; they could escape censure or blame by behaving in acceptable ways. Something more was involved when one accused a man of fault *for* a disaster or responsibility *for* some unfortunate situation. This was to connect him with a punishment which was already in existence, so that he would be punished by something which had already happened but which up until that point had not been connected with his behavior. Of course, it also meant that others suffered and were therefore in a position to punish him justly for having caused them to suffer. A good example of a tendency to act toward people as if things were wrong with *them* when it is simply their behavior that is offensive, action then being designed to change that behavior to prevent its recurrence.

In the long run, blaming a person or a nation gets nowhere; changing the situation is much more effective.

One can't, indeed, blame a people—say the Germans for the Second World War—after they are dead, and it doesn't seem fair to blame Germans now alive who were not alive when the war was started. What one does instead is to look at the behavior (but not the behavior of any person) and then at the conditions which generated the behavior, and if those conditions still survive, they can be attacked. You can blame German *Kultur* or you can undertake to change and prevent a recurrence in some other way.

In Behavioral Terms

" . . . Valery insists that Europe's position at the beginning of the twentieth century was due to the high quality of her population, which he says is marked by 'a driving thirst, an ardent and disinterested curiosity, a happy mixture of imagination and rigorous logic, a certain unpessimistic skepticism, and unresigned mysticism.' " These all need translation into behavioral terms. The driving thirst is not for alcohol or water, of course, but for knowledge—as in exploration, science, or the study of the past. Under what conditions were experimenting, doing research, and studying old texts reinforced? The same conditions explain an ardent and disinterested curiosity—disinterested in the sense that the reinforcers were not such things as food, sex, or gains in political power. Under what conditions were creative behavior and imaginative work in art, science, and literature reinforced, and were those conditions compatible with the disciplined training which led to rigorous logical manipulation? Indeed, why did logic as a discipline arise? What were the gains which led people to begin to think syllogistically, for example? "Skepticism" seems to refer to a relative freedom from verbal authority, from rules laid down by others. It was neither pessimistic nor optimistic except as people were free to respond in ways formerly proscribed by rules or unable to abide by rules which promised benefits. Unresigned mysticism could be similar. The consequences of the behavior of the mystic were certainly hard to specify, but the perpetuation of behavior under conditions in which many other people stopped behaving testify to the strength of the reinforcers, whatever they were. This is an example of the kind of writing which seems rich and full of allusion as it stands but misleading, confusing, and obscurantistic when translated into behavioral terms.

Wistfully

I was later than usual as I walked to work this morning, and as I approached Memorial Hall I looked up for the missing clock. The literary word for the manner in which I looked is, I think, "wistfully." I knew I should not find the clock, for the tower burned two years ago, but I looked for it nevertheless. My behavior was emitted, not as humor, but in a quiet submission to ancient controlling stimuli. It was a little like obeying someone who is now too weak to enforce commands, out of affection or a wish not to hurt. I did not mind the inevitable lack of accustomed reinforcement. It was not an emotional by-product of extinction, like anger or depression.

The *Oxford English Dictionary* gives as a second meaning of *wistfully*: "with expectant or yearning eagerness; with mournful expectancy or longing." It will be a long long time before a word like that is defined in terms of contingencies of reinforcement!

Skeat regards *wistful* as mainly a replacement of *wishful*, but presumably where wishing is for the unattainable. Hence a touch of sorrow, which may be simply a mild version of the depression which follows extinction—the sorrow of what might have been or of the loss of what once was.

The Chances

Adam Smith, 1776 (quoted in *Business Week*, August 4,1975): "The overweening conceit which the greater part of men have of their own abilities is an ancient evil. . . . That the chance of gain is materially overvalued, we may learn from the universal success of lotteries."

But do men gamble because they overvalue the chance of gain? Not unless pigeons do, too. The variable-ratio schedule, properly programmed, generates "behavior with negative utility." But not because anyone is calculating the chances of gain. Anyone who calculated (as by sampling a number of runs or examining the sample space) would not bet.

Chance, like reason, is a term belonging to rules and other descriptions of contingencies. Useful when rules can be manipulated to generate new rules *worth following*—i.e., having reinforcing consequences when followed. But the behavior of the gambler is either not calculated or calculated from erroneous rules, such as the maturity of the chances.

Shall I Ever Learn?

Yesterday Lisa, almost ten, was opening a new jar of mixed nuts. The metal cap was sealed with a tight plastic tape. She got a knife and began to pry one edge of the tape free of the glass on top. I was on the point of saying, "Here, let me help you," but I caught myself in time and she got the top off— and would no doubt do so even more effectively in the future because I stayed out of it.

Suppose now she had been frustrated, getting mad at the top, jabbing it ineffectively with the knife, muttering or swearing. Should I then have helped?

Definitely not! I should then have been teaching Lisa to display anger, to swear, and eventually to exaggerate these behaviors because someone then helps.

When *does* one help a child?

Pretty obviously: when the child *needs* help and before she displays behavior which, when reinforced by help from others, displaces effective behavior which might otherwise begin to be conditioned.

Don't give impossible assignments. If, by accident, one has been encountered, let any frustrated behavior extinguish before taking over and giving help.

Brave New World

A reporter asked about Huxley's book after I had mentioned *1984* and *Walden Two*. Why did I not mention it? Why had the book dropped out of sight? Did it not explore behavioral processes in building a "better world" with nonpunitive means?

I said I thought the difference between *Brave New World* and *Walden Two*, aside from the fact that the former is a satire, was the difference between a concern for feelings and a concern for action. Huxley was fascinated by feelings. The art form in *Brave New World* was not the "talkies" but "feelies." People turned to emotional surrogates. The conditioning of new positive reinforcers was the closest the book came to the use of behavioral processes.

Perhaps the current lack of interest is explained by the fact that people who are devoted to feelings avoid hearing feelings ridiculed.

Cheating the Gallows

A man who has been convicted of, say, wartime spying is dying of cancer and therefore "escapes the death penalty." Capital punishment is not death, it is death before one's time as the result of official action. But who or what is being cheated? A complete bankrupt cannot be fined. A dead man cannot be jailed, flogged, or ostracized. Society cannot, in these cases, "mete out punishment." It cannot square accounts and balance injury with injury. Hence, it cannot set up and enforce contingencies which may have an effect on others. It is being cheated in two senses: it cannot take revenge, and it cannot set an example to possible offenders. Is this why the spy is given medical treatment to prolong a life that is then to be taken, or a prisoner who attempts suicide revived so that he or she can be hanged?

A Face

I turned on Channel 2 last night and saw a boy looking toward the camera, wide-eyed. Instantly I knew the film was Flaherty's documentary about drilling an oil well in bayou country. I saw the movie at least 33 years ago and have not seen it since. It is no doubt relevant that I have seen other documentaries of Flaherty's (*Nanook of the North* and *Man of Aran*) on Channel 2 and that the quality suggested an old film. But my response was still remarkable, it seems to me. Was it the boy? There was no resemblance to anyone I know, so far as I can recall. The wonderment and curiosity? Perhaps. The boy was a good "natural" actor, and the point of the film was to show how a complex operation looked to an inexperienced boy. Still—one expression on a face—?

Care

The peasant in Europe in the Middle Ages, to some degree a slave, living a hard and unrewarding life, is said to have had a conception of Christ as a man lavishing care on humanity.

The more miserable one's estate, the more important noncontingent goods. It was easy to believe in a grace-giving God. As it was easy to *be* a Lord or Lady Bountiful.

Canned Music

When I once referred to a phonograph, Percy Saunders cut me short by saying, "I don't like canned music." His son, now called Blake, was at the time getting music on a crystal radio set, but it was not taken seriously as music. The electronics which were to follow improved the canning process, and it is now possible to hear music better in a recording than from most seats in a concert hall.

Appeasement

When we were on the train from London to Exeter, two young girls, perhaps four and two, came into our compartment with their parents. For half an hour they were beautifully behaved. Then the younger tried to get a comic book away from her sister. They fought and the younger girl cried. The parents separated them and immediately got out a bag of sweets. "To keep them quiet?" Possibly, but in any case to reinforce fighting and crying.

Protest

Bertrand Russell confined himself almost exclusively to protest as a form of social action. He made few efforts to argue with leaders. He protested the Great War when he was a young man, and nuclear war when he was old. Marching, sitting down in Trafalgar Square (with an air pillow concealed in his trousers), storming 10 Downing Street or an embassy or two, advising others to protest—it seemed to be the only social measure in which he really believed. It has democratic sanctions whenever something close to a majority can be marshalled, but Russell was always a noisy minority.

Protest, like voting, is a selective measure in the evolution of cultural practices. The initiation of practices Russell shunned. His aristocratic arrogance was relevant. Not Russell but his culture produced the social forms he tried to perpetuate. He was not a policy maker, he was a policy evaluator. He produced no mutations, he played only some part in their adaptive selection. That may also have been true of his role as a philosopher. A Wittgenstein produced novel forms. Russell supported or attacked them.

Does protest ever lead to mutations?

Sacrificial Pleasures

A newspaper article tells housewives that Friday meals may offer more to the gourmet than any other meal of the week. During Lent, articles and advertisements often explain how one may follow the letter of the law (regardless of the spirit) while enjoying many sorts of tasty dishes. Suffering is dead. Suffering *for* something has gone the way of suffering *because* of something. To the cultural practices which protect us from the hunger of poverty or famine we now add others with which we avoid the hunger of self-denial. It is probably relevant that sacrificial hunger was easier to sustain when hunger was common and people were therefore practiced in sustaining it.

Community

Seeing a small community in Amalfi again makes clear what is lacking in cities and suburbs; a *sense* of community is the cliché, but what is really lacking needs analysis.

People who have known each other fairly well over a long period of time are all a sort of common police force, censuring, commending, keeping in line. The Italians are very free in objecting to each other's conduct. (On the bus, as we started, a window had been left open and a breeze came in. Instantly there was a cry and the window was closed.) But no hard feelings, at least for long. I feel free to walk dark streets at night. A mugging would stir up the whole town (except for certain sections which may exist outside the community proper).

This general policing has its price—as all the novels about small towns show. Conformity is costly. The married women in Amalfi, all in black after a certain age, lead narrow lives, I am sure. The young girls probably divide into two parties, the good and the bad, at an early age. The good can look forward to marriage or the nunnery, with black clothing in both cases. The men stand around in groups, work in small teams, gesturing and talking.

How many Amalfians would change their lives to live in Rome? Or Manhattan? A great many, I should guess. What attracts them? Freedom from community control? The bright lights? (After all, a lot of people are constantly at work to make at least parts of cities "attractive.")

Teaching Concepts

What children are said to do "mentally" in, say, matching areas, shapes, or 3-D objects, begins as what they do "physically." The real difference is twofold: (1) in scale of action and (2) in scale of observable result. For example, to match ▨ with ▨ as its reverse and not with ▨ one would, if dealing with physical objects, turn the flag over to see where the hole turns up. A program could *use* physical objects at the beginning or it could proceed to induce "mental" manipulation via easy steps in pictured sequences.

Analysis of the covert operation could follow what happens in the overt case. How do children visually compare two curvatures such as) and ⊃ ? Do they "bend one" or "run fingers over an edge"? How do they match △ with △ and not with △ ? Do they "move the dot around"?

The Krutch-Barzun Entente

At the May meeting of the American Academy of Arts and Sciences Jacques Barzun will present the Emerson Thoreau Medal to Joseph Wood Krutch, and Krutch will then give an address. Will this be an occasion for his annual attack on me? When I met Barzun recently, his opening comment was: "Oh, you and I are always at the opposite extremes on any issue." Krutch is out at Barzun's end.

How can anyone continue to defend the Emerson-Thoreau position on self-reliance, self-sufficiency, self-determination, in the world today? Where did that position have any effect? Not in Communist countries, Barzun and Krutch would agree. But in Africa? Latin America? Italy or other European Catholic countries? Great Britain and the Welfare State? The United States with its military-industrial complex?

Strange to say, I am an Emersonian, a Thoreauvian. I want what they wanted. But I want it as part of a successful conception of human behavior. Maybe *Walden Two* was an apter title than I knew.

Precious Prose

I think it was not until the late fifties that I was able to throw away carefully written pages of a manuscript. Up to that time I had viewed each page as an achievement to be preserved and I often struggled to work a section into a text even though it did not follow what preceded it or tended to repeat or paraphrase another passage.

I have only recently seen writing as a slow process of shaping, so that a page I compose at one time is merely a version of something I shall write in a different way later. My only problem is to decide between two versions.

Unconscious Humor

In lecturing to my class in Natural Sciences 114 I used the principle of respondent conditioning to explain the fact that women's styles often move up from the demimonde. Carmen, in Prosper Merimée's story, wears red heels and smokes in public. These stimuli, paired with seductive wiles and, for Don Jose, sexual favors, acquire the power to attract (as conditioned stimuli) and are adopted for this reason by "good" women. I noted that Brigitte Bardot's piled-up hair, paired with particularly attractive nudity, was soon adopted by non-nude women. I then said, "When this happens on a *broad* scale . . . " and the class laughed before I saw the other significance of *broad.*

When "good" girls take over the style, the effect extinguishes. Something of the sort may explain the waxing and waning of styles.

Style

I have always been bothered by the fact that I have never dressed well. And I have just discovered why. Those who dress well never wear their clothing out. Yesterday I bought three pairs of shoes. (I can't get shoes in Harvard Square because my feet are size 7 and the stores seldom carry it.) I shall now throw away two or three pairs which are still good. I am planning to buy some shirts in the mode. I have not worn out my present supply, which is embarrassingly dated, as I discovered last week at my management clinic.

Of course the reason is that styles are changed precisely to induce people to throw good clothes away. Or to give them away and in doing so sharpen a class distinction. The lower classes are out of style. Perhaps that is why, recently, they have innovated a style of their own.

Avoiding Metaphors

Someone has pointed out that I do not use many metaphors. I think that may well be due to the fact that I know that metaphors may say something about the user, as Caroline Spurgeon made clear.

It is not that I mind having my personal history revealed (*Particulars* is revealing enough), it is the likelihood that my metaphors will not be helpful to people who are not like me. A metaphor showing my interest in kite-flying or building things would have a limited coverage. Metaphors about music, art, weather, etc., are usually worn out. Metaphors describe the author, and are useful only if the author is relevant to the argument.

I do accept metaphor as possibly the only good way of "describing" feelings. One has only to say "I felt as if I were . . . " and then describe a situation more likely to arouse a particular response in a listener or reader. But I am usually saying other things.

Psychology

A colleague asked me more than once where I thought psychology was going. Did I not think we should emerge as a separate discipline—where "we" meant operant people?

I have been coming close to that view. I go through programs of meetings to see what psychologists are doing. What I find is:

a. A good deal of common (but not necessarily good) sense about race, urban environments, the problems of the young, etc., but no science adduced.

b. Applied work (education, therapy, child psychology, penology, etc.). The operant formulation is emerging there and might take over.

c. Cognitive psychology. Storage of memories, search time, etc.—all on the wrong track.

d. Mathematical models. No better than the data mathematized—and often worse, sustained by a spurious prestige.

e. Mental measurement and factor analyses. But what do you do with factors after you get them?

Verbal Cost

A well-known scientist with the Bell Telephone Company has called me long-distance twice. The first call lasted more than one hour. The other has already lasted 20 minutes and is still going on as I write this note. He calls people all over the country and reads things he has written asking for comments. He talks and talks. *And all because he doesn't pay telephone charges.*

How would he *think* if he were:

1. thinking alone,

2. talking with another person or with a small group, or

3. writing what he says and looking at what he has written?

White Noise

If this is an optimal echoic stimulus—formally neutral yet insistent—it may help to explain the vogue of nature. The soughing of the wind may bring verbal responses to the surface at a time when nature is a conspicuous controlling stimulus. Hence, one talks about nature more than about other things to which one is equally exposed. It may explain some "voices"—nature speaks to us, as God spoke to Joan of Arc—but we say so only if the additional source of strength is external. But is not any strong behavior likely to be attributed to an outside or usurping spirit?

Private Stimuli

In *About Behaviorism* and elsewhere I have suggested that terms acquired from a verbal community which has access only to a person's behavior come to be used by that person under the control of associated private stimuli. Pain that begins as, for example, punishment becomes attached to the private stimuli generated. A sharp pain is the product of a sharp object, and so on.

Here are terms, often felt to pose a special problem for a behavioral analysis, which can be explained in the same way: *to wish for, to need, to long for, to yearn for, to envy, to begrudge, to scorn, to be fond of, to grieve for, to be sad, to mourn.* Are these not states of mind or feelings rather than forms of behavior? The histories of the terms to be found in the *Oxford English Dictionary* give us the answers. Each term was first used with respect to some public act or set of circumstances; it eventually came under the control of associated private stimuli. Here are some rough paraphrases.

To wish began as *to strive for* and is related to *to win.*

To need first meant *to be under aversive conditions* from which one could escape only by specific action. *To be under an obligation* was an example.

To long for began as a reference to the *length of time* one remained in a state such as a state of need. Longing sometimes suggested restlessness—aimless behavior which appeared when no effective behavior was available.

To yearn for meant *to ask for* or *to express a desire.*

To envy was *to emulate* or *to try to equal.*

To grudge or *begrudge* was *to grumble.*

To scorn was *to humiliate*, as by depriving of horns.

To be fond of was *to fondle.*

To grieve was *to bear a heavy burden.*

To be sad was *to be sated.*

To mourn was *to recall* or *remember sadly.*

In each case the term referred to a particular kind of occasion or to the behavior appropriate to it, but it came under the control of private effects which could not be observed by the verbal community. A person who learned to say "I yearn for my friend" in the sense of "I call for or ask for my friend" came to use the term to describe cognate bodily conditions when the occasion generated no conspicuous behavior. The mistake is to suppose that the condition felt may be the putative cause of any behavior which eventually appears, rather than a collateral product of the occasion which may eventually have a more conspicuous behavioral effect.

Symbolism

In *La Dame aux camélias*, Dumas *fils* says of his heroine: "Twenty-five days of the month the camelias she wore were white, and for five days they were red; no one knew the reason for this change of color, which I simply report without being able to explain it and which those who frequented the theatres where she most often went as well as her friends have also noticed." Later Marguerite agrees to become Armand's mistress, but not at once. When pressed, she takes a red camelia from a bouquet and offers it to Armand, saying in effect, "One cannot always carry out the terms of a treaty the moment it is signed." It is obvious that the red camelia meant that she was menstruating. In saying that no one knew the secret, does the author mean that she was a *femme sage?*

Allusions

Lying awake in the Plantation Inn, I suddenly realized that I could not hear the surf below our balcony.

"The sea is calm tonight," I said.

"What is that?" said Eve. "Matthew Arnold?"

"Yes," I said, " 'on the French coast a light gleams and is gone.' And you and I are the last generation to enjoy literary allusions. They demand too much *irrelevant* study."

Phony Philosophe

At a convention of the American Psychological Association, J. Robert Kantor, 80, was to speak on "Scientific Psychology and Specious Philosophy." I doubted very much whether he would make it, and, indeed, it turned out that he was in a hospital in Chicago. A former student, Mountjoy, read his paper, which was as always an attack on "spooks," with some amusing touches. When he began, there were perhaps 100 people in a room holding 600. It was not a bad audience for such a topic, and I thought Robert would have been pleased. But before the hour was half over people began to trickle in. Latecomers, I assumed. But the trickle built up into a flood. I borrowed a program and discovered that Eric Hoffer was to speak the next hour. People were coming early to get seats. I left before Mountjoy finished, glad that Robert had not been there to be insulted by that show of interest in specious philosophy.

Using One's Science

I have, I think, made good use of my analysis of behavior in managing my own life, particularly my own verbal behavior. Can the psychoanalysts and the cognitive and humanistic psychologists say as much? Did Freud ever report the use of his theory to influence his own thinking? Are cognitive psychologists particularly knowledgeable about knowledge? Are humanistic psychologists more effective in helping other people because of their theories?

Causes

The energetic activity due to an evolved genetic endowment and a personal history suggests a driving *force*. Schopenhauer's Will: "the innermost principle, metaphysical yet exorbitantly physical in its effect . . . the manifestation of one blind impulse, the impulse to exist and to secure life's continued existence through procreation. . . . " Or Carlyle's Force: "Force, force, everywhere force, and we ourselves a mysterious force in the center of that."

What chance has selection as a causal mode against such rhetoric? Even the geneticists slip when they speak of "selection *pressure.* "

The Function of a Symbol

In a baker's shop in Herculaneum there is a bas relief showing a penis in three stages of erection:

It is easy to note the similarity between tumescence and the rising of bread, before or during baking. (The loaves that survive, carbonized, are pie-shaped and divided radially, so that a resemblance to a penis—à la French bread or bread sticks—is unlikely.) But did the bas relief serve any function? A fertility symbol? What does that mean? Was it supposed that the presence of the symbol made the rising of bread more likely?

Contrast

For about ten years I have used a reel-type lawn mower, power-driven. Recently I bought a rotary mower and sold the old one to a friend. After about a month, the new one developed trouble, and I borrowed the old one for a day. I scarcely recognized it. The new one (rotary) is low and long; the old one (reel), higher and of moderate length. Seeing it again, I had the impression that it had been squeezed fore-and-aft. It was grotesquely stubby.

Did the new mower at first seem long? Possibly, but that would not have been as surprising as a change in what should have been familiar.

In a different modality, I have noticed the muffled quality of music after removing a hearing aid, although I had not been aware of that quality before putting the hearing aid on.

Universality

The less precise my verbal behavior, the more easily my listeners read something into it. Last night at the Academy of Arts and Sciences, I gave a few hurried excerpts from a paper to be published in *Daedalus*. A friend later told me he liked what I said but paraphrased it in terms I could not understand. Another friend commented at length with sentences which did not seem to bear any conceivable connection with my own. Is universality anything more than ambiguity?

Expectancy

A colleague said he couldn't understand my neglect of the concept of expectancy. Another colleague tried to be helpful by paraphrasing my supposed reaction: "It's mentalistic." I said: "Not at all. It's not a question of dimensions or nature. If you explain behavior in terms of expectancy, then in turn you must explain the expectancy, and to do that you must turn to a history of reinforcement. I prefer to go straight to the history."

The middle term does not simplify matters. Instead, it almost always misrepresents the relation between the end terms. It becomes a stopping point—a way station from which the traveler does not move on—either from cause *forward* toward effect ("The evidence leads one to expect . . . "—though the result of the expectation is not pursued) or from effect *backwards* toward cause ("I acted thus because I expected . . . "—though the sources of the expectation are not examined).

What Does Great Literature Do?

Great works of literature "add to the present value and dignity of our minds"—Santayana, quoted in *Daedalus*, Winter 1974, p. 140. But what do they really do?

For "minds" read "behavior." "After reading great works of literature we act with greater dignity and with respect to more noble consequences." Buy why or how? Because great works provide an imitative model? By suggesting action to be taken? By making it possible to form discriminations among nearly identical occasions (e.g., as in a moral dilemma)? Yes, but probably much more. We shall never know so long as we continue to talk about the value and dignity of minds.

The Selection of Synonyms I

From a review of a TV program:

"Lamp at Midnight," to put it plainly, had a touch of greatness, catching a moment of irreconcilable conflict in Catholic Church history with a burning eloquence worthy of the vast and timeless issues at stake.

Apparently this appearance of *burning. . . at stake* was quite unconscious. (If not, it is a rather macabre bit of humor.)

". . . So here we have in Freud, himself, a pessimist on the matter, an excellent case for the persistence of creativity after middle life into old age.

"Before passing on, it is noteworthy that Freud was, as aforesaid, deeply troubled by death. . . ."

Before passing on does not mean *before dying*, it means *before turning to other things.*

J. K. Galbraith in *Ambassador's Journal:* "a dog once bit me on the leg adjacent to the left testicle. . . ." Two sentences later: "They are old friends but I listened with all proper patience to the State Department view of their crotchets." Is the *crotch* of *crotchets* thematically determined by *leg adjacent to testicle?*

I had been writing about an experiment by a student, Larry Fain. A few moments later I started to make a note about simulating affection as a reinforcer. I could not get the word *simulate* and found myself writing *feign*. I examined the word intensively as I wrote it and then saw that it was a homophone of *Fain*.

After telling Deborah about my contretemps with Donald MacKay on the William Buckley show, I said I hoped nothing like it would happen on the Thames television show and that Brian McGee would keep Hampden-Turner *on an even keel*. The inept expression was pretty obviously due to the fact that I first met MacKay at Keele University.

I was writing about structuralism, Levi-Strauss, etc., and I began a kind of dictionary entry. *Structuralism was to be treated in a given place because of its kinship with.* . . . Then I saw the *kinship* with Levi-Strauss, whose major work was an analysis of kinship.

Guideposts

The Hilton Hotels give their guests a chance to read a little magazine designed "to show, by inspirational personal experiences, how men and women . . . have found strength, courage, and hope through their belief in God."

The principles described in the issue in my room are as follows:

1. God is responsible for every good thing (but the bad things are not mentioned). For example:

a. He showed James Irwin the Genesis Rock on the moon, miraculously not covered with dust. (He was not responsible for Grissom's death in another spaceship.)

b. He made a blind boy wish most of all for some Braille music for his flute rather than his sight. (He did not make the boy blind.)

c. He made a staid and dying Episcopal Church come alive with the Holy Spirit. (He is not responsible for the death of other parishes.)

d. He sends someone who needs help to give a woman renewed confidence as she recovers from an infection of the inner ear. (He did not cause the infection.)

Net conclusion: God is good. It is worthwhile to hope and ask for favors.

2. Helping others helps us.

3. Positive reinforcement is better than criticism.

Are (2) and (3) to be promoted by "inspirational personal experience" or by an effective analysis of why they are valid?

Hippies

They came into the airport restaurant for breakfast. Dirty, ill-matched clothes, his hair shoulder-length and scarcely combed, hers waist-length. The hostess showed them to a table, but they asked very pleasantly if they might have a vacant table they had spotted by the window. The hostess said they might, but it would have to be cleared first. They agreed pleasantly. When the table was ready, he slid into one of the chairs first, laughing as if he had played a trick. They sat looking at each other. In spite of their clothes they were attractive. They were young. He had no beard and could perhaps not have grown one. They showed no awareness that they were oddballs in that place. I felt very warm toward them. They had achieved a kind of happiness that seemed an end in itself.

Then it occurred to me that they were high. Had they smoked a bit of pot before coming in? Was it, after all, a synthetic happiness? Suddenly they lost all their charm. Why? What is wrong with pot-induced happiness?

In this case I think I knew. I had admired their happiness as a sign that they had hit upon a satisfying way of life. If it was due to pot, I could infer nothing.

Neural Prestige

A. "The modifiability of behavior depends on the presence of special neuronal mechanisms which possess the capacity *to store information* and change behavior."

B. *"The jackdaw's brain possesses circuitry or systems that anticipate what kinds of significant environmental information* (the visual and tactile properties of potential nest material) to acquire in a particular situation (nest building)."

How much more "scientific" and profound these sentences seem than simple statements of the facts:

A. Modifiability means that an organism may behave in a different way after contact with the environment.

B. The jackdaw does not need to learn to select appropriate nest material.

Of course neurons are involved, but in what way we do not know. They almost certainly do not store the contingencies affecting an organism; they are changed by the contingencies so that subsequent behavior is different.

Puritan?

Am I being a nineteenth-century prude in objecting to gambling? After all, isn't a national lottery a good way to make dull lives interesting? Think of the pleasure of looking at a ticket that may mean a fortune. And is not the same variable-ratio schedule at the heart of hunting, fishing, research, exploration, and writing?

Yes, but with a difference. In the contrived contingencies of a gambling enterprise, winning is not contingent on useful, let along ultimately useful, behavior. Gambling is wrong not because it ruins some people or is tabooed by a church, but because it commits a person to repetitious, stultifying behavior.

Influence

Reading a short essay on morals by Montaigne, I was surprised to see how English his point of view was. I thought I saw a bit of Bacon, a bit of Locke. Then I realized that he was 28 years older than Bacon and had been dead 40 years when Locke was born.

The influence crossed the channel in the other direction. Yet by the time of the Enlightenment it was coming back. What had happened to the continuity in France? Descartes?

Devotions

"Even the straws under my knees shout to distract me from my prayers," says St. Augustine (according to John Steinbeck in *Tortilla Flat*).

It might be interesting to search the *Confessions* or some such book for evidences of aversive control by a religious agency. Men "force themselves" to pray and to engage in pious works to avoid the consequences of sin or impiety. Hence the attribution of evil to distraction. St. Augustine at prayer is like a student over an uninteresting book.

The timing and counting of prayers is also under aversive control. One prays until an assignment is completed; one is then permitted to stop. So many Hail Marys, so many extra lines of Caesar for the English schoolboy.

The President's House

A feature of American culture, thoroughly stabilized, yet known to few, is the guest room in the home of the college president. Presidents presumably visit each other, and a certain uniformity has arisen. Invariably a touch of quiet elegance and good taste. Carpeted hallway and room. Excellent bed, with expensive bedspread. Flowers. A few magazines and books, of universal interest. Bathroom with recent plumbing. Scented soap and heavy colorful towels. Absolute quiet. Pleasant view.

Reinforcement Overlooked

I once visited a laboratory in which a research assistant was taming a monkey. He sat in a small room with a handful of peanuts, a monkey far away on the floor. The assistant chirped, clicked his tongue, and talked in a soothing voice, more and more intensively as the monkey approached. Whenever the monkey took fright and turned away, he would throw it a peanut. He apparently did this to counteract escape, but the peanuts were actually reinforcing the very behavior he was trying to eliminate, and as a result, the monkey was approaching and turning away in a rather stereotyped pattern.

The same mistake is made by the teacher who offers a treat of some kind when the class is getting out of hand. If this behavior is a kind of aggression toward the teacher, the treat may have an opposing effect. But in the long run, the reinforcement of misbehavior will offset any gain. Unfortunately, the reduction in aggression is immediate but the effect of reinforcement apparent only later. Hence, the practice may be continued, even though in the long run misbehavior becomes even more serious.

Finding the Pieces

A few months ago I memorized perhaps a dozen Shakespeare sonnets. I have not rehearsed them since. A few minutes ago, I began to recall one—with great difficulty. Pieces came back, however, in a surprising way. I may even have recalled some parts more accurately than I could have done at the earlier date. A few words stayed stubbornly beyond reach, but I think I could have recaptured them if I had continued to go over adjacent material. It was clear that I was helping myself recall by gradually amassing related intraverbal stimuli. The procedure is certainly not well described as searching a storehouse of memory for missing pieces.

Joachim in the Yard

The Divinity School, strengthened by President Pusey, must have suffered a setback at Commencement last Thursday. It had been announced a day before the ceremonies (contrary to tradition) that an honorary degree would be given to Cardinal Cushing. His Eminence arrived in the humblest of garb—a dark gray suit, hatless. He sat in the front row on the platform.

An English oration was given by a Divinity School student on "The Third Age." It eulogized Joachim, an antipapist mystic, and reviewed the argument of the Protestant reformation (as if the third age had just begun). As the Church had replaced the Temple (so much for the Orthodox Jewish graduating seniors), so the Church was to be replaced by an age in which priestly mediation would be abolished, and so on and so on. It was in incredibly bad taste. Those who could see the Cardinal reported that he grimaced wryly from time to time.

If the degree had been granted to further good relations between gown and that part of town, it was wasted. The exercises must have confirmed any suspicion the Cardinal may have had that the University was anti-Catholic.

Verbal Magic

A review of *Lore and Language of School Children* by Iona and Peter Opie reports that children "still believe that reciting the Lord's Prayer backwards makes the Devil appear and, like the Elizabethans, seldom dare try it." Are there other examples of *undoing something* verbally by reversing the order? Adding and subtracting are vaguely related: $3 + 2 = 5$ and $5 - 2 = 3$; and so are multiplying and dividing. Some questions and answers approach a reversal (*Where is Harry? Harry is here.*), but do they reverse an effect, as by resolving doubt? Taking something back is done with a different response: *Yes!—I mean, No!* Since the reverse order is not learned in the act of learning an ordered response, the behavior is likely to arise only as the result of extracting or inventing a rule.

Sources of Inspiration

The notion that Mathilde Wesendonck was not the inspiration of *Tristan und Isolde* but that Wagner was ready both to write the opera and to fall in love with any convenient woman does not rule out an environmental origin of the opera. On the contrary, it directs us toward more likely relevant environmental and genetic sources, even though not as clearly and easily specified as a person. How *could* Wesendonck have inspired an opera? By giving Wagner an occasion for being more actively in love? But the real source could have been all the love affairs, the conflicts, the frustrations, the losses, plus all the things he had read which came from the same kinds of things in others.

Wesendonck was a conspicuous part of Wagner's environment at the time. Hence it is easy to attribute the opera to Wagner's relationship with her. The rest of the relevant environment is easily missed or forgotten. As to its current representation in Wagner, we are no worse off in looking for that (or in having to give up looking) than in explaining Wesendonck's effect.

A Phrase as an Object

I had been reading *A Dictionary of Contemporary American Usage* by Bergen and Cornelia Evans (New York, 1957). Within a period of three minutes I read about *washing dirty linen in public/ washing one's hands of something/ water, of the first/ water under the bridge* (*and over the dam*). I left the book briefly. On my way back, I passed a wastebasket and on a discarded cereal box I glimpsed the words MAKE A BATCH OF . . . followed by a line-enclosed recipe, evidently part of a series. I read the phrase as I had been reading the phrases in the book and was rather startled (possibly the word is "surprised").

One reads phrases in such a book in a special way—making no effort to complete them as sentences, yet reading them as if they were parts of sentences in order to be prepared for the author's comments. I should not have been surprised by a plain sentence on a box in a wastebasket. It was my reading in a special way in an unusual situation and to no effect that startled me.

It does not help to say that I read the phrase expecting a comment and that my expectations were thwarted. It was a brief history of reading with a special kind of consequence that gave a rather similar stimulus its unusual effect. It does not help to say that I read in a special way because of a "set." It was the setting, not a set.

Rules, Models, Contingencies

The failure of many parents to have their children vaccinated shows the difference between rules and contingencies.

In the days when parents saw many children crippled by polio, they rushed for the new vaccine for their own children. Now that there are few cases, it is hard to get them to have their children vaccinated. Contingencies *grow* weak, and rules *are* weak.

What is to be done? Describe the epidemics which may come if the children are not vaccinated? Show crippled children on TV? In other words, reestablish modeling contingencies?

To what extent is one's own conduct changed upon seeing another person punished (by authorities or by nature, as in a car accident or a crippling disease)? Is nature's capital punishment a deterrent?

Gestalt

In the days of the double feature, with two different shows a week, movie houses ran "previews of coming attractions." But I was never reminded of the scenes shown in the previews when I saw the movies. There was absolutely no *déjà vu*. Yet the visual and auditory stimuli were identical, and they were presumably some of the high spots of the film. So far as I was concerned, they were swallowed up by the continuity, by the plot. (Eve says she almost always did recognize the preview scenes.)

Courtesy

In Russia in 1961 one could apparently not visit an institute or laboratory without being received by the director. The reception almost always meant refreshment—tea or wine and cakes—and remarks, often extensive, about work in progress. (I blush to recall how impolite I must have seemed upon many occasions when Russians have visited my laboratory.) Occasionally one gets the impression that the reception is a security measure: some of our party were unable to visit a laboratory because the director could not be located, and it is easy to imagine that he insisted on approving all visitors. But in general it seems to be a social ritual.

In Prague our plane was late, and Anatol Rapoport and I were rushed to the Institute where we were scheduled to speak. The audience was assembled and had been waiting for some time, but we had to go first to the director's office, where we talked about trivial matters for ten minutes. Only then was it proper for us to go to the auditorium and give our lectures.

Guaranteed Gratitude

Touring Cape Cod in a leisurely fashion with friends, we stopped at a tourist home for the night. I went for some ice cubes before mixing a drink. The man who gave them to me said jovially, "Of course, there's an extra charge for this."

It is a fairly common kind of joke. In what sense is it "meaningful"? Did he *want* to charge me for the cubes? I don't think so. Possibly he was promoting a return favor—a tip, or, more likely, an invitation to join us for a drink. Possibly he was setting the stage for reciprocal joviality, establishing an equality of status.

I suspect the remark is usually strong simply because it makes a reinforcing expression of gratitude almost inevitable, such as "We appreciate your *giving* us this."

Verbal Miscellany I

Waiting at the optician's with a prescription in front of me from Varant Hagopian, M.D., I glanced at a copy of *Life*, the cover of which referred to a story on Runaway Kids. A typed ad read, "Police want you only for questioning. We love you. Call collect. Mother and Dad." I turned to the prescription and read it with surprise as VAGRANT.

Reaching a restaurant in Soho where I had an appointment for luncheon, I started to ask the head waiter for a *tailor for Mr. Iceberg* instead of *a table for Mr. Eisler*. Possibly because I had just come from a fitting at a tailor's, I converted *table* to *tailor*. This robbed *Eisler* of the *l* and left *b* to be used. *Eis-er* plus *b* gives something close to *iceberg*. The example is unusual because the interchanged consonants come at the beginning of unaccented syllables.

I told my class about hearing a rabbi on Long John Silver's radio program. The class pointed out that it was Long John Nebel's program and that the rabbi's name was Silver. What was the name of the character in Stevenson's *Treasure Island?*

I was reading an article in *Science News* which began, "The emerging earth sciences program of the National Aeronautics and Space Administration is a many-headed, multidisciplinary effort. It deals with hydrology. . . . " I immediately thought *Hydra!* Had *hydrology* triggered *many-headed* in the writer, as well?

The Uses of Complexity

Cognitive psychologists, particularly psycholinguists and linguists, like to point to the extraordinary scope and subtlety of human behavior. The child soon becomes able to respond to "a potentially infinite number of sentences."

This is offered as:

1. implying the inadequacy of any behavioral account, and

2. proving the scope of cognitive analysis.

There is no question of the extraordinary complexity of human behavior, but should we not conclude that any formulation which now appears to dispose of the complexity is likely to be spurious and that the best criterion at the present time is the adequacy of an analysis in dealing with some part of the field?

Unreal Life

Why do we applaud actors at the end of effective scenes? Probably for the reasons for which we applaud other performers—in music, ballet, the circus; they have done a good job and we thus make other good jobs more likely. Applause may be related to the unreality of the life on the stage. Actors are not really getting anything out of it except their salaries and acclaim. We contribute a bit of reality, not only by applauding but gasping in surprise, crying out in fear, or hissing the villain, though it is less likely that these are exhibited *in order to* reinforce the actor's behavior.

Why do we not applaud in church, at weddings and funerals and on other ceremonial occasions? Because the performers are felt to be genuinely involved and hence do not need our applause? Note that weeping, wailing, and keening during a funeral oration are acceptable in many cultures. And so are paid mourners, who are close to actors.

Theory of Subjective Values

Ludwig von Mises, according to the obituary in *The New York Times* of October 11, 1973, "developed the theory of subjective values to explain the demand for cash balance as a basis for expansions and contractions in economic activity. . . . stressing the causal role of individual human decisions, Professor von Mises observed that changes in the amount of cash individuals want to hold would cause expansion and contraction in economic activity."

I daresay this is much oversimplified, but possibly near enough to make a translation worthwhile. I assume that the immediate cause of expansion and contraction is the amount people do hold. Holding money reduces the amount in circulation. But why do they hold it? Because they *want* to hold it? But why do they want to hold it? The available facts are: (1) how much money is held, and (2) the environmental conditions responsible for holding. No subjective value there. When they say they like to have cash reserves, people are commenting on these facts, and they may report the condition they feel as "liking." But the condition is not among the causes of holding; it is one of the effects of those causes.

Misreading II

Waiting for a train, I looked at magazines in a rather poor light. On a cover I read *income tax* only to discover it actually said *extra income*. Note that *tax* is in *extra*. But the reversed word order? Yet I could conceivably have read *income tax* in *tax income*.

A line began: *manners, customs, folkways, and . . .* I read *monkeys* so strongly that I looked for the word elsewhere in the text but could not find it. There were intraverbal variables, however. The passage was about the evolution of behavior and about dominance and submissiveness, relations which have been studied in monkey colonies. Formal sources of strength were also there; as in:

m   om k ys
or
man   k ays

The word BONNEVILLE seen from a taxi on the back of a car had an emotional effect which I immediately associated with a vaudeville performance I had once seen in which a one-time child star, now in late adolescence, made a personal appearance. She had been given bad lines, written to remind the audience of her early triumphs. Her reception was chilly, but she carried on as a good trouper. I recalled that her name was not Bonnie but Bonita. Some vague search for the etymology of Bonnie (as in *bonnie lass*) and Spanish-Hollywood *Bonita* followed. Then, but only then, I remembered her last name: Granville.

BONita   GranVILLE
BONne   VILLE

On the window beside our seat in the Metro was a sign indicating that the seat was reserved by priority to certain groups:

1er AUX MUTILÉS DE GUERRE

I had my cane with me and said to my companion, "I could pass for a *mutilé*." When I looked at the sign again I read it as

FAUX MUTILÉ

Epistemology

A long review of Popper and Eccles (*The Self and Its Brain*) in the *Times Literary Supplement* (February 17, 1978) goes into Cartesian Dualism, Parallelism, Interactionism, and more, without a glimmer of the formulation open to a behavioristic analysis. But at least the reviewer, D. M. Armstrong, seems to agree with Popper that "We may perhaps say that at the time of writing, radical materialism or behaviorism seems to be the view concerning the mind-body problem that is most fashionable among the younger generation of students of philosophy."

This Side of Heaven

Nine of the Ten Commandments are negative. "Thou shalt *not* . . . " The sanctions are not specified. The voice of the Lord, or at least of Moses, was enough.

But one is a positive injunction: "Honor thy father and mother." And the positive consequences are specified: "that your days may be long in the land." The contingencies are not clear, but they are this-worldly. Presumably a natural consequence, with no divine intervention needed.

Context

Toilet paper is useful—to wipe pens, clean eyeglasses, dry fingers, and so on. A roll is a more convenient form than a box-fold of tissues. Yet one resists mounting a roll of toilet paper near one's desk or worktable or even in a machine shop.

Knowing and Understanding People

Biographers often say that they feel they have come to "know" or "understand" the persons whose lives they are recounting. Clinical psychologists say the same thing about their clients, and so may everyone about friends or colleagues.

The effect is close to understanding as I analyzed it in *Verbal Behavior* (page 277). The listener who understands "says it along with" the speaker, and biographers come to *respond* along with the people whose lives they are recounting. They know how and why their subjects respond because they have become disposed to respond in the same way themselves. For the same reason, they are not surprised by what their subjects do. Eventually, they *are* their subjects, in the sense of possessing the same repertoires.

Recording a Distortion

I was dictating from a handwritten text, but improvising a new sentence: . . . *leaves less to be explained than the standard definitions given above.*

I said *diffinition* and had to wrestle with the word to get *definition*. I was at once aware of *dictionary*. Had I chosen *standard definition* in place of *dictionary definition?* Note that the short *i* appears almost immediately again in *given.*

The recorded passage (on tape) is approximately this: *standard dif-di-standard diffinition* where the last word is close to *definition* but still quite clearly shading into a short *i.*

Concealed Intraverbal

"We'll toss a die 1000 times. I calculate that the odds are one to three for five sixes in a row."

How many people reading that sentence aloud will discover that they have been counting—1,2,3,4,5,6?

Science Fiction

Science fiction is close to scientific hypothesizing. It is a speculation to be replaced by observation. Or a proposal to be carried out. In its extreme form it is brainstorming— proposals unrestrained by any fear of absurdity or possible failure. In its milder form it is Karl Marx and an inchoate science of economics, or an application to NIH to study "thought control" *via* electrical or chemical means.

Walden Two lies between fiction and fiction-come-true. Bits of it have come true. More will do so.

Getting and Saving

"No man was born a miser," said Dr. Johnson (*Boswell's Life*, April 25, 1778, vol. V, p. 24), "because no man was born to possession. Every man is born *cupidus*—desirous of getting; but not *avarus*—desirous of keeping." Was he right? Other species *hoard*, and hoarding is far from getting. Bees get honey, but build honeycombs because they are *avari*. Squirrels bury nuts, which is just the opposite of getting. The long infancy of the human child makes it difficult to check on the human case.

Keep Your Eye . . .

. . . not on the ball, but on the words in bold-faced type at the top of the page in a dictionary when you are looking for a word. They are much easier to see, and one can find a word more quickly by following this rule. But it is hard to follow. One looks at the words alongside their definitions because that is where one will find what one wants, just as golfers or baseball batters or tennis players find it almost irresistible to take their eyes off the ball in order to be ready to see where it goes after it is struck.

Oaths

Acontius induces Cydippe to read an inscription: "I swear by the temple of Artemis to marry Acontius." This is accepted by the goddess Artemis as an oath, and the marriage is arranged.

A verbal response is accepted regardless of the controlling variable—in this case, a text. In English courts a witness takes his oath by reading a text, in some American courts by assenting to a question. Other oaths, as in marriage, are made by repeating a spoken passage. The supporting textual or echoic stimuli are regarded as prompts, not as primes—that is, the speaker is assumed to be stating or asserting what the oath says for other (and better) reasons.

Self-Management and the Will

How to remove oneself from a situation in which one behaves in ways having aversive consequences is sometimes a problem. Apparently one cannot simply remain in a situation and stop responding. Some autistic children cannot stop punishing themselves but may act in ways which appear to be reinforced by constraint. The solution to many neurotic problems often consists of doing something to bring behavior to an end instead of simply ending it. Is this the difference between self-management by exercising the "will" (just stopping a bad habit) and by changing the environmental contingencies?

Verbal Values

One of the school administrators I met in Brookline asked why, if some 20 to 40 percent of students cannot be taught to read, we should continue to teach verbally. I came up with two spur-of-the-moment answers:

1. Thinking is mostly verbal behavior, and we need to teach thinking.

2. The rules which are so important in the transmission of a culture are verbal. Without the verbal help given by others, we should be little more than feral children.

Dangerous, Troublesome Growth

. . . is beautifully illustrated by education.

The private tutor gives way to the public school, and the academy of Plato to lectures. Large universities, city school systems—all suffer from bigness. Technology gets far away from the individual student; it is a matter of finances, organization, logistics of supply—with almost no attention to what is happening as a student learns.

The programmed text and the teaching machine go back to the individual, and are damned for "neglecting individuality"!

The Loved One

A man whose father had died was told by the funeral director that, since his father was six feet four inches tall, a special coffin would be required which would cost an extra $50. The man said:

"But can't you cut off his legs?"

The funeral director was horrified and a moment later reported that there would be no extra charge for the larger size.

Saving the World

"If the world is to be saved, men must learn to be noble without being cruel, to be filled with faith yet open to truth, to be inspired by great purposes without hating those who try to thwart them."

How vicious one seems, how inhuman, to call that nonsense, yet nonsense it is! To say so does not mean that one does not want a world in which people behave in ways called noble and not in ways called cruel, or act "with faith" but only insofar as they have the facts, or energetically without spending time in attacking those who try to thwart them.

Assign and Test

I keep forgetting how ubiquitous the principle is. Yesterday in going over a "basal reader" I found a modern version of the Pestalozzi sample I used in *The Technology of Teaching*. The fourth grade student is to read a story—about the Wright Brothers—and then to answer questions. What was the first problem they met? How many men helped them? And so on.

A horrible kind of "motivation." Read *carefully* so that you can answer questions! Of course, a student who reads the story with pleasure might recall facts of this sort, but with the questions in prospect pleasurable reading is impossible.

Paradise

Members of the Stanford faculty have houses set in small lush Gardens of Eden—green grass, exotic flowers, odorous trees and vines. And always, somewhere—as a reminder that man has fallen from grace—a long, loosely coiled, sleeping snake, the Garden Hose.

Labor

How pleasant it must have been when one could, like Wordsworth, imagine that

> *Maids at the wheel, the weaver at his loom,*
> *Sit blithe and happy.*

Can anything like joy in one's work ever be assured? Was it assured in Wordsworth's day? I doubt it. If maids and weavers were happy at their very repetitious tasks, it was because they saw other people in much worse condition.

Young people today, out of tune with the world, are choosing to be

suckle'd in a creed outworn.

Useful Symbol

A sea gull high against a sky of gathering clouds—how different it seems when listening to the last act of *Parsifal!* What kind of symbol is it? Probably not very different from that of music itself or abstract art—in other words, a symbol of nothing, and hence useful in all moods.

Sense and Nonsense

"All utopias are fed from the sources of mythology," says Arthur Koestler. (Quoted by Robert C. Elliot, *The Shape of Utopias.*)

What can that mean? A utopia fed . . . ? And from the *sources* of mythology, not the mythology itself?

Can he mean that those who write utopias are conversant with mythology? That can be checked. But why "sources"?

Can he mean that those who write utopias are moved by the same forces as those who composed mythology? Utopias *are* mythology?

Then why not say so?

Spoiled

The attractive person who receives attention and other favors because he or she is attractive, or the child who receives them from a doting parent or sibling, is an excellent demonstration of how damaging noncontingent reinforcers may be. We call such a person "spoiled."

Freedom from Coercion

Those who oppose governmental action in, say, fluoridating drinking water on the grounds that personal freedom is infringed are simply expressing a preference for noncoercive control. But people are also not free to use or to refuse to use fluorides if the facts have been made clear and if their teeth and their health are important to them. Persuasively advocating fluoridation and opposing it are both attributable to circumstances. In general, the difference between education and law is not a difference in the extent to which people are free but in the kind of control to which they are subjected.

Les Enfants de Dieu

An acquaintance asked me for advice. His youngest child, aged one, is mongoloid. He and his wife are, I believe, Quakers. In any case, they plan to raise the child at home. They have three other children, all in school. What could they do for their youngest?

I suggested various devices which might give the child something to do for long hours each day. Toys and games— foolproof to avoid frustration, paying off on the generous schedules needed to control the retardate. I warned him of the social demands which will not only increase but become harder to satisfy as the child grows older. People are very reinforcing, and they reinforce appealing behavior. The retardate responds to those contingencies, and acquires behavior that is hard to resist. It resembles the affection-getting behavior of the intelligent child, yet it may be no more necessary, may satisfy no more real need for personal attention, than mechanically arranged reinforcing systems. The retarded child should not be allowed to damage the lives of the older children and the parents. There is no cruelty here. A repertoire of behavior must not be rein-forced which can be supported only by exhausting labors, because once these behaviors have been allowed to develop, only sacrifice or guilt-ridden remedial action will follow.

Initiator

Newspapers typically report that "a car went out of control" rather than that a person "lost control of the car." In a fatal accident this may be kindness, in a near-fatal one, an avoidance of charges of libel. "The driver allegedly lost control" or "police said the driver lost control" would be safer but awkward.

In general, it is a good example of the effort to absolve someone of carelessness or to avoid allusions to probable environmental causes (alcohol, high speed, etc.).

A car *may* go out of control if the steering gear locks, or the brakes fail, or a tire blows at high speed. In such a case the fact is mentioned.

A sound car with a defective driver is another matter.

Radical but Popular

By the early teens most popular song books and "best loved" piano collections contained "Evening Star" from *Tannhauser*, the "Pilgrims' Chorus" from *Tannhauser*, and the "Bridal March" from *Lohengrin*.

The march was probably used at a majority of weddings. The "Ride of the Valkyries" was, as I recall, played by the orchestra when I first saw *The Birth of a Nation*.

This is possibly more than any other single composer of the nineteenth century could show. Yet Wagner was an innovator, a musical radical.

Enterprise

The unproductiveness of people in warm climates is often attributed to the weather, but the persistence in Egypt of beggars and peddlers is phenomenal and seems clearly due to reinforcing contingencies. A party of tourists disembarks at a temple, and the beggars and peddlers converge on them. They hold out hands for "baksheesh," offer for sale strings of beads, postcards, and half-concealed, forged "illegal antiquities." To say "no" is to encourage them, and they redouble their efforts. The reinforcing schedule is clear. Occasionally tourists change their minds, or grow sorry and capitulate.

The schedule is a variable ratio, but the effect is due to "stretching." The children are attractive and quickly learn to display melting expressions and attitudes. At that stage they are often successful; a few responses mean reinforcement. But as they grow older, and lose teeth and hair and brightness of eye, more and more begging is needed.

It is true that the labor of begging is not great. There are no marked aversive consequences, and it is only episodic. Yet it is not easy, and the dedication to the task is intense. Climate has evidently little to do with it. It is never too hot or debilitating for a beggar.

Trust

From the *San Francisco Chronicle*, January 23, 1972:

U.S. military authorities denied claims by Russian defense experts in Red Star, the top Soviet military publication, that there were American plans to use skunks, sea gulls, dolphins and bats as weapons of war.

This is the sort of thing that weakens credibility. Perhaps we are not "planning to use" animals in warfare but we are investigating their use. We also may not have "planned to use" biological warfare, but we investigated it.

A better answer would be to describe the Russian use of animals in World War II.

Misinterpretation

When Eve put one drop of a pilocarpine solution in my eye, I felt it going out one corner and turned my head quickly so that it would flow the other way. Eve interpreted the movement as a sign of pain, and she said, "Does it smart?" The movement is the same in both cases; the independent variable makes the difference. The actual variable was uncommon, and it was much easier to infer a commoner one.

Wisdom

Two or three years ago I began to translate La Rochefoucauld into behavioral English. I lost interest when it became repetitive and mechanical. Now I have been reading Frame's biography of Montaigne and will pick up his translation of the *Essays*. A complete translation "into behavior" is out of the question because of time and energy, but I should like to sample it to find out just what sort of wisdom Montaigne was dispensing.

So much goes back to identifying reinforcers (as it did in La Rochefoucauld) that I feel particularly the need of an alternative vocabulary. There is surprisingly little about process: Rulers should make themselves loved rather than feared—but how? By giving subjects occasions to love them, by clemency, by magnanimity? But what will subjects then do? Variables interact (as reported in terms of emotions, wants, etc.), but according to what laws?

Feigned Laughter

Stendhal (*Journal*, 17 *janvier* 1805):

> "*La manière la plus sûre d'humilier celui dont vous riez est que votre* rire *ait l'aire le plus possible independant de la volonté.* . . . "

A good respondent laugh, rather than a social operant.

In an essay of Max Beerbohm's, a butler flatters a guest by appearing to turn away to avoid laughing at a joke he has overheard, but to which, as a butler, he should have been deaf.

The Design of a Person

We first met her when we were waiting for the special bus that was to take us to the inaugural meeting. She was well-groomed, good looking, very pleasant. Her husband, in tails and with his CBE cross hanging just below his white tie, was very English and very distinguished. We were on our way to the Free Trade Hall. On the bus I said to her that I supposed there must once have been an active society here advocating free trade and mentioned how much alive the issue now was with the Common Market. "Oh, yes," she said. "My father got into parliament on free trade."

Later I tried to imagine what her life must have been like. She had no doubt been a beautiful, well-educated girl. Did she find her husband herself or was he chosen for her? From how large a group of eligibles could she have chosen? Where had her children gone to school? Was this inevitable, or had she had a hand in it? Was she simply the product of a culture or in some sense free to be herself? But who or what was the child who was "free to be herself"? The woman I saw was the product of well-controlled genetic and environmental histories. If she ever revolted or tried to revolt from the culture which shaped her, it was not because of something *in her* but a flaw which permitted a fragment of another culture to break through and take control.

Euphoria and Ecstasy

In the Dedication of his *Idea of a University* Cardinal Newman refers to his conversion to Catholicism as breaking "the stress of a great anxiety." Billy Graham, and Protestant evangelists in general, speak of being *saved*—presumably from punishment for nonbelief. This reduction in powerful conditioned aversive stimuli—felt as anxiety—seems to generate an unusual euphoria or joy, all the more moving for being misunderstood as a presence.

The euphoria of satiation may be a release not from aversive contingencies but from the possibly exhausting (and hence aversive) effort of positively reinforced behavior. Is the feeling of accomplishment commoner in the compulsive worker?

Since there are many ways of being released and many kinds of aversive conditions from which to be released, there are many kinds of euphoria and ecstasy.

Anxiety-reducing drugs seem to produce all of them in appropriate doses.

Reinforcement of a Mand

A boy traveling with his younger sister on a plane was clearly the dominant sibling. But he was late in getting back to his seat when the seat-belt sign lighted up, and his sister said, with obvious delight, *"Fasten your seat belt!"* He complied because of the sign, but there was a special strength in the girl's response; for once she would be obeyed.

Pheromone

I think it was Freud, or at least a follower, who suggested that otherwise inexplicable personal attachments might be due to unconscious reactions to odor. There are conscious reactions which work in the other direction. Our rubbish cans are used in the summer for grass clippings, and inevitably a shallow layer of damp grass collects at the bottom. It rots within a day or two and is often left in the bottom of the cans after the rubbish is collected. It stinks in a most unpleasant way.

Yesterday, waiting for a young woman who was helping me with a lecture *en français*, I started to put the cans back after collection and saw that they needed hosing out. When I had finished, my hands stank, and I washed them thoroughly and added a few drops of shaving lotion. After the woman had arrived, I discovered traces of odor on my right hand. I excused myself and scrubbed up again. But throughout our discussion, I was aware of faint traces. I might have splashed some of the dirty water on my shoes or trousers. It was clear to both of us that it was a session *manqué*.

Mind? No, Matter.

A writer on hypnosis says that "a part of the patient's mind is *en rapport* with the hypnotist." Why not say a part of the *patient?*

What the patient *does* is *en rapport* with the verbal (not necessarily vocal) behavior of the hypnotist. Why not say so?

A historian says that "Since the Muggletonian sect continued to exist, to argue its ideas, and to publish, throughout the eighteenth and well into the nineteenth century, it represents a possible 'carrier' for certain ideas."

But what it "carried" were certain kinds of verbal behavior. Why not say so?

The Sabbath as a Cultural Practice

A hard-working people will welcome a taboo against working on every *n*th day. Any religious reason should be readily accepted. (Did the account in Genesis precede the practice of a Sabbath or was the Lord's day patterned after Man's?) But the strictest enforcement may be needed: God says, "Do absolutely *nothing!*" Impressed into slavery, the group may suffer in order to maintain the practice, and members may therefore be particularly grateful for those who suffer for them and be all the more likely to believe in the validity of the taboo and to observe it more strictly in order to maintain it against encroachment. "You can't ask me to work for *you*, we never work even for ourselves."

As soon as other days of leisure turn up—among the wealthy or with a five-day workweek for everyone—a Sabbath loses force. A taboo is no longer necessary to avoid being forced to work. Moreover, being idle is no longer strongly reinforced. There must be something to do for fun, and the other free days teach one what to do. Hence the breakdown of a Sabbath as it yields to travel, visits, do-it-yourself work, games, spectator sports, movies, and advantageous trade.

Behavioral Unit

At the top of the basement stairs I turned to shut the door to the basement. Instead I shut the kitchen door, which is at a right angle to it. The kitchen door has a baseboard clasp, and as the door came free I saw that it was the wrong door.

"Closing a door" is a behavioral unit acquired with respect to hundreds of doors. "Closing the basement door" is a special case under special stimulus control. I emitted "closing *a* door" by responding to the first door that came to hand. (I was turning around and closing the basement door as an afterthought.)

This kind of analysis is needed, but I am afraid that we won't see much of it for a long time.

Traits

Chapter XIII in *Science and Human Behavior*, "Function versus Aspect," may offer an escape from the racist implications of mental measurement. Selection of the right people grows less important as we begin to look at control. Is the problem to find better students—or to provide better teaching? To find more energetic workers—or arrange better incentive systems? If we could stop looking at the person and look instead at antecedent histories, genetic or individual, we could begin to act more effectively.

Love as an Archetype

The extraordinary frequency of successful courtship in literature suggests the extraordinary power of sexual reinforcement. The problems of courtship range widely—from Emma to Humbert Humbert and beyond—but the central theme is always winning a man or woman.

There may be other reasons for its relative frequency:

1. Sexual deprivation is maintained in modern cultures by limiting consummation. Only under unusual circumstances is hunger or thirst or escape from danger similarly exalted.

2. The consummation of courtship takes time and may be devious and that usually means a story.

3. Techniques of courtship are familiar in daily life and hence easier to make plausible and interesting than scholarly or scientific problem solving.

4. The solution is clear-cut. The lady (man, boy, girl) yields, says yes.

War and other kinds of struggle for power are perhaps equally frequent themes in literature and for similar reasons.

Word Play

One does not need to see or "get" Joyce's verbal tricks to be affected by them. The underlying sources give an impression rather like *déjà vu*, which after all is one object of a prose style—particularly in gaining an uncritical acceptance.

The sentence "Someone was playing the *Ophyria Mazurka*" gains something (for the reader or listener familiar with French) from the outlandish and farfetched resemblance to *au fur et a mesure que*. It does not matter whether there is any relevance (whether the performer, for example, was playing hesitantly or with limited ability) or whether the French parallel is spotted.

"Behavioral Science"

We are told that business is looking to "behavioral science" only to discover that it is looking at sensitivity training, encounter groups, and psychoanalysis.

The Possessed

In Chapter 9 of *Contingencies of Reinforcement*, I mentioned the Goncourt brothers' description of their mistress as she talks in a drunken sleep: "a cadaver possessed by a dream."

Any behavior taken out of a normal setting may suggest possession. Facial expressions produced by drawing out the skin for shaving, or by tics or sharp pains, sometimes suggest invisible outside forces. The dog that suddenly growls and bristles for no observable reason is responding to a ghost.

Yesterday on the bus I saw a girl, perhaps in her twenties, who startled me because I had never expected to see anyone like her outside an institution, or at least unattended. At times her eyes were rolled upward so that only the whites showed, her jaw sagged, and her mouth was open. Yet from time to time, she composed a normal face. Relaxed, she became an idiot. I could not imagine how she might respond when spoken to. Would she reply in a dull mechanical lisp with the hollowness of a cleft palate or in a normal way? Which of her two selves would reply?

Speed of Writing

The great letter writers of the past may have been skilled penmen, but even so, they could not have written as fast as they spoke. A quill pen on comparatively rough paper, sputtering, quickly running out of ink—how crude a means of behaving verbally. Did they think ahead, or did they gradually adopt a slower tempo of verbal thinking? How fast does one *dictate* letters when one has been accustomed to *writing* them? Is there an acceleration of thinking—or mere prolixity—when one begins to correspond with cassette recordings?

I used to think that italic, which is a slow hand, gave me an advantage by making revision less necessary. I am not sure. Do my notes during the italic phase show a difference?

What Can We Say About Groups?

We are alert to the dangers of stereotypes—the Japs are not tricky, the Germans not bellicose. But we don't carry through. What did the American people "really think" about Vietnam? Is there any possible answer? Say, via a poll? In what sense can a large number of people think—or act?

Many historians make no claim to the practical usefulness of history. Yet we all go on talking in historical analogies, as if they *were* useful.

It all keeps coming back to scientific method. Fictions are still in fashion. In practice we have to say *something* about groups. We change economic, political, educational practices. We rationalize our changes, in the sense of giving reasons, valid or not. But what are the real reasons why we change practices in a given way?

Can we change the nature of the concepts we use through quantification? How *many* members of a group say something, respond in a given way, emit behavior reinforced by a given event? By counting we reach a number of cases, but not a "group mind." The mode of behavior is one thing that is left out. How does a *group* behave?

Records

In choosing employees we need to know something about their previous experience, not only with respect to skills or knowledge, but schedules of reinforcement. Teachers need to know a great deal about the past educational history of their students, and much of psychotherapy consists of exploring histories. Something better than a casual impression of the behavior of the individual is important in all these fields. We speak of police *records*, employment *records*, *records* in school and college, though comparable records are seldom available to the psychotherapist. In particular, attention must be paid to reinforcement. What happens when people behave legally or illegally, work hard or idly or carefully or carelessly, when students succeed or fail, and patients adjust or fail to adjust?

"Playing God"

On a television show, Margaret Mead responded to something I said by telling the audience that she didn't want to play God. She did not want to "control people." Everyone applauded.

But the Christian God doesn't want to control people, either. That is quite explicit in Christian theology. If He controlled us, He would be responsible for the mess we are in. He's leaving it to individuals to control themselves.

When you act to control yourself and other people, you are doing "what God allows you to do rather than forces you to do." And you do it by constructing a *situation* that controls you or the others. Frazier does not control the members of Walden Two. The world which he designed and which they maintain is the controller.

Stone-Dead Metaphors

In "Figures of Speech in the Social Sciences" (*Proc. Am. Phil. Soc.*, October 1974), Alexander Gershenkron complains of the use of metaphors, but he himself uses them with abandon when speaking of verbal behavior.

Metaphors, he says, are "well-worn," "dead," "limping," "stone-dead," or "revived." The hero of Thomas Mann's *Magic Mountain* "swallows the organistic theory . . . hook, line, and sinker." An otherwise meaningless concept has a "thrust." A rhetorical figure and a logical figure are "stewed together" in a "ragout." A metaphor "seeps into" a language. A metaphor "suffers difficulties." A technical term can be "softened or diffused" in its meaning. A quotation "sheds light." The use of metaphor is "pregnant with difficulties."

A beautiful demonstration of his point. Very few behavioral scientists can talk about verbal behavior in unadorned prose.

The Story in Les Miserables

A young married woman was slapped in the face by her husband. Furious, she went to her father. "Will you stand for this? He slapped me! You must revenge yourself!" The father thereupon also slapped her. "Tell him if he has slapped my daughter, I have slapped his wife. We are quits."

The triumph of rule-governed over contingency-shaped behavior. It is only because the two slaps are *described* that a relation between them seems *rational.* If the husband had slapped his wife in the presence of her father, the father would have slapped the husband.

The Tangled Web We Weave

The way in which LSD breaks up the patterns of webs built by spiders was once taken very seriously—as if the pattern represented a cognitive structure that could be destroyed as such. The unconventional sequences produced by schizophrenics in guessing tosses of a coin were also said to be tangled webs.

Dangerous Fiction

An article on freedom begins: "You have chosen to read this sentence." A clever rhetorical device, but misleading. I was not reading the sentence when the author wrote it. He was predicting my behavior, not describing it. Even so, he had evidence for nothing more than: "You are reading this sentence." Perhaps the sentence "caught my eye" when I had nothing else to do—when there was no competing behavior. Perhaps I had been assigned the article by a teacher. Even under the "free" conditions assumed by the writer, my history and the current circumstances need to be taken into account. How important were earlier instances to which the title of the article, the name of the writer, and the layout of the page bore some resemblance? To bring my personal history, my present state, and the current situation all together in an act of choice is the kind of simplification that makes cognitive psychology so futile.

The Meaning of Meaning

The sounds represented in English orthography as *cat* or the marks CAT have no meaning *in* them; nor is it possible to put meaning *into* them, to invest them with meaning. As stimuli, auditory or visual, they may have a place in contingencies of reinforcement, and as a result special responses may come under their control in those who hear or read them. Producing them under certain circumstances is also reinforced in special ways. As responses, the circumstances controlling their appearance *are* their meaning. As stimuli, their meaning is the behavior under their control.

Feeling Old

An article discusses what it means to begin to "feel old." The feeling is put first. At issue is what a person who feels old does. But the essential fact is that the body begins to *be* old, and two things then follow: (1) behavior changes (reinforcers change, aversive consequences pile up, skills and power decline), and (2) one responds to all this by "feeling an old body and its characteristic behavior."

Pre-Baconian

Francis Bacon, a lawyer, is said to have been the first to speak of the laws of nature, but in *The Rise of the West* McNeill makes the point that the Greeks could conceive of laws of nature governing the world because they had the model of man-made laws governing the polis. The existence of a law prior to the behavior governed by it encourages a belief in Platonic ideas, which are said to exist prior to their embodiment in reality. It also seems to support the mistaken view that we behave by applying laws or rules, rather than by conforming to contingencies, even when the laws or rules have never been formulated.

"Knowing They Know"

The example of catching someone's eye, as I analyze it in *Science and Human Behavior*, has a parallel in what happens when two people know about a common event. Jack and Jill have kept a secret from Tom.

1. Jack then tells Tom. (Jill doesn't know Tom knows.)

2. Jack then tells Jill that he has told Tom. (Tom doesn't know that Jill knows he knows.)

3. Jack then tells Tom that he has told Jill that he has told Tom. (Jill doesn't know that Tom knows she knows.)

4. Jack then tells Jill that he has told Tom that he has told Jill that he has told Tom. (Tom now knows the secret and he also knows that both Jack and Jill know that he knows it.)

Every stage is distinct and exemplifies an important arrangement of "knowings."

A Many-Splendored Thing

"Do you love me?" One of the commonest of questions, but how is it to be answered? What do you examine before reporting "Yes" or "No"? Do you check your "feelings," as you might do in answering "Are you cold?"

The answer may be an evaluation of the probability that you will say "I love you." In fact the answer "Yes" may be followed by "Well, say so then." What does the response "I love you" do? Is it a verbal caress? Is it reinforced when it evokes the same verbal response or a caress? It is more than a report of feeling. It is a little like saying to someone who has just prepared a meal, "I'm hungry [and you may be sure I will enjoy this]."

If "I love you" is not a description of an autonomic pattern, and if it is not a kind of mand ("Love *me!*"), what is it? A description of the probability of behaving in a given way? "Yes, I *do* want to please you, make love to you, make you happy, be nice to you. . . . "

If *that* is the answer, loving is perfectly visible to the one loved. The behavior is there or it isn't. The question concerns either a possible probability of action not now manifest because the behavior is ambiguous or weak, or an assurance that controlling variables are still in force.

Hitler's Traits

In *Spandau: The Secret Diaries* Albert Speer says that Hitler was "cruel, unjust, unapproachable, cold, capricious, self-pitying, and vulgar." "He was also the exact opposite of almost all those things—a generous superior, amiable, self-controlled, proud and capable of enthusiasm for beauty and greatness."

What he means is that Hitler behaved in ways attributed to all these traits. The behaviors were often quite different, but not because of different characters. Hitler behaved differently to different people and under different circumstances. That his behavior was due to changes in traits is absurd. It was due to changes in environments.

A Reminder

In England the turn-signaling lights on cars tend to be yellow-white rather than red. I have seen hundreds in operation, particularly because they are used in pulling out of line before "overtaking," but this morning, in a heavy mist, a light blinking on a car some distance ahead reminded me of a lighthouse.

I did not seriously "think it was a lighthouse," but in some sense, I "saw it as I have seen lighthouses." The simple fact is that a flashing light, its edges softened by fog, is more like a lighthouse than a turn-indicator on a clear day.

Corpus Dei

In his *Memoirs* Casanova tells of being asked by a lady he is courting to suck her finger, which she has pricked.

"You will easily guess the manner in which I performed my delightful work. What is a kiss? Is it not an ardent desire to inhale a portion of the person we love?"

When he finishes, he is told to spit out the blood, but he has swallowed it ("God alone knows what happiness it has given me!"). "Are you then a cannibal?" asks the lady.

Do Freudians say that "You look sweet enough to eat" is a generalization from one deprivation to another? Certainly the Catholic mass is a ritual of love, in which one ingests a part of Jesus.

Incidentally, would a "lady" have asked a man to do this or was it, perhaps, incitement? And in that case did Casanova misunderstand his own response?

Nonsense About Time

From an article in *Harpers*, January 1974: "Man's perception of time, his knowledge of cyclic change, and his belief in permanence is one of his most powerful tools. Just as the capture of time's flow within the clock and the calendar is fundamental to civilization, so the individual's grasp of past, present, and future is basic to his personal identity."

Time's flow is not captured in clock or calendar. Clocks and calendars are devices for changing the environment with respect to time, making that property more conspicuous. It is not man's perception of time but the behavior he acquires under the control of temporal aspects of the environment which is his most powerful "tool" (the word is still misleading). The power is in behavior, not perception. Personal identity does not depend upon the "grasp" of anything—let alone past, present, and future. How could one grasp them? Identity refers to persistence in time, and what persists are repertoires. They are the products of past contingencies and their appearance in current settings may have important future consequences.

The passage continues: "Time is the healer, the builder, the thief, the destroyer." But what can that possibly mean? Wounds heal in time, things are constructed in time, things disappear in time and are destroyed in time, but this is not what time *does*.

Oedipus

In choosing that name for the complex, Freud recognized that the theme had long been known. But that Oedipus committed his parental crimes unknowingly and that this might show that his wishes were unconscious was an additional point for which Freud might claim credit.

But there were more explicit anticipations—for example, in Diderot's *le Neveu de Rameau:*

"MOI. Si le petit sauvage était abandonné à lui-même, qu'il conservât toute son imbécillité et qu'il réunît au peu de raison de l'enfant au

berceau la violence des passions de l'homme de trente ans, il tordrait le cou à son père et coucherait avec sa mère "(Payot, Paris, p. 133).

This has been translated in a published version as follows:

"MYSELF. If your little savage were left to himself and to his native blindness, he would in time join the infant's reasoning to the grown man's passions—he would strangle his father and sleep with his mother."

It is a bad translation. *Imbécillité* is not blindness. Diderot is saying that if the violent passions of a man of thirty were as unrestrained and *irrational* as the behavior of a baby, the man would kill his father and sleep with his mother.

Ratio Schedule with Counter

Saving money in a conspicuous form has the effect of reinforcement on a ratio *with counter*. Banks would do well to supply some conspicuous indicator of the amount saved.

George Eliot describes the beginnings of miserliness in *Silas Marner* (Chapter 2):

"Marner wanted the heaps of ten [guineas] to grow into a square, and then into a larger square; and every added guinea, while it was itself a satisfaction, bred a new desire—."

Building bigger squares is an example of working on a stretching ratio, stretching very rapidly.

George Eliot is aware that it is the contingencies, not the guineas, which build the behavior. "The same sort of process has perhaps been undergone by wiser men, when they have been cut off from faith and love—only, instead of a loom and a heap of guineas, they have had some erudite research, some vigorous project, or some well-knit theory."

Memoranda

We make memoranda in order to respond to them usefully at a later date. Having counted a number of things, we jot down the number and thus save the labor of counting them again.

But some memoranda are not constructed in this way. If we are to remember to take a book back to the library, we may make a note to that effect on a desk pad, *or we may put the book where we will see it as we leave.* We construct a memorandum only in the sense of putting a stimulus where it will probably be effective "as a reminder" in the future.

The Effect of Competition on Design

The new cars are full of gadgets. Motor-driven screens cover the headlights except when in use, the tailgate of a station wagon opens on either horizontal or vertical hinges, steering wheels can be pushed out of the way, windows open and close and headrests rise or fall at the touch of a finger, and so on, and so on. The gain in convenience and comfort is slight—indeed negligible—compared with the increased need for maintenance, but the really startling contrast is with what could be done in most homes, apartments, kitchens, public transportation, airports, stores, hospitals, and schools. The economic forces behind the designers of cars are fantastically powerful. When will the design of a better way of life be as strongly supported?

Fat

A psychiatrist friend insists on "displacement." The person who isn't loved takes to food and grows fat. But how many other causal relations can be pointed out between lack of sexual gratification and overeating? (In the first place, are the facts as stated? The Sultan in his harem is usually pictured as fat. There have been fat wives and mistresses sexually replete, and fat men are familiar to prostitutes.)

Those who allow themselves to get fat are less likely to be loved, in which case cause and effect are reversed. Those who are not loved have more time to eat. Those who "give up on being loved" may escape entirely from social control including the negative reinforcement and punishment which restrict eating. The funny behavior of a fat person is socially reinforced; it is easy to be funny. An unhappy person may be especially susceptible to reinforcement by any available reinforcer. Is it displacement when one who is not loved turns to masturbation, prostitutes, or an unattractive lover?

"*Thinking in Rope*"

The lid of a lobster shipping crate is tied shut with small lengths of rope attached for that purpose. I have seen the gearshift lever of a diesel engine on a fishing boat held in any of three positions by loops of rope, the original ratchet having broken. Rope does not rust in salt water and is almost always at hand but, given free access to other means, a fisherman is still likely to "hold something in place" with rope, where a carpenter would use blocks of wood, nails, and screws, or a metal worker wire hooks, solder, and bolts. A repertoire appropriate to a special field is generalized to other circumstances.

Backward Child

In a filmed version of *Pride and Prejudice* made, I think, in 1939, the fawning, pompous, foolish Mr. Collins was very well done, but he was represented as the *librarian* of Lady

Catherine de Bourg, rather than a cleric. The church was secure enough in 1800 to survive the honest portrayal of a silly curate, but not today.

The minister in Somerset Maugham's "Rain" became a fanatic faith-healer in the movie version, although his lines and action would be unexceptional in any Protestant missionary of the period. Would an immoral minister offend too many potential customers, or is the offense all too real in a moribund institution?

How long will Friar Tuck remain a religious?

(I believe Aldous Huxley wrote the script for the filmed version of *Pride and Prejudice*.)

On Rereading

I have just read a detective story which I had read no less than—possibly longer than—three years before. I must have read 40 or 50 pages before it began to seem familiar. It was only with the mention of a place in France with an odd name, the Ferme du Grand Puits, that I was sure. I vaguely sensed the violent scene into which the hero was walking and had a rough idea of the nature of the intrigue behind the murder to be explained. I could not at any point describe what was coming or "who dunnit."

What had I remembered? The prose seemed to move logically, efficiently, easily. It may have done so on the first reading, but I doubt it. In a sense it was now the recreation of something once known—though this fact was not conspicuous enough to be remarked for a long time. To some extent the writing must have been a little closer to my behavior, intraverbally, autoclitically, etc., as the result of my having engaged in it all at least once before. It was familiar in the sense in which heavily reworked prose, or prose influenced by another language (in a poor translation or in the writing of someone, e.g., Conrad, whose native tongue is different) is unfamiliar.

Some of the comfortableness of rereading a favorite book could attach to rereading a nonfavorite with little recognition that it has been read before. A popular author may exploit this so long as he does not lead the reader all the way to *déjà vu.*

Temporal Conditioning

Suppose the radio people decide that—in the United States as in Britain—a bit of silence is a good thing. Perhaps advertisements would be less aversive and more effective if the sustained sound were broken up. Some programs—such as broadcasts of games—need not be continuous, for the listener has learned to wait for the next play, but in most programs a silence of, say, ten seconds would make thousands of viewers change stations and thousands of others grow uneasy about their sets. Announcements that periods of silence are to occur would have little effect unless made frequently, but a program of gradually lengthening periods of silence would do the trick.

A scheduling system could be arranged so that, when an opportunity for silence arose, the speaker would press a button and not speak again until a signal light came on. The device would automatically time silences of variable lengths, with an increasing mean value. Many days or weeks might be needed to reach an occasional silence of, say, half a minute, but the result would be a great relief and might increase the effectiveness of programs and advertisements.

Gender

Making a possessive pronoun agree with the gender of the thing possessed instead of the gender of the possessor can be inconvenient. I have noticed many examples in Françoise Sagan's *La Chamade*, much of which is concerned with pairs of people of different sex. It is often an important question whether something is *his* or *hers* but all we learn from the pronoun is the gender of the *thing*. Thus, *"Il dinait chez 'ses amis,' il dormait dans 'son appartement,' il vivait 'sa vie.'"* Or, in English, "He dined at *her* friends, he slept in *her* apartment, he lived *her* life."

Do We Really Want to Save Labor?

What do we do with the time? Is not the alternative to aversive work nonaversive work? Until it has been shown what people in general might do with their lives, can a culture safely give them leisure?

It is no answer to point to the great artist, composer, writer, or scientist. That is a very special use of time. And it is, as artists, composers, writers, and scientists will insist, *labor*. What we want is labor that has reinforcing consequences—labor that is not performed to escape aversive consequences. Like absolute freedom from aversive control, absolute freedom from work would be a dangerous condition if it were not an illusion.

A Novel Defense of Capital Punishment

A public execution in Communist China (a man shot to death by a soldier in a public square) was explained ("justified"?) by saying that people were outraged by his double murder. In other words, the execution was to affect the feelings of law-abiding citizens rather than the behavior of potential criminals. The government was not punitive; it was simply concerned for the happiness of its people and did not like to have them suffer feelings of outrage.

Sciurine Matador

The bushy tail of the squirrel is probably a stabilizer in climbing and jumping, but on the ground it seems to serve as a decoy or diversion. How many predators have failed to capture squirrels because they have attacked the big flicking tail rather than the sleek body? (There must be a military term for a worthless lure which draws fire from a vulnerable point.) The matador's cape and muleta serve the same function. Something conspicuous, in almost constant motion, is set up as the primary object of attack.

(The matador's *costume* attracts *our* attention more than the cape or muleta, but the bull may have inherited a disposition, or learned, to avoid variegated surfaces which, like boulders in a pasture, are more likely to be solid and have sharp points. Of two large objects, one plain and one braided and sparkling, which will an enraged bull more often attack?)

Freud and Mothers

At the Massachusetts General Hospital Grand Rounds someone asked whether there might not be some special innate relationship between mother and infant that had survival value and would confirm the Freudian formula. (I had said that if a man raised an infant, things would be different.) But I raised the question of the "innate" environment. How much of what a mother does in a two-room apartment with modern furnishings could be innate?

Nausea

Digestive distress is a negative reinforcer. It is dramatized as such in television advertisements for antacids. Swallowing a bubbling drink is followed by "relief." One escapes from nausea by ingesting a remedy, and takes the remedy again when in distress.

But one produces nausea by ingesting indigestible or poisonous food. Nausea is thus punishing. One is then less likely to eat that kind of food again. It is not a *reinforcer;* it does not strengthen the behavior. How does it weaken it? By reversing a process of conditioning? No, by making the food a conditioned aversive stimulus to be avoided.

Music

Only by listening to a piece of music until it is perfectly familiar can we hear it as the composer heard it—or "meant" it. Wagner evidently composed large blocks of music in something close to the finished form in one session, but how much revision, alone or in rehearsals, must have gone on even so, and how much familiarity with one part went into the composing of another? The promptings and probings of musical form change drastically upon rehearing, and even more so upon memorizing. To the composer it was all memorized.

Museum Management

There is a problem in arranging displays in a museum. Assume that you have ten things to be displayed and that the public is interested in them (and will spend time looking at them) to degrees indicated by the numbers 1 to 10. Assume that they must be arranged in line. Visitors are to enter at one end and leave at the other end. In what order do you display them if a crowd around an item is to be avoided? If you isolate the three most interesting items, as in—

$$1-10-2-3-9-4-5-8-6-7$$
$$\text{or } 1-8-2-3-9-4-5-10-6-7$$

you will get crowds, because the preceding items will lose newcomers to the interesting ones, and the following items will fail to pull them away.

There is a case to made for

2–4–6–*8*–*10*–*9*–7–5–3–1

as minimizing the crowd around 10, and encouraging people to leave the room after 1.

Verbal Expansiveness

In the midst of an enormous flood of verbal behavior, a friend frequently loses strength and ends a sentence with *and so forth and so forth and so forth* or with *and this and that and the other*. Content runs out, but the sentence lingers on. In the end, the behavior is under the exclusive control of space-filling contingencies.

Utopia

George Eliot, *Felix Holt the Radical* (London: Panther paperback, p. 333), first paragraph of Chapter 38:

" . . . her little private Utopia, which, like other Utopias, was filled with delightful results, independent of processes."

That was Marx's point: Utopias are easy to enjoy but not to produce. The behaviorists are on the same side: one can picture a good life by analyzing one's feelings, but one can achieve it only by arranging environmental contingencies.

Superstitious Generalization

Our gasoline lawnmower is started by winding up a stiff spring which is released when, as one folds back the handle, a pin on the handle disengages a pawl. The student who had trouble starting it banged down the handle as if he were spinning the shaft. Nothing he could do by way of a forceful blow would alter the speed with which the shaft turned, yet he threw the handle down with greater and greater force as the motor failed to start. There were no relevant contingencies. Evidently there was induction from starting comparable motors by pulling a cord or from starting anything that refuses to start—say, a balky mule or a stuck door.

Salestalk

Eve and I decided we needed a new vacuum cleaner of a particular type that is sold door-to-door. By chance a salesman turned up shortly thereafter.

"Could I interest you in a new vacuum cleaner?"

"Yes. Come in. We'll take one."

The salesman was thrown completely off balance. He went into his salestalk, demonstrating various advantages of the model, refusing to be stopped when, again and again, we said, "Fine! We'll take it." He kept on to the end and seemed genuinely puzzled as he made out his sales slip and took our check.

Miscarriage

At the conference on *Beyond Freedom and Dignity* at the Center for the Study of Democratic Institutions, I was asked to make some closing remarks. I ended by saying how much I appreciated the fact that the Center had arranged the conference and how much I had enjoyed and profited from it. Then I added:

"That is why I was surprised by the message in the Chinese fortune cookie at dinner last night, which read, 'Won't you join me in a cup of Eucalyptus?—Socrates.'" (The Center is surrounded by Eucalyptus trees.) There was laughter and applause, but Harvey Wheeler was deeply puzzled.

The next day he said that his wife had explained it to him, but he added, "Eucalyptus is a poison." "So is hemlock," I said, and he fell back into puzzlement.

What I had meant was that if the conference had gone the way criticism of my book had gone, it would be appropriate for Socrates to ask me to join him. But it had not and that was why I was surprised.

The South Seas

"Natural man" was discovered in Tahiti and elsewhere in the South Seas, and "self-sufficient man," the master of all he surveyed, was cast up on an uninhabited desert island. Both enjoyed a successful anarchy, but for different reasons.

Travelers like Marco Polo discovered nothing comparable. They found other ways of life but on familiar patterns, with a ruling class and peasants, a code of morality, and so on. That people could live well and happily without oppressive government and could behave well without Western morals came as a surprise. Diderot had fun with it in his *Supplement to the Voyage of Bougainville*.

If Locke, Rousseau, Voltaire, and Diderot heard about these examples of real natural men and real simple societies (much exaggerated, alas), how much credit can we give them for what they wrote?

States of Mind

"Lack of faith in ourselves and in our institutions and the tenets upon which our way of life is founded." Is that what ails us? But if so, why the lack?

The phrase is really intended as a description of current behavior. We do not act as successful people act; we do not follow the rules and principles laid down by government, religion, or ethical groups.

If we are to say why, we must look at the contingencies of reinforcement. Our everyday behavior is not productive. We have no reason to conform to rules and principles. The world has changed. It is no longer reinforcing our behavior.

Unclear Stimuli

Being deaf, or listening to faint speech at a distance, is like being half blind or reading bad handwriting. One can hear and see phrases which have strength from other sources—familiar intraverbals, memorized passages, and so on—but a new response, like an unfamiliar name, cannot be heard or read.

Developmental Contingencies

At a certain age (3½ for Lisa), a child begins to speak in mature ways which surprise, amuse, or impress adults, who then show astonishment, laugh, or compliment the child. These responses do not shape behavior in any useful way. A child has to put up with a great deal of irrelevant reactions at this stage. He or she would be better off if adults restrained themselves, responding only in ways appropriate to the behavior.

Impressionism

How much of the extraordinary productivity of the Impressionists was due to the quicker reinforcement and the reduction in aversive attention to detail which followed when photographic realism was abandoned? Cézanne worked hard, there is no question of that, but he could still produce a picture quickly. Could Picasso have done half of what he has done if he had done it "photographically?" Someone like Dali, who remains compulsive about details, has produced very little.

The startling discovery that detailed likeness was not necessary in a beautiful picture made a picture more immediately reinforcing and freed the artist from many hours of busy work.

The Language of Music

When Julie was 21, she and I were listening to a recording of *Tristan und Isolde.* She was not at all familiar with the opera and speaks no German. When the duet between Tristan and Isolde was interrupted by the entrance of the King, Wagner had conveyed the change in situation and mood so accurately that Julie cried out: "What happened?"

Deep Structure

An account in the Sunday *Times* suggests to me that Chomsky's deep structure is what I have been calling primordial verbal behavior—before autoclitics are added. At least that is true of the examples given in the article.

One "psychologist" is said to have argued that the developing child feels a "language pressure." What is felt are the growing demands of a verbal community to which the child's verbal behavior becomes more important.

But deep structure is really the nonverbal situation giving rise to verbal behavior, rather than the primordial responses which first appear.

Noncontingent Reinforcers

"After all," says Frazier, "what is love but positive reinforcement?" "Or vice versa," says Burris.

They were both wrong. They should have said "an act of love." Love as a state is a disposition to act toward another in ways which are reinforcing but *without attention to any contingencies.* In love we act to please and not to hurt, to be nice and not to be mean—but we do not act to change behavior. No doubt we change it, since we are more likely to act in reinforcing ways when we have just been treated in such ways. Reciprocal action may escalate, quite without an implied contract (neither party says, "I'll love you more if you love me more").

In therapy and education genuine affection cannot be *used* to solve problems. It cannot be turned on or off at the right time. But what about avoiding its use? Suppose you discover that in loving someone you *are* reinforcing harmful behavior; can you withhold signs of your love while continuing to love? Would that not simply be a slightly more farsighted form of doing good to someone—i.e., of loving?

Multiple Causation

Yesterday, in my seminar, while reporting on Gilbert Ryle's lecture the night before, I developed a theme I had previously missed. When you read a paper you yourself have written, you are presumably combining textual behavior with behavior very close to that which produced the text. You are reading and at the same time asserting what you say. You once asserted it without supplementary strength before there was a text; now you use the text to prompt yourself so that you can assert it all in good order upon a specific occasion.

Ryle was scarcely asserting anything. He was reading. He would interrupt a sentence between words as he turned a page. He would skip a word, find he was not emitting a sentence at all (he *was* functioning as a listener evidently), say "I beg your pardon," and try it again.

At the other extreme would be using the text as the skimpiest of prompts, *speaking* the lecture sentence by sentence, probably departing from the text a bit here and there, "carried away" (from the text?) by the excitement.

Morphology

I tried to get a student to see the emptiness of mere form by asking him how he would define a plural. "In English, as added *s's*," he said. "As in *run, runs?*" I said.

In field work, the linguist asks an informant, *Is this a sentence?* and then after rearranging the words, *Is THIS a sentence?* But no *arrangement* of words is a sentence at all. No one has spoken it.

Book is not a word if it was composed by drawing letters from an urn. Neither *He did not go* nor *He go did not* is a sentence if it was composed by picking words out of a hat.

We want to study not *forms* but verbal responses having form.

Obeying a Rule

The superiority of positive reinforcement is evident even in mediated consequences. I have trouble remembering to put drops in my eye, in part because they sting. If I forget them I may lose more of my field of vision, but even so I forget. The immediate aversive consequence is prepotent over the avoidance of loss in the future. The last time I was tested, however, I had a very *good* reading, an especially low intraocular pressure, and since then I have remembered much more easily to put in my drops. Why?

There is only a remote connection between putting a drop in my eye and a reading of reduced pressure. The behavior is rule-governed. The rule is laid down by my oculist, and I follow it either because he warns me that I may become blind or because he assures me that I will continue to have useful vision. The assurance appears to be more effective than the warning.

Freedom

One who writes fiction can describe characters behaving in ways which escape the criticism one would receive if one acted in those ways oneself. Actors can also behave publicly in possibly censured ways while "being unaccountably themselves." Of course it is the reader who is most likely to do this. One searches for characters to act with and speak with, with little or no risk of censure.

Yet one cannot go too far at any given time—except in a completely permissive culture in which outright behavior would also probably not be censured.

Sources of Poverty

Karl Marx (*The Paris Manuscripts*) paraphrased by David McLellan (*Marx before Marxism*):

"Marx contrasts the socialist attitude to the wealth of human needs with the attitude brought about by private property which artificially created needs in order to bring men into dependence. As a result, poverty increased as men and their needs were at the mercy of the money market, and eventually men's living conditions became worse than those of animals." (p. 263)

What about the rancheros around the city of Caracas (and Rio de Janeiro?)—have their needs been artificially created? Are they *dependent* on capitalists? (They have no jobs.) Are they at the mercy of the money market?

One could say they are deprived of land they can work, and of the things to work it with, but most of them came into Caracas and left land and things behind. For what reinforcers? Other people. Crowded housing but plenty of sex, including incest. A chance to go into a glamorous city. A small chance to beg or earn a pittance. Not designed control, certainly. Much more like the accidental contingencies of physical and undesigned social environments.

"Experimenting"

Critics often say something like this: "In the sonnet, Shakespeare was experimenting with new rhythms." But what does "experimenting" mean? Trying new rhythms to see if they work? Starting with stress patterns and finding relevant words to fit them? Something else seems to me much more likely. Various current conditions and recent verbal and nonverbal histories contrive to produce verbal behavior having new rhythms. The creative act came when Shakespeare allowed some of the results to stand and rejected others.

In *Men of Good Will*, Jules Romains has his poet, Strigelius, discover a way to be creative which was almost wholly a question of selecting or rejecting.

Imitative Model

If other people are more likely to behave in a given way when we behave in that way as a model, we may use the effect for purposes of control. Thus, teachers model the behavior their students are to display, verbally or nonverbally, and by providing reinforcement when they do so, they strengthen both the behavior and their imitative repertoires. The control is quite explicit: The teacher acts because of identifiable consequences. But we may also serve as an imitative model "unwittingly"—that is, without noting or being able to say that we are doing so. The referee's gesture of both arms in the air, which signals a touchdown, is highly reinforcing to members of the team that has scored. When the result of a play is not immediately clear, a player may himself signal a touchdown, just because doing so creates a similar stimulus. If the referee then also signals, the player has seemed to supply an imitative model, even though the referee's behavior was quite uninfluenced by the player. Gesturing a touchdown becomes a superstitious way of "getting the referee to make the same gesture."

Reasoning Defined

"As C. S. Lewis has pointed out, reason itself is one of these fundamentally non-analyzable traits, because by attempting to derive it from irrational factors we destroy its claim to correspondence with objective truth." (Letter to the Editor, *The Sciences*, January/February 1976.)

"A trait derived from factors claiming correspondence with objective truth"—what can *that* be?

Reasoning as an activity can be defined. It is not a trait, a factor, or a corresponder with objective truth. It is the analysis of contingencies of reinforcement, by the help of which the reasoner may satisfy the contingencies without being directly affected by them. Instead of throwing dice with a likelihood arising from the frequencies encountered in a long history of throwing, one "examines the sample space" and acts "rationally" with respect to a given setting.

The Ghost of South Station

This is Saturday morning, not a day for commuters, but it is also bad flying weather and some of the people here have been grounded. Of thirteen ticket windows on the concourse side, three are open. In the waiting room a long string of windows which used to be reserved for Pullman and long-distance tickets are permanently closed. The benches, which used to fill the room in rows, have been reduced to a single long row down the middle. If this was done to facilitate cleaning, it has failed. At ten o'clock this morning the long bench covers a trail of candy wrappers, beer cans, and old newspapers, kicked under the benches by customers. In the concourse a man pushes a broom ahead of him down the middle of an area, leaving edges and corners untouched. The platform alongside the train is covered with slushy ice. The train has three parlor cars, in which there are seven or eight passengers. I suppose it may pick up more. I asked the porter for a table ten minutes ago. He is standing around at the far end of the car. I shall be interested to see when he brings the table. We are pulling out eight minutes late.

The porter was pleasant and apologetic when I eventually asked again for a table. Why had I not reminded him?

The roadbed makes it impossible to write. Freight does not care about the roadbed, and the railroad does not care about passengers.

The Wrong Word Written II

I wrote *The student must be thought—taught to think*, where the conditions leading to *think* presumably contributed to the strength of *thought*.

I wrote *The two are, of close . . .*, where I had started to write *The two are, of course, closely related. Close* has the strength needed to displace *course*.

I wrote *A series of triangles of different sizes may seem to be represented by length of size* and corrected the last word to *side*. Was *size* a self-echoic response? Might it not have appeared even if *sizes* had been, say, *magnitudes?* If so, the slip was due to both formal and thematic variables, combining to strengthen *size* to the point at which it displaced *side*.

I started to write *While planning to write this note.* Instead I wrote *While planti* and then broke off. I had been recalling a lecture in which I discussed the horticultural metaphor of guidance. Did that strengthen *plant?* But note that all four of the words following *planning* have a *t* in them.

I wrote . . . *when analyzing what when does when doing nothing,* in which *when* displaces *one*. It has already appeared and is due to appear two words later. It is also a near rhyme.

Under a line beginning *Includes covert problem solving* I wrote *Rules not known to the person so* . . . where *so* was the beginning of *solving them*, which I then corrected to *following them*. *Solving* could be a simple transcription of the word in the preceding line, but it resembles *following*. Did I change my covert "oral" response to *solving* and then "take dictation" by writing it?

From my notebook: *I am slowing seeing that.*

Topless

When the topless shows first hit San Francisco, I went to one with two friends. The student-working-nights who parked our car recommended Off Broadway as the best. A barker urged us in: "Show in progress." We were taken to seats at a table with a white plastic top, on which a girl was "dancing." From bottom to top: gold shoes with very high heels, gold bikini pants, very sparse but held firmly in place by strong elastic straps at the sides, bare breasts with large areolae but no visible nipples. "Dancing" consisted of walking without going anywhere, occasionally clapping hands. My friends looked at her *face*, and she stopped still, pointed to them and drew a square in the air. Five other girls were dancing on other tables in the room.

There was a change of guard. The girl asked me to let her use my chair to step down, and a replacement took over. This time the music was, significantly, "He's got the whole world in his hands." Meanwhile dozens of barebreasted waitresses served drinks. Big breasts were supported. Small ones had metallic nipples glued on.

Later there was a fashion show, with models wearing rather attractive gowns with exposed breasts. Bright spotlights. One gown cut very low in back—the spotlight "irising out" on the buttock cleft.

Finally the "star"—naked except for a very small flesh-colored bikini—cavorting on a bearskin rug, making the most of her large but well-shaped breasts, motioning to male customers to come up to her, pretending to push their hands away.

Then the girls climbed up on the tables again, and we left.

The Value of Design

When evolution is redirected by breeding cows that give more milk and horses that run faster, no one asks "design for what?" The "values" are clear. When the genes are changed, as in recombinant DNA work, the values are again clear (less sickle cell anemia, for example).

When teachers use contrived contingencies to build behavior that will be effective under the natural contingencies of early life, the "values" are also clear.

Is the design of a whole culture any different?

Contingencies, Plus and Minus

"It is said that Thales was once in charge of some mules, which were burdened with sacks of salt. Whilst crossing a river, one of the animals slipped; and the salt consequently dissolving in the water, its load became instantly lighter. Naturally the sagacious beast deliberately submerged itself at the next ford, and continued this trick until Thales hit upon the happy expedient of filling the sack with sponges." (H. W. Turnbull, "The Great Mathematicians," in *The World of Mathematics*, vol. 1, p. 81.)

A likely story! Wet salt, even if partly dissolved, is heavier than dry; the load was not "instantly" lighter— though the storyteller evidently thought this the important point. A load of sponges would not be aversive enough to generate escape by falling—and the change would in fact represent a great victory for the mule.

Looking

It was in the thirties or forties that I first realized that the behavior of "looking for things" is reinforced. The idea seemed quite radical. One looks about because the behavior, topographically specified rather than defined by purpose, is reinforced by finding things.

The other day a friend and I were throwing a tennis ball for his young poodle to retrieve. The dog would find it only if he raced after it just as it was thrown. If he lost track of it, he stopped immediately and came trotting back. My friend would then go after the ball. No exploratory behavior on the part of the dog was reinforced by finding the ball. (I tried gesturing another throw, to get the dog to run into the area where the ball lay, but generalized running under the control of that stimulus had been extinguished.) Pointing was, of course, useless. (Karen Pryor says porpoises follow a point "as dogs do not," but I am sure a dog could be taught to follow a point.)

The notion of reinforced looking now seems to me commonplace.

Sh!

In *Verbal Behavior* I note that putting a finger on one's lips as a gesture is similar to the mand *Be quiet!* One may put one's finger on the lips of another (if close enough and if personal relations permit) but not in quite the same way. On one's own lips, where no real blocking is needed, the finger is in profile; one could blow along the nail. One puts the *ball* of the fingertip on the lips of another, and this is closer to physical blocking.

Partial Paraleipsis

It was my pleasure [or privilege] to address a large audience . . .
What is the function of the phrase *It was my pleasure?* It shifts the assertion from *I addressed a large audience,* and hence makes it less likely to sound like boasting or conceit. It is partial paraleipsis in the sense that it says something without saying it very strongly.

Translation Translated

George Steiner's *After Babel* is about translation, and I cannot see that it says anything more than that a translation is something which has the same effect on readers in a different language as the text has upon readers in the original language. A musical setting can be something of a translation in that sense. So can a parody; though written for a different effect, it depends upon having something in common with the original.

Perceiving

For onto- or phylogenic reasons, we see and hear what *usually* happens in a given setting. An object moves from spot to spot through the intervening space, and we see it move even when it appears disparately in different spots in quick succession. A bird flying behind a dimly perceived tree, the successive frames in a movie—these are rare exceptions to the rule that things pass *through* space, and we see the rule rather than the exception.

Speech or music fed into alternate ears in succession is heard in one or both ears as continuous; that is the way speech and music is almost always heard. Photographs of bumps on a surface are seen as bumps or depressions depending upon the position of the lighted edge; light almost always comes from above.

The photograph of the concave back of a mask of a face is seen as a convex face; such a pattern of planes and lines is almost always seen as convex.

We can add details—run the film slowly, alternate the segments of speech slowly, supply other information about the bumps, look at a real mask for a long time, and in doing so we may change our perceiving to some extent (and we do this in part when we "try to see" the nonmovement or try to hear the alternating segments).

Avoidance Learning

"Knowing it's time to change the record" (while playing an opera one has played many times before, without an automatic record changer) would seem to include (a) listening more closely to the music as it approaches a given point, (b) responding to it as a preaversive stimulus (where the aversive stimulus is the rough scratching of the eccentric end groove), and (c) starting up to change the record. When different recordings of the same opera break at different points, the result can be quite distracting. The temporal stimuli cannot easily be verbalized (by me, at least, though an informed musical theorist would have less trouble: "It breaks at the end of the recapitulation"), and they build up as in any avoidance contingency.

Just now I noticed a related but reciprocal effect. The second movement of the Bruckner *Fifth* ends halfway through Side 2. I got up and approached the phonograph, gradually "knowing" as I did so that the third movement was about to start. There were preaversive effects here: I was about to appear to have done a needless thing. I also saw that I was slowing down in my approach and in my reaching toward the cover of the cabinet. I had it slightly open, as if merely peeking inside, as the third movement began.

The Plain Mistress

Stendhal's point in *De l'Amour* is that a woman who has given reinforcing "favors" becomes beautiful via conditioning. Her face and voice, seen and heard during moments of sexual excitement, acquire some of the same reinforcing power. Later they excite, as conditioned stimuli. "Come on" expressions and tones of voice are discriminated from "not interested." They reinforce daydreaming. They also acquire power as stimuli controlling the behavior of making advances, and this may generalize. One who has enjoyed *plain* women may become interested in a new plain one and make advances toward her.

Though Stendhal would not have mentioned it, the same may be said of women and plain men.

Pattern

Looking down on the farming country between New York and Baltimore I saw a piece of woodland shaped like a piece of the Phoebe Snow jigsaw puzzle I had as a child. Views from the air often resemble jigsaw puzzles and probably strengthen all such reminiscences. I had a feeling of satisfaction, of familiarity, of knowing where the piece went, of knowing it was the right piece.

I remember many details of that puzzle, especially the pieces showing parts of the polished brass fittings of the rear platform of the train. All this in a puzzle I played with as a child a great many years ago. Why do I remember it?

Putting a jigsaw puzzle together is a good example of perceptual behavior reinforced with respect to shape and pattern. "Looking for" a piece to fit in a given spot is reinforced when a piece with the proper shape and pattern is found. Does this explain why a subtle shape evokes similar behavior years later?

Attracting Attention

"Waving to attract attention" may be simply using a conspicuous stimulus. We wave more noticeably when a response is important (a castaway waving at a passing ship or a friend warning a person of danger), and when there are competing stimuli (waving from the deck of a boat when others are waving, too).

But waving may become a stimulus to which one pays attention because it has been part of important contingencies. A person selling hot dogs at a ball game notices a waving person, as a fire warden notices a wisp of smoke, even though the stimulus would not otherwise get attention.

The Driver's Self-Control

When driving in city traffic, one is subject to the remote consequence of arriving where one is going, but certain behaviors, such as starting quickly after a change of light, blowing one's horn at a slow driver ahead, or moving into a faster lane, have effective immediate consequences, and as a result, the driver who is in no particular hurry to reach a destination may nevertheless drive intensely, generating many aversive by-products.

One solution is to adopt a set of contingencies similar to those of a bus driver. One simply "keeps moving," filling up the space ahead of one's car. The remoter consequences of arriving at one's destination then resemble that of the bus *rider*, who except under strong pressure accepts the prevailing movement of traffic.

The solution could be said to "split one's personality," in the sense of splitting apart two sets of controlling variables. The bus driver is free of the ultimate contingencies of getting somewhere at a certain time; the bus rider is free of the immediate contingencies of moving as rapidly as possible.

Russell on Storage

Russell (*Philosophy*, in a chapter called "Memory Objectively Considered") raises the objection to Watson's view of memory as retained habits by pointing out that if someone asks me to recall what I had for breakfast, I shall use words I did not use at breakfast. Hence my memory was not the retention of a verbal habit formed at breakfast. Russell feels that "meaning" must be brought in. But:

1. if meaning is, in this case, the breakfast (which my memory was about), and

2. if, when asked to remember my breakfast, I simply *see* it again (not conjure up a copy which I then inspect), then I am behaving in "describing the memory" as I should have behaved if I had been asked to describe the breakfast at the time.

Agency

When we say that a man moves his arm, we imply that the rest of his body either is, or contains, the man. When a man moves his body (along a bench, say), who or what is the mover? There seems to be nothing left of the body to be a mover; hence, it must be a noncorporeal agent. In "the arm of a man moves" or "the body of a man moves," the phrase "of a man" simply identifies the arm or body. "Joe's arm moved" or "Joe moved" describes the observed fact.

All the more reason for saying that the movement is reinforced, not the mover.

Contingencies of Blaming

As Choderlos de Laclos's Presidente managed to think about her illicit lover by constantly praying to God to help her cease to do so, so de Sade attempts to allay his own and his reader's guilt by deploring the sexual excesses he describes. It is the technique of the self-righteous gossip, and it succeeds to the extent that punishment is contingent on the conditions under which behavior occurs rather than on the behavior itself. No blame is attached to being forced to "enact" a crime, or to committing one accidentally ("negligence" refers to a different topography), or to displaying comparable behavior under contingencies not involving punishment (killing in warfare). Describing the behavior for which others are to be blamed, unlike describing the same behavior for, say, pornographic reasons, is itself not blamable.

A simple example to be explained by conflicting positive and negative contingencies, rather than by unconscious activities.

Confession

Several psychologists appearing before a committee on which I served made abject confessions of stupidity, oversight, blindness—but always followed by reports of wisdom or clarity. I did not hear a confession where a problem remained unsolved or was solved by someone else. The confession was thus frequently reinforced, although it had the nature of a submission to punishment. If the sin had already been expiated, the wrong righted, the omitted act committed, the net consequences were reinforcing. The confessant was seen to be humble and insightful. Confessing to stupidity has few aversive consequences if wisdom is displayed or reported at the same time. Is this true of confessing sins about which you are now sorry?

Dos Passos, the Behaviorist?

Edmund Wilson, writing to Dos Passos, July 16, 1939 (*New York Review*, March 3, 1977):

To begin with, I don't think your account of what you are doing in your books is accurate. You don't merely "generate the insides of your characters by external description." Actually, you do tell a good deal about what they think and feel. "Behavioristic" only applies properly to the behavior of rats in mazes, etc.—that is, to animals whose minds we can't enter into, so that we can only take account of their actions. Maupassant, in the preface to *Pierre et Jean*, announced his intention of abolishing "psychology" and using something like this method for human beings; but even he, as I remember, cheated; and in any case, how much or how little (in point of quantity) a writer chooses to tell you about his characters, or how directly or indirectly, is purely a technical matter.

But how do we enter into the minds of others? (1) Others tell us how they feel, as they have been taught to do by those who have seen only their behavior upon given occasions. (2) We feel events in our bodies when behaving in the same ways upon similar occasions, and hence suppose that that is what others are talking about. (3) One way of "describing" a feeling is to describe an occasion upon which people would presumably feel that way. "Then felt I like some watcher of the skies. . . ." "He felt as if he had been physically struck. . . ."

I have tried to remain "behavioristic" in writing my autobiography. *Some* readers have been deeply moved—*as I was*—both when I wrote and when I lived the life I was describing. (Dos Passos had met Pavlov—with Horsley Gantt—and *was* writing behavioristically.)

Meditation

When I listen to music while not reading, I sit up, my earflaps on (sound-reflecting surfaces held at angles to my ears by a wire frame fitted on my head), and I get a "sense of self." I am not sure that it is different from lying awake listening to music in the middle of the night, but at least I do not read.

Someone should study the social history of "things to do." What is one escaping from in pure leisure? Women who knit or crochet can also think. Men who whittle or smoke a pipe can think, too. But magazines, books, pictures, and television induce behavior which displaces the weak behavior that would otherwise appear as thought.

Music leaves room for many kinds of behavior, but why do I not simply sit in silence?

"To Thine Own Self Be True"

What can it mean? Let thy behavior be determined by a Thee? By a Self? Or by the history of reinforcement that has made thee a *person?* To act to please another person is being true to oneself if the other person then does one a favor. To please someone you like is being true to yourself because ὁ φίλος ἐστιν ἀλλος αὐτος (a friend is another self). And it is being true to oneself to please and hence appease one who threatens. But these are pretty surely not what Polonius meant.

The relation of current reinforcers to a person's history is the issue. One who has acted for the good of others all one's life and now betrays a friend to avoid punishment is *not* being true to oneself though it is the self that seems to gain.

Slips of the Pen

I wrote *more effective in ducing men to behave well* where *in* preempts the *in* of *inducing.*

Particularly when I am in England, I am aware of giving special attention to the way I pronounce *u* (as in *student*). I have just discovered that a few days ago I wrote *What people due when conscious of pressure*, where *due* is a better transcription of what I try to say than *do*.

I started to write: *2 small checks*, but I made the *2* rather like a *z* and then wrote *mall*, yielding *zmall*, where the *z*-like *2* seemed to be functioning as an *s*.

I wrote: *Did the Greeks no all wee . . .* I then caught and corrected the double *ee* and continued: *. . . need to know.* Only later did I spot the *no.* Did I begin a blend of *we need* because *no* had disturbed me? When shall we be able to answer a question like that? But meanwhile, it is worth asking.

In discussing intraverbals I started to write *higher order*, referring to supraordinate stimulus control. I was going to mention the possibility of several levels. As I wrote *higher* the subvocal response *hierarchy* broke in, almost leading me to write *hier*.

Rumor

At Cambridge University I was scheduled to speak to a group of students in education on a Friday night. Eve was in Ireland at the time, and I had been in Belgium earlier in the week. Efforts to get in touch with me to make sure I had remembered the date naturally failed. Suddenly the report started that I had not given my lecture in Edinburgh (though I had) because I had slipped a disc. I soon heard it from three different people, and it was mentioned later as I was introduced at another meeting. I expected it to hop the Atlantic, but I think it did not.

The Individual and the Culture

We take credit for our culture, but if any credit is to be taken, the culture should take it for us. We like to think we differ from savages, but not because our world differs from theirs; we feel our *minds* must be superior. It is no adequate corrective to acknowledge that there is some of the savage in us all. When we concede the irrational in our behavior, we are not disclosing a vestige or throwback. Humble though the acknowledgment may seem, we are saying that in other respects we *are* superior. And, indeed, we have built a superior world.

A Lengthening Variable-Ratio Schedule

Bill's truck is his only means of support—like a fisherman's boat or a small farmer's cow and plow horse. The island salt air, badly maintained roads, and the abuse of a drunken driver have nearly finished it. The windshield is full of small holes with radiating cracks. The fenders are rusted to thin sheets, bent and torn. Only fragments of padding remain on the springs of the seat. All dashboard instruments are gone except the all-important choke. The gearshift lever rattles into place—and out again if not held. The gears groan and crack. The badly timed explosions of the motor can be heard for half a mile.

I asked Bill to help bring our boat down the hill. The truck was parked on a downgrade in front of the village store. I got in and sat on what was left of the right side of the seat. Bill gave the truck a push, jumped in, set the gear, and, as we picked up a little speed, let in the clutch. A violent jerk, and the motor began to cough. Bill put on the brake (to save the rest of the grade if needed) and pumped the accelerator wildly, keeping his hand on the choke. Satisfied that the motor was started, he reversed and backed rapidly to the store to turn around. The truck stalled, across the road. Three or four of us pushed, including two young men from a car whose way was blocked. We had to push back and forth several times because the steering gear was damaged and the wheels would not turn very far. We went downgrade again, starting and stalling. From time to time Bill would jump out, open the hood, and adjust something with a wrench. We worked our way a tenth of a mile in the wrong direction, the engine coughing and exploding and refusing to race as Bill pumped gas. Eventually he explained that his starter was in for repairs. It might come back on the excursion boat. How would it be if he came up for the boat in a couple of hours? He did not come. Forty-eight hours later he was still parking his truck on downgrades. No one would tow him anymore.

Why does he go on? For one thing there is no alternative. He drinks away his income. He has no capital and not even a decent used car for a down payment. He is currently the "truant officer"—for a school with ten pupils—but he is probably paid by forgiveness of taxes. The lack of alternatives is not the whole story. His zealous preoccupation with the truck is the result of a stretched variable-ratio schedule. Any deteriorating mechanism "stretches" a ratio, as more and more tinkering is needed to finish a day's work. Bill will not take No from the truck. If it were a horse, he would have beaten it to death long ago, for it is also the lot of an aging horse to reinforce the behavior of its owner on a lengthening ratio of work per task. Bill's truck is being beaten to death, too.

(A month after this was written Bill was taken off the island to a state hospital, where he died of alcoholism.)

Verbal Strength

On Tuesday evening, reminiscing about our graduate student years, Eddie Newman and I tried to recall Dave Wheeler's name and failed. Later, possibly the next morning, I got it. I planned to tell Eddie when I saw him. Just now, about 40 hours later, I caught a glimpse of WHEELER in the program of a meeting and instantly recalled our effort.

The fact that I had recalled the name did not cancel the heightened condition of my textual response. My plan to tell Eddie apparently kept it alive.

Playing Fair

The control exercised by religious agencies through a promise of paradise is particularly unfair in the sense that one does not even find out too late that the promise is never kept. By definition one is never in a position to collect until it is impossible to discover that one can never collect. Think of the millions of corpses at the end of pious lives—cheated but never to know!

The only justification for such control is that the good life *has* paid off. But if it has, why could its natural rewards not have sufficed?

Satiation

Does the word mean the same with respect to food and sex? Can a person be surfeited with sex (in the literal sense of having had too much) as one who has overeaten is surfeited with food? The phylogenic "purpose" of sex has not been altered, but the ontogenic "purpose" of food has been. In a monogamous species there may be no reason for further copulation at the moment, since any available egg has presumably been fertilized, but that is a statistical issue, and multiple copulation may still have had survival value.

This is a matter of need-reduction, but not to a "felt" need; rather, to being *satis*-fied, in the literal sense of having had *enough*.

Mass Action

I was once showing the Minnesota animal laboratory to a visitor. We stood looking at perhaps a hundred small cages with one rat in each. I clapped my hands, and all hundred rats leaped up together as if I had moved a great frame on which they were mounted.

I remember lying in the grass at dusk when clouds of gnats would form above any light-colored object. By moving a sheet of white paper one could move the cloud back and forth.

"Wanting It to Be Over"

At a concert or in listening to recorded music I have often found myself impatiently waiting for a piece of music to end, even though I am enjoying it. In part I may be inclined to escape from an uncomfortable seat or to get to bed, since the tendency is strong when the seat is noticeably uncomfortable or the hour late, but it is also a matter of the relative importance of the end of a piece of music. The music builds up to a termination which is maximally reinforcing. (I have noticed that the end of one sonata induces me to start playing another even when, midway, I am bored.)

There are many activities in which the major reinforcement comes at the end of a long chain of responses. In sex the activity is repetitive and in scientific research it is often diverse, but in both the great moment comes at the end. The end competes with the beginning and middle.

I now see that I have been discussing large fixed ratios.

Role and Rule

The "role a person plays in life" is a repertoire of behavior, not a "self" or "personality." It is more than a structural concept because it implies an effect. As its theatrical origins suggest, it has something to do with one's place in a group, with the part one plays in order that some social function may proceed successfully. It strongly suggests rule-governed behavior. The role of Hamlet is the behavior executed by an actor in response to a script which instructs him what to say and do. To assume "the role of mediator" is to act as mediators are told to act—to act to specifications. The behavior one exhibits in playing a role is not the behavior shaped by the contingencies responsible for one's genetic endowment or the uncodified contingencies in one's personal history.

Shaping

Bergen Evans, *Dictionary of Quotations:*

"From the time of Plutarch and Pliny and probably long before, it was believed that young bears were brought forth as shapeless lumps and that the mother licked them into shape. From this came the idea of licking some young 'cub' into shape, and since the chief shaping object, formerly, was the rod, the word 'licking' came to mean a beating."

Must the "shaping" of behavior suffer from the ubiquity of punishment?

Science and the Human Condition

On a television program relayed by Telstar II, I have been watching people pass by the bier of Winston Churchill in Westminster Abbey. A woman wipes away a tear in

London and within a split second her handkerchief flutters on our screen. It is easy to pooh-pooh the scientific achievement. What has it done for us? Yet it is thrilling. And what could more immediately point up the contrast between physical and behavioral technology? The man was great because he rallied a discouraged people in a decisive war. When can we dispense with that kind of hero?

Why does war "bring out the best" in people, and why is it often justified for that reason? Is it simply because the aversive contingencies in warfare are much more powerful, subtle, and sustained than positive contingencies can ever be? But given a wise and skillful design of positive contingencies, can we be sure that we shall not see even finer hours?

Healing a Feeling?

When I was a child my mother used a kiss in a ritual of healing. If I pounded my finger while driving in a nail, she would say, "Here, let me kiss it. That will make it better."

Was this an example of generalization? A kiss made one feel "better" in general. It often healed "mental" suffering, why not medical?

Very different was the philosophy attributed to American Indians of "No smart, no cure." The iodine or peroxide hurt, but it prevented infection. If there is generalization here, it is to the rod which must not be spared if the child is not to be spoiled.

Tea and Madeleines

This morning, washing my face in the bathtub, I felt an irregularity in a tooth and immediately concluded that a filling must have come loose. I had smelled oil of clove, which the dentist often uses. Then I realized that the oil of clove was in the soap, and immediately the filling went back into place. Neither the oil of clove nor the irregularity in the tooth alone would have suggested a dental problem. Combined, the conclusion was almost irresistible.

Person

How can you "discover the real self"? What does it mean to discuss a "real you"? Genetic considerations aside, the real you is whichever of two or more selves, in the sense of congeries of responses, is most likely to be effective in your future and hence most worth building up. Or, in an extreme case, if an earlier self cannot be sufficiently attenuated, it may have to be salvaged and the environment redesigned.

The "reality" is a practical matter of dealing with behavior traceable to two or more conflicting sets of variables.

The Negative Audience II

An example of "negative strength" in the multiple causation of a verbal response, as I discussed it in *Verbal Behavior* (p. 235), is the rejection of a name because of aversive consequences. A child is not given a family name if it is also the name of a strongly disliked person. If two or more names are available, the least aversive emerges. Names which become aversive may be changed. In the first World War, Americans renamed hamburg "victory sausage." After a revolution, there may be sweeping changes in names away from those of earlier heroes or favorites. The French Revolution rejected royalty so violently that, according to Crane Brinton (*Anatomy of Revolution*, p. 188), the suggestion was made that *reine abeille* be changed to *abeille pondeuse*.

I resisted using the initials *HB* to stand for *human behavior* for several years after being rather badly treated by a company the name of which began with those letters.

I avoid *lab* as an abbreviation for *laboratory* (e.g., *lab. res.*) because it is a verbal response used colloquially—going *to the lab*, *a lab coat*, etc., and is not in tune with my current writing.

Rituals

. . . are clearly rules. One observes a ritual. In doing so one may simply play a role, a part, as in a play, where the script is the rule, dictating (good word here!) the speed and action of the character.

But an actor, or one who plays a role in daily life, is not necessarily merely a role player. The role (rule?) may describe contingencies (or behavior normally due to contingencies) similar to those which have a part in the actor's life.

A helpful ritual prompts people to do what they tend to do anyway but at a time and in a pattern which make for a smoother ceremony.

A New Year's resolution, like a party platform, is a rule prompting appropriate behavior. It may serve an aversive function if behavior which breaks the resolution or violates the platform is punished. The role player in a ritual and the actor in a play are also subject to punishment if their behavior does not conform to the script.

Progress?

I wrote *Some people take it upon themselves to change the environment with the intention of changing the behavior of other people.* Then I noted that a definition of intention would be helpful. I roughed out a definition but found that it was much easier simply to drop the word: . . . *to change the environment in such a way that the behavior of other people changes.* But that is not exactly what I first said. The second version lacks the reference to past contingencies implied in "intention." I should have to add: *because of what happened when they behaved in the past.*

Philosophies as Descriptions of Contingencies

"The doctrine of fatalism [has lulled] its adherents into an apathy in which they fail to avail themselves of existing opportunities, and fail to create new ones." —H. J. Muller, "The Meaning of Freedom," *Bulletin of Atomic Scientists,* XVI, no. 8, 1960.

But surely the *doctrine* has not had this effect. Some people may not act—to earn a living, say—and may not create anything by exploring or inventing. They may subscribe to a doctrine, which they have probably not originated, to the effect that nothing is of any use, but they do not fail to act because they subscribe to it. The doctrine is merely a description of the contingencies: "Behavior has few, if any, reinforcing consequences."

This makes a difference. To change people who hold to a fatalistic philosophy, we should not try to change beliefs about the consequences of actions, we should change the consequences. We should arrange contingencies of reinforcement which generate productive and creative behavior. The people will then not describe the contingencies by saying that nothing is of any use; they will not "subscribe to the doctrine of fatalism."

The Cognitive Appeal to Ignorance

A review in *Scientific American* (January 1974) of *The Psychology of Anomalous Experience: A Cognitive Approach* indicates that the author (Graham Reed) is willing to let some unidentified inner determiners explain a lack of normal (nonanomalous) correspondences between behavior (experience) and a current setting. Thus:

Hallucinations: "It is the absence of recognition of the subjectivity of the perception that makes the difference." But how and why do people recognize that perceptions are subjective? Do they *say* that something is really there though it isn't? "The belief in the external correlate . . . marks the true hallucination." Belief? A tendency to respond to an external stimulus? In one case an "experience was . . . no percept at all but a projection from internal ideas." But what is done in projecting an idea?

Delusions: "The environment presents a world of new meanings." How does an environment present a world? And where are meanings? When we see a box on a table, "we normally . . . perceive and classify it appropriately, in a useful hierarchy of relations." Does this mean more than that we respond to it according to past contingencies? But we may suffer a "slippage. We search experience to find among familiar structures a novel fit for the novel meaning." Does this mean more than that if, for example, we are afraid, we may say something about the box that we tend to say about things we are afraid of?

The point of the book is that we do not function as recorders or cameras. Quite right, but it is not a useful alternative to say that we function by actively assembling a tiny sample of cues from the world into a working model of the world. That is also too close to a stimulus-response formulation. The contingencies of reinforcement are the missing key.

"*Verbalize*"

I find myself avoiding or canceling "verbalize" as not only vague but vague-for-purposes-of-escape. If it means *name* or *describe*, then why not say *name* or *describe? Can he verbalize his anxiety?* What does that mean? *To describe a state accurately* obviously means more than *to name or report it correctly.* "Verbalize" masks the distinction.

Auditory Imagery

I have very weak auditory imagery. I can seldom recall a musical theme unless it is very well known. I can read a page of familiar music in a vaguely spatial way, though with little auditory effect. But if I play it on a dead keyboard (say, my electric organ not turned on), I *hear* it. The movements of my hands and fingers seem to be better correlated with auditory stimuli than visual notes.

Text and Context

Shortly after reviewing a section in *The Shaping of a Behaviorist* about L. J. Henderson, I drove down Brattle Street. My eye hung on the sign "Willard Street" as I passed. I have passed it many hundreds of times. I noted my interest and then recalled that Henderson had lived on that street. I had dined with him there.

The simple fact was the heightening of textual control. I had not used the words *Willard Street* in what I was writing, nor had I recalled the dinner. (Just now, in preparing to write this note, I could not recall the name. I knew it began with *M* or *W*, but that was all.)

Jean Renoir

Last night I saw *Le Déjeuner sur l 'herbe.* As in his other films, Renoir directs so carelessly that the viewer is always aware of direction. His characters often have no reason to behave as they do except that they have been told to behave that way. Near the end the hero and the girl whom he is, surprisingly, taking as his bride, burst in on the waiting wedding party. The girl dutifully falls into a front rank while the hero goes through a series of maneuvers turning to first one and then another of the company; then suddenly she steps forward, joins the hero, who has not once looked in her direction, and they march toward the camera. She is doing, not what a girl in her position would do, but what she has been told to do—taking her cue from a well-rehearsed routine or directly from Renoir. In another scene the hero is being sought by his fiancée and vice versa. The fiancée crosses from left to right and leaves the picture; immediately the hero comes from behind a tree and moves right to left. Impossible to suppose he would not have seen her. Of course the whole thing is a farce and was obviously composed on location and as you go, as were early movies generally.

For Better or for Worse

When two people of very different ages marry, there is necessarily an inequality in the exchange of vows. "For better or for worse, in sickness and in health"—the chances are very much poorer for the younger; he or she is much more likely to suffer from the illness of the other. Any other imbalance—say, in wealth—may offset or intensify the difference. The situation becomes more and more improbable as differences add. Thus, it is extremely unlikely that a sick, ugly, and destitute old man will marry a healthy, beautiful, and rich young woman—even though, if love is as free of all this as they say, two such people might fall in love.

The Rebel

"Would the rebel have a place in your world?" is a question I have heard three or four times in the past two weeks.

I tend to compare it with a question asked of a physicist: Would there be a place in your world for a body that moved the wrong way in a gravitational field?

In the past rebels have been important—because the system has needed change, and rebellion may have been the only way to bring it about. Systems will always need change but not necessarily in the style of rebellion. Rebels are defined by their aversive techniques, not by the fact that they try to change things.

"*Discovery*"

Socratic irony—"the assumption of ignorance for the purpose of leading (or misleading) another into an untenable, absurd or embarrassing position"—is part of much current maieutics. Teachers must conceal the fact that they do know so that the student's response will appear as true "discovery" (and to avoid explaining why they do not help). They must then simulate surprise and delight when the student makes a discovery. A frank "*I* know but *you* must find out" is felt to be unhealthy.

The same is true of nondirective therapy. Where the Socratic teacher must conceal the fact that the student is misunderstanding something or making a mistake, the therapist must pretend not to see that the patient is describing an instance of a well-known personal problem. It is no answer to say that *every* act of thought is *in some sense new and peculiar.* To refuse to classify because of small discrepancies is to forego a productive strategy. The teacher and the therapist *do* know what is going on much of the time, though details differ, and to refuse to say so in order to let students or clients "discover it for themselves" is to misrepresent. If the practice taught problem solving, so that both student and patient would be more effective in other matters, it could be defended, but there are better ways of achieving that result.

A Baby Cries

In the Boston airport a family was waiting to board a plane. A baby—possibly nine months old—was held by its father. It cried, with varying intensities, most of the time, and I could not see why. The room was not hot, the baby was comfortably dressed, and it did not seem hungry. But I noticed that the father would respond to each burst of tears by shifting the baby in his arms, jiggling it, or lifting it high in the air. The following day I heard Yvonne Brackbill describe the reinforcement of smiling in a four-month-old. The contingencies were almost identical with those in the airport. The father was reinforcing the baby's crying!

Why had the baby started in the first place? Waiting is a special kind of activity which displaces many standard responses. It is quite possible that the family's normal responses were suppressed, and the standard repertoire with which the baby controlled the family was undergoing extinction. A by-product of extinction is aggressive emotional behavior.

Ear

Follet (*Modern American Usage*) speaks of the "ear" as the organ with which we judge a sentence well or badly composed. Only a person with a "bad ear" will accept such and such a way of expressing something. It is a particularly unhappy term when one is judging a written sentence. It is like the intuition with which a person is said to see that a sentence is not grammatical. Neither expression gets very close to what the listener is doing, or not doing, or not being able to do when hearing a badly composed sentence. One must go more deeply into the contingencies, rather than into the mind, to get at the behavior of the listener.

Robins Calling for Rain

If it is true that robins make some special sound when it is likely to rain, why do they do so? Rain brings earthworms to the surface, and robins eat them. Is there a selective advantage for the species in alerting other robins to the imminence of food? But that would not be a call for rain. Ontogenic contingencies may strengthen a true call (possibly building upon such a phylogenic base) if rain occasionally follows. The "call" is then adventitiously reinforced, like the human rain dance, which is clearly a call for rain.

Elevators

An elevator is a labor-saving device—essential in a tall building. It has aversive properties, such as acceleration (once rapid and disturbing to small children, but now well engineered) and confinement (particularly aversive to the claustrophobic), but in general, if going up or down is reinforcing, then so is entering an elevator.

The operator's "Going up" or "Going down" are important stimuli, as are colored lights, coded or shaped like arrows pointing up or down, or bearing the words UP or DOWN. We step into an elevator appropriately labeled, are taken to our floor, and move on to other reinforcements.

Pressing a button beside the door of a shaft is reinforced by the arrival of an elevator, but not immediately or inevitably. In early elevators, pressing set a telltale in the elevator which the operator might reset or ignore. Some other signal might take precedence, the elevator might pass the floor on its way elsewhere (if loaded to capacity) and clear the telltale, or the button might not work, either because it was out of order or because the elevator was in use and had no memory. Under these contingencies a button tended to be repeatedly pressed or held. An elevator which becomes available as it goes out of use but which may be put in use by someone else maintains the contingency called "limited hold."

Since all this is aversive, improvements have been made. A memory which stores commands eliminates the "limited hold." A report to the user that a command has been registered (as when the button lights up) eliminates other aversive features of intermittent reinforcement.

Racial Unconscious

It is raining again and very cold for May, and our flat at Churchill College is depressing. It has just occurred to me how nice a fire would be, and how important it must be, living in England, to have a fireplace.

But *why* is a fire reinforcing? How long has fire been controlled and used in ways in which it is likely to be steadily watched? Long enough to select and breed those whose behavior is particularly reinforced by fire? (Some recent medical stuff about the dangers in being cold applied only to people past breeding age.)

Can you show that people whose ancestors lived mainly in the tropics do not like fireplaces when they live in temperate zones? How about the Indians, Egyptians, or blacks living in England?

In Love with Wagner

The intimacy of music is like affectionate massage—the composer, helped by the performer, is doing things which feel good to the listener. If they did not feel as good to the composer, there is no "sympathy," in the sense of "feeling with," and the composer is merely a professional masseur, not to say whore.

The Supportive Autoclitic

A speaker may invoke a second speaker to support a remark made to a third party: *She was an interesting old lady, wasn't she, John?* The *wasn't she, John?* is added to strengthen the effect on the third party. The supportive autoclitic often turns up when the third party has not been responding satisfactorily—when bored or skeptical, for example. *As John says* has the same effect, and can be used when John is absent. Literary allusions have the same effect—*as Tolstoi says* or *as the Bible tells us.* One may seek one's own support at another time—in *as I say in my treatise on probability* or *as I have long insisted* or *as I have said a thousand times.*

Killing the Bearer of Bad News

A simple example of a conditioned aversive stimulus is the person who says something aversive. We tend to avoid the doctor who has given us bad news, the dentist who has advised us of work to be done, the gossip who tells us tales heard about us, the critical friend, the psychotherapist who stirs old wounds—and the bearer of bad news. Medical and dental schools advise their students about this.

The jeopardy of the ancient messenger carrying news of defeat to his king is shared by the barber who comments on the customer's falling hair, the insurance agent recalling burglaries in neighboring houses, the priest and his *momento mori*, the tailor commenting on the asymmetry of his customer, the dentist noting the bad breath produced by unclean dentures. All are in danger of commercial death. As the messenger attenuates the reported disaster, so the businessman uses "tact," offering compensating good news, favors, and alcohol to avoid the consequences of avoidance conditioning.

The teacher, the policeman, and the priest must be carriers of bad news so long as education, government, and religion specialize in punishment. The avoidance takes the form of truancy, vandalism, crime, apostasy—from the mildest protest to the ravings of the psychotic.

Second Nature

In his biography of Montaigne, Donald Frame writes
(p. 263): "[Montaigne's] method is *habit*, whose power for
goodness he stresses more and more. After Aristotle he calls
it 'a second nature' and he adds: 'and no less powerful.' It
has made him what he is, turning 'this form of mine . . .
into substance, and fortune into nature. . . . What those
men [the Stoics] did by virtue, I train myself to do by
disposition [complexion]'—meaning that he does this by
habit, which forms a second nature." (Montaigne apparently wrote the quoted material in 1578–80.)

We might translate: Montaigne recognizes the sources
of good behavior in genetic endowment and in environmental history. The former is first nature; the latter second
nature. A person is the product of both. The Stoics may
have been born to behave virtuously; Montaigne finds it
necessary to arrange an environment which induces him to
do so.

Straw in the Streets

I was casting about for examples of protecting people from
reality and came up with the practice of putting straw in the
street to silence horses and carriages passing the houses of
the ill. I thought also of hearing aids and was puzzled by the
fact that I had done so, until I realized that I had jumped
ahead to a common effect. Both those measures, undertak-
en to alter the magnitude of a product of behavior, probably
work mainly by changing the behavior and hence the
product. A hearing aid makes speech louder because the
speaker, seeing the aid, speaks more loudly, just as the
coachman, seeing the straw, reins in his horses and drives
quietly.

The blind person's cane is another example. It is used
to discover objects, including pedestrians, but it actually

gets pedestrians out of the way when they see it in use. Painting the cane white intensifies the effect, as concealing a hearing aid weakens it.

Reduction in Stimuli

The blinders on a carriage horse were designed to eliminate distracting stimuli. The horse needed to look only straight ahead. Some racehorses wear a doughnut-shaped device, a "bourrelet," below the eyes to keep them from being frightened by their own shadows on the ground.

Evidently a horse lends itself well to blinding as a measure of control. In rescuing one from a burning stable the first step seems to be to throw a blanket over its head.

Aggression

From my hotel window I have been watching the wrecking of a building. The wreckers break windows, smash doors, pull down sections of a wall, and smile at each other with satisfaction as a whole wall goes over. Their behavior is highly reinforced by the destruction they work. Are they more or less inclined to be vandals in off hours? Is there satiation or a whetting of appetite? What happens to the employee of the abattoir who spends his day killing animals with a club? Someone who visited a Bruderhof in Paraguay many years ago told me that the Brothers discovered they found that they enjoyed killing their livestock and therefore hired native Paraguayans to do it for them.

Prepared for Recall

During the night I speculated on how little of the world of my childhood I should find after 40 years when I return, as I plan to do, to Susquehanna. Just now, cleaning out some space in the basement, I picked up a long broom or rake handle and suddenly saw it and felt it as my Boy Scout staff. I was in many ways myself of 45 years ago as I took hold of it. It is probably relevant that I have recently seen a television news account of a Boy Scout encampment at Valley Forge, and that my secretary told me that Tom Lehrer was not allowed to sing his "Be Prepared" in New Zealand because New Zealanders respect the Boy Scout movement too highly to permit anyone to make fun of it.

Harrumph!

Raising one's voice in order to be heard is an example of the differential reinforcement of energetic verbal behavior. Changing pitch to overcome a particular masking noise is another. The composer is affected by similar contingencies at the beginning of an opera. A great crash brings the audience to order.

Some Spoken Blends

A television announcer describing the condition of a football playing field said *sloppery* and corrected it to *sloppy, slippery*.

Just making an early plane, I said to the man at the gate, *You stop at San José, I hust.* I was too tired to correct it to *hope* or *trust*.

A newscaster: *the Miami Beast—Beach bus strike.*

Baseball TV announcer: *He went in as a pinch rinner—a pinch runner—for Petrocelli. Pinch hitter* is a much commoner term. In this case *hitter* was no doubt strong—in the eighth inning of a game—but not just at the moment.

Rinner is pretty clearly a blend of *runner* and *hitter*. The short *i* of *pinch* could have made an echoic contribution.

In hastily referring to *Daniel Deronda* I mentioned the character *Gwendoleth*. I knew it was not right but let it pass. Hours later I said to myself *Gwendolen Harleth* and recalled, and thus corrected, the mistake.

TV election reporter: *He was resoundly (s* pronounced *z) beaten.* A blend of *soundly* and *resoundingly?*

That is all for the present time. A blend of *for the present* and *at the present time?*

A speaker said, *Please bear me out.* Presumably a blend of *Please hear me out* and *Please bear with me.*

Fiction

If I argue that only limited things can be done about anything as vast as human history because we are in contact with so small a sample, I shall be told, "Yes, but one may go beyond the facts by using one's imagination!" That is said to be done, for example, in theoretical physics. What is the evidence?

The facts: What is said cannot be traced to a situation of which it can be called a description. It is about things not (or not yet) seen. Therefore, it must be due to some inner process of construction. But where does that come from? Why does it operate?

The real distinction is not between behavior attributable to "sense impressions" and behavior attributable to a "creative imagination"; it is between control by immediate stimuli and control by conditions resulting from an environmental history.

Imagination, like other faculties, is a name for origins of behavior which are found in a person's history rather than a current situation.

Stimulus Generalization

For years we kept our kitchen clock ten minutes fast to help get our daughters through breakfast and off to school on time. It is said that the great clock in the Edinburgh railway station has always been two minutes fast, presumably to get passengers into their trains on time. I know of a restaurant at an airport where an electric clock is set five minutes fast.

A stimulus is thus moved along a continuum in the direction of a more powerful value. The clock is a white lie. But why do we not form a discrimination between such a clock and others which are accurate? Certainly train-goers in Edinburgh must know of the deception, yet it is probably effective, as our kitchen clock was. It is possible that there are so many different clocks, so different in size, shape, and location, that a sharp discrimination is never formed.

The Invention of Myths and Rituals

Raglan's argument in *The Hero* against folk invention of folk tales, myths, etc., and in favor of origins in ritual doesn't get very far. After all, the stories, if not historical accounts, must have been invented by someone. Under what circumstances? And what does "invention" mean? Here are some relevant speculations suggested by parts of Raglan's book:

A ceremonial parting may have been derived from a genuine parting, as before a human sacrifice. Part of the spectacle is the behavior of the victim in saying farewell: Are there signs of fear? Bravery? Tenderness? Which will the spectators applaud? Which will they boo? A role is shaped, as part of a ceremony. When the practice ceases (why?), reminiscent stories are told about it. When "going to sacrifice" becomes meaningless to listeners, it may become "going into danger" and then ". . . into battle," and we get Hector and Andromache. (These stages need to be explained.)

"Armed dances" are connected with "military defense" (war?). When danger threatens, the warrior takes up his arms. The more powerful he looks, the more the spectacle pleases the old, the too young, the women. Looking and acting fearful are reinforced even when not in combat. Frightening makeups, masks, helmets which greatly increase height, skillful flourishings of swords and shields, like parades of tanks, soldiers, guns, missiles, and space technology, pay off, not in scaring the enemy, but as the effect of ritual on the group itself.

Frightening gestures may be induction from, or preparation for, action, but this too may be distinguished from ritual ceremony.

Ring magic and fertility. Sexual induction? (Details are not given.)

"The *Iliad* is an account of a ritual." But a highly elaborated one. And whence the ritual?

The installation of a king involves the theory that the king (1) dies, (2) is reborn, (3) as a god. This may be an effort to explain the difference between a man before and after he becomes king (especially if he is chosen from the people). Surely it is the previous king who dies. There is no longer a man called So-and-so. Although he resembled the new king, he is no longer the occasion for the old salutations, approaches, and joint actions. One must get rid of him with a decent burial. The new king has "magical" powers not possessed by the previous king; his commands are obeyed; he impresses people with mysterious prestige; he is permitted to wear distinctive garb. He must be brought into the world with care.

Barbarus

The barbarians of the steppes, skilled in horsemanship, easily invaded the effete culture of the cities. Their way of life put no premium on the survival of their culture, offered nothing more interesting than rough, day-to-day survival of the members of a group. And that was a source of strength.

Urban life became strong through the invention of methods of defense and warfare requiring industrial skills not possessed by barbarians (though taken over quickly enough by them) and by the invention of civilization. The intelligent are the gentle.

Barbarus hic ego sum quia non intelligor a quoquam.

Paraphrase

I started a note:

"In trying to think of the word *prodromal. . .*" I fleetingly noted my use of *think* and reflected that to paraphrase it as *behave* would have been awkward to the point of ridiculous. "Trying to *say* the word *prodromal*" would not be much better.

Yet *think of* is not only misleading in suggesting nonphysical action, it forces a reification of the word. It suggests that I was trying to see what the word looked like. A visualizer might "think of a word" in this sense—and then it would be even more difficult to show that he or she is engaging in perceptual behavior.

"Trying to respond by saying *prodromal*" is awkward but worthwhile. For one thing it reveals the misuse of *by*.

"In casting about for conditions under which I would say *prodromal*" is closer to the facts, though metaphorical.

What progress we should make in understanding these difficult matters if we insisted on throwing off traditional metaphors and ellipses!

Compare "to come up with the word *prodromal*," the metaphor of dredging.

Theoretical Models

A remark by a student suggested one of the best arguments against "models." They evoke contemplation rather than action. The theoretical physicist wants to *represent* reality;

the laboratory physicist wants to *do something* about it. One changes a model to produce a different *picture;* the other manipulates independent variables to change a dependent variable. A model is what something is to be done about; it is not what is to be done. *Model* is little more than another word for *idea*—something known by acquaintance.

I look forward to greater recognition of the importance of laboratory scientists. The theorists have been sponging on them for decades and getting most of the credit.

Reporting Behavior

Gerald Durrell, in *The Overloaded Ark*, attributes human expressive gestures to his animals.

Item: A drill (monkey) afraid of a dead chameleon eventually screws up his courage, reaches out, and touches it—"quickly, then drew back his hand and wiped it hastily on the ground." The chameleon may have been sticky or in some other way currently aversive to the touch. If not, is Durrell simply adding a human gesture to make it clear to the reader how the monkey felt?

Item: A group of drills, thrown together with a baboon for the first time, are fascinated with its "long, sweeping, lionlike tail ... they would examine it for a long time with intense interest, and then turn around and gaze at their own blunt posteriors." Is this simply another human gesture thrown in to point up the curiosity of the drills?

Some behavior which could be easily interpreted in this way may well have occurred, but Durrell could have read into it the behavior he reports.

Current State

Behavior may be determined by phylo- and ontogenic histories, but do we not need a systematic description of the resulting current state of the behaving system, and is this not what mentalistic psychology is all about?

Such a description would be useful:

1. if it did not appeal to nonphysical events. "How does a thought cause a nerve impulse?"

2. if it did not assume that mind is directly observable through introspection (some self-observation might have arisen from its usefulness in the evolution of the species, but there is no reason why it should have embraced all the facts about any current state),

3. if it did not assume that the nervous system was equally accessible to observation,

4. if it did not see a useful similarity in computer models, cybernetic systems, information-processing theories, none of which recognizes selection as a causal mode.

I have not faced up to the demand for a useful set of concepts. However, I can claim to have clarified such things as:

1. strength or probability of response,

2. stimulus control, and

3. various "states" associated with schedules of reinforcement.

Raking and Sweeping

Our gardener has been raking up the leaves on our lawn. As usual, the conspicuous reinforcement from moving a large pile of leaves dominates. As in sweeping, raking is a matter of getting enough together to make picking up worthwhile. At one extreme each leaf might be picked up separately; at the other, all the leaves on the lawn might be raked into one pile. Somewhere in between is the optimal size of the pile. But moving a large pile is more reinforcing than moving a small one, although the same leaves are raked again and again with no gain in convenience in picking them up.

I have seen a man sweep the whole floor of a restaurant the morning after a big night, pushing ahead of him an increasingly satisfying pile of paper, cigarette butts, and dirt.

Useful Fantasy?

From a dictionary of usage: "The story [of the ugly duckling] owes a great deal of its popularity in the nursery, as does Cinderella, to the unconscious appeal it makes to children's egotism and self-pity."

At what age do children like to hear about the poor who become rich, the ugly or plain who become beautiful, the weak who succeed, or the miserable who emerge happy? Should we say that it is when they are able to "identify" with the characters in stories? But does that mean any more than that they then behave as the characters behave or undergo the same changes in those bodily states which are felt as "feelings"?

There does not seem to be anything unconscious about this; nor, given the fact that the story evokes similar behavior in the child, is there anything unconscious about the reinforcing value of reassurance after being frightened, enlightenment after being puzzled, or success after struggle.

Examples of Feelings and Intention

A long article on an important subject repeatedly asserts that we "seek community" but that we "love privacy." Community and privacy are made into things. An environmental analysis gains by reducing these things to social reinforcers.

Other people are positively reinforcing when they help, support, applaud, protect, approve, and show affection.

They are negatively reinforcing when they annoy, demand, take things away, criticize, blame.

We seek or construct an environment in which people are positively reinforcing and avoid or escape from one in which they are negatively reinforcing.

By isolating ourselves we escape from possibly negatively reinforcing people at the cost of abandoning positive reinforcers. By joining other people we may achieve positive reinforcement but run the risk of negative.

Privacy in community (or community with privacy) could be said to be characteristic of a world in which one's behavior is positively but not negatively reinforced by others. *Walden Two* was an exercise in that direction.

Getting Attention

The "walker on before the king" is a sort of visual blare of trumpets. Something is going to happen; watch!

The "walker on" need not be as attention-getting as the king. Indeed, he had better not be. He is effective simply because he comes first. The trumpet is effective not only because it comes first but because it is auditory rather than visual (the audience need not be looking). Processions are generally organized with "walkers on before." At commencement, the most important personages appear last in the procession.

The word "climax" began as a metaphor—a ladder on which the top rung was presumably the only important thing. Its use to describe the step-by-step buildup in music and sex seems to have come later. Should we use the word if the preliminaries do not contribute to the culmination except as attention getters?

Teaching a Sheepdog

A French woman who runs a restaurant in Vermont sold some young dogs to a farmer, who later complained that they had attacked, killed, and eaten a young lamb. She was sure this was because they were starving; they were given a commercial dog food and were too thin. Then she said that in France when a dog kills a sheep, all the other dogs are brought together around the dead sheep, and there the offending dog is "beaten to death and shot." And she insisted that the other dogs knew why it was being punished.

This desperate effort to teach animals, accentuating all the details of the human parallel, could at most have the effect of making a dead sheep a conditioned aversive stimulus. Would it work? I doubt it.

Why are people different? Or are they?

"Storing" a Poem

When I memorize a poem, I do not store it as a copy of the text which I go back to and read again as I recall the poem, but the storage *seems* to be in that form if I recover it mainly by seeing it ("visualizing it"), as I sometimes do. It also seems to be stored in the form of an audio recording when I recall it by hearing it. I can also recall it simply by saying it, in which case it is more clearly the behavior that has been "stored." But seeing or hearing it is also behaving. It is what I did when I first read or heard myself reading the poem, in the latter case possibly subaudibly.

"Operant Conditioning"

In Russia we saw an experiment in which a dog responded to half a dozen levers under the control of as many stimuli. A young woman, sitting alongside the enclosure and peeking in through a window, presented the stimuli by squeezing rubber bulbs. The dog was taken through a sequence of responses by presenting the appropriate stimuli. It was described as an experiment on chaining. But the only organism with a well-established chain of responses was the woman.

The Mind of a Group

A reviewer of a book called *The Mind of America* notes H. S. Comminger's *American Mind*, Perry Miller's *The Life of the Mind in America*, and W. J. Cash's *The Mind of the South* and asks why Americans speak of the mind when in other countries historians are more likely to speak of class cultures. Here is a good example of internalizing. A culture as a social environment, like other contingencies affecting the individual, is moved into the head as mind. But into whose head? A generalized American?

It all comes out right if we speak of what people do in reinforcing the behavior of others. Texts are part of the "mind of America" if they are read, cited, supported, or attacked—in other words, if they play a part in the contingencies of reinforcement affecting Americans.

"Mind" in such a case is a structural concept: *what* people "thought" (said?) not *why* they "thought" it. If we define a culture as a set of contingencies of reinforcement maintained by a group, the "motivating force" that is lacking in structuralism is restored.

Holding the Audience

The commitment of those who watch football on TV, especially professional football, is extraordinary. Winning or losing is not the issue. Viewers quickly take sides, but unless they have bet on the outcome or have a strong loyalty to the sponsoring organization, city, or region, a preference for one side can scarcely explain the fascination. The play is exciting, sadistic, tense, often surprising. It is sometimes skillful, though nothing like, say, ice skating in that respect. The important thing is the schedule. Football resembles a slot machine. A few yards gained is two cherries; a first down, three cherries; a long gain, three plums; a winning touchdown pass, the jackpot. Both the game and the slot machine maintain a variable-ratio schedule with a set of reinforcers of varying magnitude.

Comedies, variety shows, quiz programs, and serious drama seldom use the same schedules. But producers want more than sustained viewing. If they are to catch and hold the channel-sampler, something interesting must always be happening. A period during which nothing happens is fatal. Yet there are dull periods in a football game and the audience is not lost. Viewers have come under the control of a "stretched" variable-ratio schedule. Time out, dull plays, measurements, huddles, and so on take a great share of viewing time, but devotees hold to a channel showing any part of a game. Their behavior is sustained through long, dry periods.

Big moments, moving episodes, really funny remarks or actions can't be rapid fire. They would not get the effect of a variable-ratio schedule if they were. They must be scheduled—carefully.

A variable-ratio schedule is effectively stretched in a single program. An opening scene is sexual or violent. Similar scenes recur but they are spaced farther and farther apart and still hold the viewer. Alas, a late tuner-in finds the material boring.

(Truly continuous viewing confounds time and "number of looks" and requires a different analysis.)

"Forgetting the Past"

The defender of free will says, "Here I am. There are many different things I can do. I am free to choose among them." To say this is really to confess that one's current state inadequately represents one's past history. Cognitive psychologists point out that since a past history leaves its effect on an organism, the current state can be used as a kind of summary of the history if one is interested in explaining behavior, and that is why so much more attention is given to feelings and states of mind than to histories.

If our information about our current state were adequate (if we had "nerves going to the right places"), we should know at any given time what we were going to do and hence we should know that we were not free to choose. It is our ignorance of our past history and of our current state that misleads us into thinking we have many possible futures.

The Don Juan Principle

A Don Juan begins his amorous life as a handsome young man on a variable-ratio schedule: The mean ratio gradually increases as he grows less attractive (assuming a population of women of varying susceptibilities). In the end he is a pathetic old man whose amorous advances *seem* wholly out of proportion to the results but can be understood in terms of a stretched mean ratio.

Emergence of a Causal Relation

At the National Academy of Sciences I spent a spare hour at work in an office provided for members. Across the room another man was at work facing me. A door to my left was open. I knew that an old friend worked at the Academy and hoped to see her. When anyone passed the door, I glanced toward it. I was aware that this made me appear easily distracted, and I began to pretend to be glancing away from my desk in thought, wrinkling my brow, chewing the tip of my pencil. I am not sure that the other man paid the slightest attention, but if he did, he must have felt a causal relation slowly manifest itself, as I myself did. Though I might disguise the *form* of my behavior so that it did not appear to be "glancing at all passersby," a response followed the sight and sound of someone passing. I could have masked this relation to some extent by glancing occasionally at the door when no one was passing, but a glance at every passerby could still have been detected.

Over the Wall

A survey of nuns who have left their orders is said to have shown that tension and a lack of a sense of identity were responsible. These feelings or states of mind presumably preceded the act of leaving an order; hence they are said to have caused the act. But what caused the feelings and states of mind? What is tension? The effect of ambiguous, punitive contingencies under which no one course of action is easy and natural? Or of punitive sanctions restraining strong behaviors? Something of the sort could have been aversive enough to lead to escape (and simultaneously to feelings of tension). What is a sense of identity? Is one less a person when behaving by rule rather than because of contingencies of reinforcement?

Fatigue

My reaction to shaving varies greatly. At times I go through my morning routine scarcely noticing what I am doing; at times I resent the chore. I had long since thought of the latter—like making too many mistakes at the piano—as a sign that I was tired. Recently, on sabbatical, I've confirmed this. Being thoroughly rested, I have found it easy to do chores. When I finish shaving and wash out the bowl with scouring powder, it is almost a pleasure. I find time for even the most routine correspondence, for check-writing, and so on.

There is a parallel in social behavior. How often I observe the amenities is a matter of how rested I am, and only indirectly of whether I "have the time." Now I find myself writing fairly long letters to old friends. I have always "had time" in the evenings, but something besides time is needed. The life of the upper classes in the eighteenth and nineteenth centuries is unrealizable today. No Lady Mary Wortley Montagues; no Horace Walpoles; no long visits; no brilliant evenings. We can find evenings—but we can't find ourselves. A way of life that reduces both aversive stimuli and the senseless reinforcements which exhaust people should mean a return to adequate social behavior and an adequate daily routine as well.

Self-Programming

I took Lisa at age two to the swing across the street. She had seen other children swinging and obviously wanted to do the same, but it was clearly frightening. (The swing was a bow of rather stiff fabric attached to stretchable rubber thongs and then by rope to rather high branches.) She let me put her in, and she clung to the rubber thongs tightly. I pushed her very slightly. She programmed the aversive consequences as follows:

1. She looked straight down at her body. I could not get her to look at me. This minimized the visual stimuli from the movement.

2. She began to look toward my feet (in front of her). Slightly more stimulation.

3. Then, as she "extinguished her anxiety" she looked higher, and finally at my face. No smiling.

4. She looked slightly to one side, where motion was most clearly visible. Then squarely to one side.

5. Finally, she looked straight up.

Meanwhile I had increased the size of the arc. As she began to smile, I pushed in such a way as to jounce her slightly. She stopped smiling at once. Later I put some jounce in, and she continued to smile.

Superstitious Topography

Listening to a piano concerto on television, I could see the pianist's hands close up. There were occasional single melodic passages with the right hand alone. The pianist (Russian, I think) definitely "drew out the tone," pressing his finger on the key until it was bent sharply backward.

The key was at the time wholly disconnected from the sounding string, of course.

Had he played a clavichord and was this induction? Or had he played a stringed instrument and was this a more far-fetched induction? Or was it an even more general induction—from pressing doorbells, or stamps on letters, or balance pans on scales, or tiddlywinks, or measuring tape to prevent sliding? Or was it the bowler's "body English," superstitiously reinforced? Or was it just the exaggerated avoidance of the noise of the damper returning to the string when a key is released carelessly?

Opening Shot

Fog. The figure of a small boy emerges, coming toward the camera, driving a soccer ball before him. He twists and turns, kicking the ball in a zigzag path. The camera moves back as he comes on, passes above and beyond a goal net, through which the boy is still seen. The murmur of a crowd builds up. With a quick, whirling kick, which trips him so that he falls down, the boy sends the ball into the net. He jumps up, sees that he has scored, shouts in victory, and jumps into the air, his arms and legs spread-eagled in a great X. The roar of a crowd is heard. The boy claps his hands, jumps again, shouting—then quiet. Slowly and sadly he goes into the goal, picks up the ball, tucks it under his arm with difficulty, and starts to walk away. The camera moves back, showing an empty, foggy expanse, the boy now a tiny figure, plodding slowly off a deserted field.

Knowledge by Acquaintance and Knowledge by Description

The distinction seems to be between behavior shaped by contingencies and behavior governed by rules (descriptions of contingencies). But I haven't the patience to read Russell et al. and work out the details.

According to Ronald Clark, Ryle says that Wittgenstein had generalized the rule provided by Russell's Theory of Description: "All logic and all philosophy are inquiries into what makes it significant or nonsensical to say certain things. The sciences aim at saying what is true about the world [describing contingencies]; philosophy aims at disclosing only the logic of what can be truly or even falsely said about the world [rules]."

But how far can logic go in deriving new rules from old? Can it arrive at descriptions of contingencies not yet experienced by manipulating descriptions of contingencies experienced? Or must that be left to the extrapolations of science—which are, of course, rules?

Hope for the Future

There is mugging and murder in our streets, and pornography rather than love, according to an article in *Newsweek* by Marya Mannes. It would be good, she feels, if the "muscle of conscience could be trained in earliest childhood," if people learned to distinguish between good and bad, to recognize immutable standards in traditions and conduct, to recognize beauty and reject ugliness. But how is this to be brought about? "Our hope," she says, "is in a new breed of young men and women who will follow their intense hatred of war with an equal disgust of daily murders on neighborhood streets and for nightly 'entertainment' by mass violence and loveless sex."

Here again is that consoling appeal to feelings. The reference to new breed does not, of course, mean a genetic program; we are to breed feelings, not people. But the important things are the conditions that breed feelings or, what is more to the point, that make people more likely to do something about current moral and ethical problems with some of the intensity they displayed with respect to Vietnam. References to "intense hatred" and "disgust" help us to picture vigorous action, but they give us little help in producing it. Our "only hope" lies not in making people feel emotional but in showing them what can be done and giving them reasons for doing it.

Delayed Action of Formal and Thematic Prompts

Here are some examples collected over a period of about eight years:

I tried to recall the name of a wildflower I picked as a boy but failed and stopped trying. At least 24 hours later, possibly as many as 48, I heard someone mention honeysuckle and immediately recalled my earlier attempt and knew that *honeysuckle* was right.

One night I tried to recall the name of Oscar Levant. Something about Gershwin had brought it up, but it stubbornly refused to appear. I went over all the relevant material I could think of: the "Information Please" panel, Clifton Fadiman, F.P.A., and John Kiernan. I visualized Levant's boyish smile, the way he played the piano, his adulation of Gershwin, his alcoholism. I went through the alphabet a dozen times. I kept getting *Alex*, with complementary last names like Guiness. I got *Eric* and *Ernie*—clearly wrong. Then I went to sleep. When I awoke, I did not immediately remember my search, but eventually I did, and I started through the alphabet again. At O, rather to my surprise, I stopped, clearly getting close. Then it came easily, though I was surprised that *Oscar* was the first name and was not sure it was right. It is probably relevant that I had no particular interest in recalling the name. I worked at it as an exercise in using a technique of recall.

I tried to recall the name of a broker. I used a number of techniques, such as fantasying a telephone call beginning, "Let me speak to Mr. ———, please." I was pretty sure of the ethnic character and length of the name. Then I began to go through the alphabet. After several run-throughs I got *Palmer*, *Potter*, and then finally *Perry*, which I saw at once to be correct. Just now, about 20 hours later, I was leafing through the telephone book, and the name *Perry* jumped out at me. After recalling it yesterday, I did not use it or, to my knowledge, repeat it, but the formal and thematic prompts I had been using were apparently still active.

I had tried several times to remember the last name of John and Marion ——— whom I knew in Greenwich Village in 1928. I used several tricks of recall—going over scenes with them, recalling the names of others in the group, trying to visualize the reviews John wrote in the *Saturday Review* years later, recalling the children's book-store Marion later worked in, and so on. All without success. Then one day, waiting in a doctor's office, I went through some copies of the *Saturday Review* and saw the name *Vance Woodward*. Immediately I got what I had been looking for: *Woodburn*. I suppose the issues of the *Saturday Review* may have revived my concern, though I did not think of *John Woodburn* until I saw *Woodward*.

In the middle of the night I tried to recall Stuart Margolies' name. I could visualize him clearly. I thought of his company, and I recalled Charles Walther's reference to his part in the reading program. It took me a long time but I finally got *Stuart*, and then, almost instantly, *Margolies*. The next morning, in the *Times*, I saw a headline announcing the marriage of a Morganthau. The name leaped out at me, with nothing more than *M-rg* and a stress pattern to strengthen it.

I tried for some time to remember the name of a young psychologist at Minnesota who was a close friend of Heron's. His name was Bill—what? Olson, Johnson—a Scandinavian name. Then I dropped it. A day later I opened the *Times*, saw a headline reading "Senator Carlson Hints Career End," and knew immediately that it was Bill

Carlson. The variables I had manipulated in trying to recall the name remained operative for 24 hours to combine with the textual prompt when it appeared.

One evening, dictating a letter to Deborah, including a transcription of an early note, I wanted to add something to explain a reference to a family she stayed with when she was ten, but I could not remember the family's name. I recalled the first name of a daughter, now working in a store in Cambridge, but it did not seem to help. The next morning, about twelve hours later, I was painting a small set of bookshelves I had made for my desk. Suddenly I knew I was going to recall the name, and it came: *Gray.* Then I saw at once and without "searching for causes" that I was painting the case gray. There was no textual prompt; the label on the can of paint was CHARCOAL. But *charcoal* and *gray* have been, of course, intraverbally related in my history.

States

"At least you are willing to refer to states of the organism."

Yes, but only if "state" is wholly noncommittal. I condition a response on Thursday and extinguish on Friday. I change the organism on Thursday, and I see the effect on Friday. The only thing I know about the "state" produced on Thursday is how I produced it. Any other property (such as its location in the nervous system, its susceptibility to decay, or its response to drugs) must be independently established. If the term "state" suggests any of this, without further evidence, it is dangerous.

Selection

In commenting on a new Swedish law that requires worker participation in management in industry, I tried to distinguish between the design of the policy maker and the selection exercised by those whom the policy affects, and I said I thought the worker was qualified for the latter but not for the former, except in small details concerning the conduct of work. And in democracy, the people are authorities on how policies work; they exercise selection at the polls, and they keep the policy makers in power or throw them out. But they are not qualified to design policies and do not do so. Those who work through the people—for example, by arousing concern about pollution—simply prepare for the selection of policy makers who may change policies accordingly.

A government may put a new policy into effect and the people may approve or disapprove because of the natural consequences. Or a policy may be approved or disapproved because of statements about what it will do—advice or warnings about consequences not yet encountered. The propagandist may work directly on the policy maker—"The people won't like it"—or on the people—"Don't let them do it"—or on both. This is possible because one may design a culture either by introducing new practices or by changing contingencies of selection.

Rules More Powerful than Contingencies?

In a detective story the housemaid refuses to sit in the chair of a man who has just committed suicide.

"I'll not set in his chair . . . The chair of the dead!"

Some of the aversive effects of the suicide may be exerted by the chair. A vague tendency to avoid doing anything which "reminds one of the dead." But the statement makes the effect more powerful. This is not simply a chair to be avoided because it reminds one of a suicide, it is the Chair of the Dead.

The practical advantages of clarifying contingencies by formulating rules have their parallel in the strengthening of conditioned stimuli. The formulation which explains "why I do not want to sit in the chair" gives sitting much more aversive consequences and hence makes it less probable.

Making Rules

I have never properly developed the theme that myths arise when people "explain" their cultural practices. The practices arise from natural contingencies (naturally), but natural contingencies cannot all be analyzed. Many lead to superstition because they are adventitious, but tend to be given logical explanations. A ritualized rain dance brings rain (often enough to maintain the dance as a ritual), but how or why? One answer is that the dance influences *someone* who responds by sending rain. The personified may be as much god-the-listener as god-the-doer.

God-the-doer appears as part of a system of rules derived from contingencies. Why does it rain is a question about the reinforcing "equipment," the operant apparatus of the world. A myth arises when people are asked to explain their behavior by describing the contingencies responsible for it (see Raglan's *The Hero*).

Symbols of Submission

"Then spake the Chaldeans to the king in Syriach, O King, live forever: tell thy servants the dreams . . ."

Prostrating oneself, salaaming, bowing, curtsying, not turning one's back, not preceding, speaking only in reply—these are all pretty obvious forms of submission, indicating a willingness to serve. "Long live the king" may be a magical mand, and reinforced by the king as a gesture of deference or as a denial of plans to assassinate. It thus serves the same purpose as prostration, indicating the absence of any tendency to dominate.

Finding

When someone or something important is lost and being actively sought, people commonly fantasy or dream of being the finder. Put more generally, the behavior of finding is strong. (Note that finding is reinforced looking; making contact with what has been lost or showing it to others is the consummation.) A fantasy of finding a person who has never been lost before must be constructed from materials which go back to actual episodes or episodes learned about in other ways.

The behavior of searching frequently takes place in company, and the larger the group and the longer the search, the greater the acclaim the finder receives. This may explain the tendency to join in any search in progress. The searching group is an occasion upon which looking is optimally reinforced.

Efforts to stimulate search often consist of making searching conspicuous (say, by organizing parties) and by increasing the importance of finding (say, by offering a reward).

Bribery

The issue of contingency-shaped behavior versus rule-specified behavior is relevant to bribery and its weakness. Bribery includes or implies a specification of behavior to be emitted "in order to obtain" a reinforcer. Sometimes the reinforcer may be the same as that which would shape the behavior without a rule, but not often—especially since the bribed behavior usually has aversive consequences.

Concern for Others

What seems like a concern for the welfare and happiness of others may be entirely selfish. "Am I boring you?" checks on prospective reinforcement. "Do you mind my saying that?" "Am I driving too fast for you?" "May I smoke?" and "May I ask you a question?" are questions not so much about whether the listeners are or will be happy as about whether they will complain.

Topography

I have been dictating a good deal lately, using my compact cassette recorder. Just now I was dictating part of my paper on education (for the Yearbook). Something turned up which I started to put in a note. I finished *writing* a sentence, paused before seeing just how to go on, and *reached to turn off the recorder.* In spite of the difference in topography between speaking and writing, I transferred from speaking to writing a compulsive husbandry in the use of tape (and the time of the typist who will eventually transcribe).

The Pleasure of Anticipation Realized

A statement in terms of feelings is easy. "We like music which comes up with the note we anticipate." Rock music does it by endless repetition. "Modern" music fails to do it for many people. Baroque music is a golden mean: only slight changes in anticipated notes. It once struck me that Brahms deliberately frustrated expectations.

Technically we tend to (1) imitate, and (2) execute learned sequences (they would be intraverbals in verbal behavior), as we listen to music.

The composer supplies the next note (or group of notes) at just the point at which the listener is ready to—what? say, sing, think them?

Dreaming

. . . is almost always weak behavior and hence determined by trivia. Even when strong variables appear to be at work, they are attenuated in sleep; hence, the chaotic, illogical, fragmentary character of dreams. And hence, too, the fact that dreams are so often perceptual rather than motor? Sleep is a lowering of motor activity, and perceptual behavior may be the only behavior available when one cannot move. (Note that a common theme in a nightmare is not being able to move.)

Myths, Rituals, and Drama

These may have worked as rules about situations rather than about behavior or its consequences.

In most climates the seasons are important occasions for action. There are behaviors appropriate to winter, spring, summer, and autumn, and the consequences are also characteristic of the season. Changing from one to another must have been important. When the seasons were given names, one could simplify the change: "It's Spring!" A ritual would help in making the change. One *marks* the arrival of spring, celebrates it, and one then stops behaving in ways appropriate to winter and begins to behave in ways appropriate to spring. A leader, political or religious, may *stage* a ritual, a drama, at the appropriate time. The effect is much like that of being told the weather before one goes out; hearing "It's warm!" one dresses for warm weather. At one time straw hats were *never* to be worn after Labor Day, no matter how hot the weather.

Survival and Beauty

Why have people made statues and paintings of the human body for thousands of years? Presumably because the human body is beautiful in the sense of reinforcing. Looking at the body is strengthened by what one sees. But why? Is survival value the explanation? Some aspects of female beauty in our culture seem unrelated to survival. How can a pale delicate skin, easily torn, vulnerable to wind and sun, have had survival value?

One answer is sexual selection. Characteristics which lead to mating are particularly likely to be transmitted to offspring. Soft delicate skin has survival value if it reinforces looking and touching as steps toward copulation. But in that case soft skin must have been reinforcing before it was favored by selection. Its reinforcing power could have arisen for some other reason. In a culture in which a man chooses a woman, or a woman a man, as a servant or slave, and in which different traits are therefore selected, the prior reason for selection can be identified.

Our version of a beautiful woman appears to be a product of affluence and leisure. What we feel when we look at a nude by Michaelangelo, Titian, or Manet is much more salient than the evolutionary history which has made what we see reinforcing. Our feelings therefore appear to be the important thing, and they are easily mistaken for an explanation of reinforcing power. And if we then overlook the evolutionary history, we may dismiss a reference to survival value as crass, philistine, or incompatible with sensitivity.

Consider a different example. Why are flowers beautiful? Because they attract bees? If so, our standards of beauty are evidently similar to those of bees; we "go for" the same things. But when we start to breed flowers, we select other colors, shapes, and sizes—and again for reasons possibly irrelevant to survival. When we look at a rose, we are aware of what we feel, but we can easily neglect the reasons why we feel as we do. And why did bees find flowers attractive?

Do the abstractionists have the answer? Or are they simply raising the same question?

Production Line

The pacing device of the production line (invented by Henry Ford?) seems very modern. The worker must work at a pace determined by the line. In *Modern Times* Chaplin satirizes the employer's tendency to increase the pace.

Yet most work is scheduled.

A farmer must milk a herd of cows on schedule and plant crops before a given date and whenever the weather and soil are right.

All hunting and fishing are on a variable-ratio schedule.

Incentive wages contain ratio elements. The craftsman or private contractor is essentially on piecework.

In short, systems of pay with no such contingencies are rare. They must be arranged by people, and by people who do not base their reinforcers on temporal properties of behavior.

Bombast

The word once meant "cotton or any soft fibrous material used as padding or stuffing." Now it means a "pretentious inflated style of speech or writing" (definitions from *Webster's Third New International Dictionary*). Here is a sample: According to General MacArthur's biographer and confidant, Major General Courtney Whitney, the family often repeated this prayer during early morning devotions:

"Build me a son, O Lord, who will be strong enough to know when he is weak, and brave enough to face himself when he is afraid; one who will be proud and unbending in honest defeat, and humble and gentle in victory.

"Build me a son whose wishes will not take the place of deeds; a son who will know Thee—and that to know himself is the foundation stone of knowledge.

"Lead him, I pray, not in the path of ease and comfort, but under the stress and spur of difficulties and challenge.

Here let him learn to stand up in the storm; here let him learn compassion for those who fail.

"Build me a son whose heart will be clear, whose goal will be high, a son who will master himself before he seeks to master other men, one who will reach into the future, yet never forget the past.

"And after all these things are his, add, I pray, enough of a sense of humor, so that he may always be serious, yet never take himself too seriously. Give him humility, so that he may always remember the simplicity of true greatness, the open mind of true wisdom, and the meekness of true strength.

"Then I, his father, will dare to whisper, 'I have not lived in vain.'"

(*The New York Times*, April 6, 1964)

Why is this so objectionable? It is composed in such a way that the listener (God?) is ready for much of it long before he has heard it. It reminds one of Kipling's *If* and for good reason. There are at least fifteen pairs of opposites: strong-weak; brave-afraid; proud-humble; unbending-gentle; defeat-victory; wish-deed; know Thee-know himself; ease-stress; comfort-difficulty; stand up in storm-fail; master himself-master other men; future-past; sense of humor-serious; humility-greatness; and meekness-strength. After one has heard two or three pairs, the first members of the others prompt the second, which, as a result, may seem natural, correct, *juste*, but also superfluous. The advance preparation does not yield plausibility or credibility (scarcely a consideration in a prayer) but simply a certain readiness to make responses along with the speaker. When the responses are too easy, the preparation is not worthwhile.

In addition, of course, the text confirms a well-known belief that MacArthur was himself proud, unbending, and humorless, and that he seldom merely "dared to whisper." If he were to be remembered *only* for having fathered such a son, would he really regard himself as not having lived in vain? What is the word for it? "Pharisaical" is not quite right; "sanctimonious" is not broad enough.

Plus and Minus

A familiar example of conflicting contingencies is seen when a man is looking over the edge of a cliff or rampart. He must get his head out over the edge to look down, but the rest of his body is held back as far as possible. The neck is stretched and the head is advanced only as far as necessary to get a view. In addition, the hands and arms may be placed in position to execute a backward push.

Cf. handing something to someone you want to keep away from. (The bribe being *pushed across the table* to the Informer in that old movie with Victor McLaglen. The gold louis *thrown* to the man who operates the guillotine.)

Cf. the purely verbal case, giving information to someone you don't want to speak to, as in speaking through a third person. This could be exaggerated for dramatic purposes.

Physical Dimensions

A basic principle of behaviorism which has guided me throughout my professional life but which I have neglected to emphasize in my writings (it is neglected in *About Behaviorism*) is the importance of converting mentalistic terms to alternatives which refer to things having physical dimensions. *Verbal Behavior* was my most serious work in that vein, but it was largely confined to the physical dimensions of the evidence for meaning, ideas, information.

Cognitive psychologists use these terms, and many others, without placing their referents in centimeters-grams-seconds space. Where and what is knowledge, for example? Is there any definition that fits all the expressions in which the word is used—"acquiring knowledge," "possessing knowledge," "using knowledge," "communicating knowledge," and the like?

Or, where and what is "information"? When it is said that the consequences of behavior "give the subject information," what passes from the contingencies to the body or "mind" of the subject?

Wish Fulfillment

If a dream is a fulfilled wish, *what* is fulfilled? Is there gratification in a dream or is dreaming simply a form of wishing? Is dreaming consummatory? The same question may be asked about sublimation. An activity which is strong because it resembles a strong activity but is not reinforced in the same way offers no fulfillment.

The trouble with talk like this is that it is in part about goals. "Consummation" is satisfaction, not reinforcement —but strength of response is due to reinforcement. An act of sublimation does not reduce deprivation, but it shares some of the reinforcement.

How much needs to be done! Who is bothering to make these distinctions?

Disturbing Irrelevancies

From an article by André Gide: . . . *art was not destroyed. . . . It did not die, because the laurel of Apollo is hardy, and will not perish. . . .* How can a Laurel and Hardy fan not run off the track in that sentence?

Picture caption in a news weekly: *Would steel follow the lead of aluminum?* How should one pronounce *lead? Steel* and *aluminum* strengthen *lĕd. Follow* strengthens *lēd.* The past tense of *lead* is *lĕd.* I was aware of the conflict as I read (rĕd).

From *Term of Trial* by James Barlow: *What a psychiatrist would say about Mitchell Weir did not know.* A difficult sentence for anyone familiar with the name of the American psychiatrist Weir Mitchell.

The Origin of a Culture

We explain the achievements of contemporary people by showing how the social environment shapes and maintains their behavior, and we explain a contemporary social environment by analyzing the behavior of those who contribute to it. In other words, given existing social institutions we can account for existing social behavior. But we ought to show that a social environment could have arisen from nonsocial precursors. Otherwise we should have to suppose that society began, as Rousseau supposed, with some explicit social contract. An analogy may be taken from technology. We observe in the world today the existence of almost perfectly turned metal cylinders. To explain these, we show how a cylinder is turned on a lathe. But the lathe itself contains turned cylinders. We have explained one instance but not the existence of all turned cylinders. It is not difficult, however, to imagine the development of the lathe and the bootstrap operation which led to more and more perfect turning. We could even begin with crude materials and construct a series of lathes ourselves, recapitulating the evolutionary process. The origins and selection of cultural practices leading to a "smoothly turned" society may be similar.

Distant Recall

On Sunday I had Sultana Roll with claret sauce for dessert. The sauce was thick and red. It covered the middle of the slice of ice cream, leaving the green edge. At the first taste of the almond-flavored ice cream I vividly recalled our 'ritual of making fondant at Xmas time in Susquehanna, at least 40 years ago. As far as I could tell, the flavor was not unique. It was certainly strong. I can't recall whether we flavored green fondant with almond—though it is possible, even likely. The red-green pattern—Xmas—was probably relevant. Also, that we were eating at an apartment-house restaurant, which may have reminded me of the last ten years of my mother's life when she lived in a hotel and we dined with her in a similar restaurant.

Seeing "Guilt"

Y says: "When I came into the room, X was at his desk writing, but I had the feeling that he had been at something else, had heard me coming, and had taken his position at the desk just before I entered. He showed a certain embarrassment, a certain guilt. He was certainly not wholly at ease."

Whether or not there is any trait called guilt to be attributed to X, certain aspects of his behavior could have given Y certain "feelings":

a. X will notice Y when he enters and attempt to do so "casually," but Y's footsteps and appearance will be stronger stimuli than usual and X will, with difficulty, simulate an ordinary reaction time, greeting, and return to work.

b. X may blush or blanch, fumble with his pen, or give some other sign of poor coordination.

c. X will respond too quickly (or, covering up, too slowly) to any remark of Y's.

Double Meanings

In writing about an article in a magazine, I hesitated to say that several readers had "noticed" something. I considered saying "told me" about it, and then vacillated between *noticed* and *told me* until I came up with *had observed*, which did both jobs. For *observe*, Skeat's *Etymological Dictionary* gives only *heed*, *regard*, *keep*, none of which has ever come to mean *say*. But *remark*, says Skeat, means *take notice of* and came to mean *speak about*, too. I should have used that.

Reformation

I have often wondered how a people can give up licentious living and turn to Puritanism, as in England in the seventeenth century. In *Adam Bede*, Dinah ends an evangelical sermon in this way: "I am poor, like you: I have to get my living with my hands; but no lord nor lady can be so happy as me, if they haven't got the love of God in their souls."

Not everyone was able to be licentious. The discovery that one could be happy in a superior way *by foregoing pleasures* may be the clue. Religion as the pleasure of the people?

Police State?

Everyone watched me as I walked through Kalamata. No one spoke. There were no friendly or unfriendly gestures. Many signs reading "Long live the 21st of April," but none reading "Long live the king," as there had been two years before. Several placards with statistics showing progess during three years in agriculture, sports stadiums, buildings, medicine, etc. A larger panel in the square with photographs of officers walking and talking with church officials. New buildings going up. Clean streets. Dozens of taxis but no one using them. (No one tried to sell me anything.) One street crossing had stop-and-go pedestrian crossway signs and an officer supervising the people, who did wait, though the street was narrow and there were no cars. Elsewhere people crossed anywhere at any time.

Our ship is carefully guarded. I had to show my embarcation card to a soldier at the foot of the gangway before I could leave to walk through the town. No revolutionary is to enter (or leave) by the Ankara!

(Later, in Athens, the menu in a restaurant said, "Prices are controlled by competent authority.")

The Uses of Decision Theory

Marcus G. Raskin, in reviewing Anatol Rapoport's *Strategy and Conscience* (*Scientific American*, August 1964), asks why the Department of Defense and large business operations "flirt with [decision] theories when they have only marginal utility." (He does not mean the economist's marginal utility; he means borderline usefulness.) He says that Rapoport's answer is that these organizations are "insatiable consumers of scholarly knowledge, ideas, and theories." The computer is useful as a symbol.

The explanation neglects an important effect of a theory. It resolves doubt. The water diviner is not taken too seriously, but if you are going to dig a well and do not want to be blamed for choosing a bad spot, five or ten dollars to a diviner is well spent. Tossing a coin has the same effect whether or not one believes in luck or any other determiner of the fall of a coin.

A theory may actually work for accidental reasons. The tribe that spins the shoulder bone of a deer and accepts where it falls as pointing to a good hunting ground randomizes the area it chooses for hunting and avoids exhausting an area to which it would otherwise go because hunting has been particularly good. Astrologers are flourishing in Washington as in other parts of the world where important decisions are made. Evidently the search for absolution is universal.

Outside Ghosts

How much is gained, in designing techniques of self-control, by moving the tempter outside the body? If it clarifies the struggle by separating the contestants, it makes a battery of responses available: Inkpots can be thrown at the Devil, Devils can be frightened away by charms, witches can be burned or hanged, and the Devil can be ordered about ("Get thee behind me!") and preached against. But the separation means that one may join the Devil or sell oneself to Him or Her. Resigned evildoers have "gone over" to the Devil. The physical separation has given them a chance to move toward rather than away from the tempter, and so far as well-wishers are concerned, they are "lost."

The real tempters, the contingencies of reinforcement, are almost always outside the body, and they are not ghosts.

Atoms

The light switch in my bedroom works as a push button. As I came into the room, I reached for the switch just as I closed the door and pushed the button on the knob which locks the door. I rarely lock the door when closing it. I had transferred the "push" of turning on the light to the button on the door.

Is "Need" Needed?

To say that people eat because they *need* food is convincing because we can easily imagine (and to some extent observe and measure) a bodily condition quite reasonably called a *need*, in the sense of a want or a shortage. Yet we observe only that people eat when they have not taken food for some time (limiting the case to a single food). We induce people to eat by depriving them of food, and we stop them from eating by giving them food until satiated. The need, as a state, is not observed. It is inferred, either as an effect of deprivation or as a prior condition of action. We feel a need ("hunger") under the same conditions, and it is easy to suppose that we eat to reduce the feeling of hunger, and that we "need" to be nonhungry.

More often, a mere consequence is said to be what is needed. We need the food we eat. But not all consequences qualify. That people sometimes act in ways leading to their death does not mean that they have a need for self-destruction. That people so easily fall victim to confidence men does not mean that they "have a deep need to be deceived or tricked." We are not in need of deception any more than we are in need of death.

Misdirection

There are many examples of the practical misdirection wrought by an obsession with feelings.

In industry, workers are made to *feel* happy by piping in soothing music, while the "feelings" associated with achievement, not so easily explained or described, are overlooked.

In education, the student is encouraged to *feel* curious, interested, or enthusiastic while the contingencies generating the behavior said to show curiosity, interest, or enthusiasm are neglected.

Economists who explain their failures by appealing to "psychology" are usually appealing to feelings—fear, panic and so on, while the environmental variables which account for the behavior said to show fear or panic are not mentioned. They generally lie outside the bailiwick of the economist. (Strangely enough, if psychologists explained failure by attributing behavior to economic factors, it would be pretty clear that they were talking about the environment.)

Autoclitics and Freud

Ernest Jones (*Freud*, vol. II, p. 310): "Freud observed that dream language was unable to express any negative concept, that the words 'no' and 'not' were simply omitted in it. . . . the 'primary process' differs from the 'secondary process.'"

A rather curious parallel to primary and secondary language. In *Verbal Behavior*, I argue that negation is autoclitic. *No* and *not* are added to primordial verbal behavior. "Omitted" suggests that dreams are careless rather than that they do not move on to a second stage. Dreams are similar to protocol-sentences—not yet edited by a speaker.

Social Behavior

J. P. Scott in *Animal Behavior* cites as cooperative behavior two horses standing in such a way that the tail of each flicks flies away from the head of the other. What are the contingencies?

If a horse in a fly-ridden field flicks its tail to brush flies from its own rump, then there is a small area where a second horse may stand and escape from flies around its head. It might hold its head near a moving branch of a tree for the same reason.

If both horses have been conditioned to seek such areas, the position Scott describes follows, but there is no cooperation in the sense that tail flicking is reinforced *because* it flicks flies off the head of another horse. As in crowding together to conserve heat, each behaves entirely for itself. But another contingency may control not only standing in this position but also moving the tail. If flicking the tail is not a reflex out of reach of operant reinforcement, then A's tail-flicking is reinforced because it maintains B in such a position that B's flicking drives flies away from A's head. The same thing holds in the other direction, and this contingency may be needed to explain the mutual character of the performance.

The grouping is self-sustained. One horse at right angles to another, or in tandem, would have to keep moving as the other moved. The parallel position keeps both still. This is also incidental rather than cooperative.

Contradiction

In Henry James's *Portrait of a Lady*, Caspar Goodwood is speaking:

"The world's all before us—and the world's very big. I know something about that."

Isabel gave a long murmur, like a creature in pain; it was as if he were pressing something that hurt her. "The world's very small," she said at random; she had an immense desire to appear to resist. She said it at random; to hear herself say something; but it was not what she meant.

Not quite at random. She was "set" for opposites and finding herself unable to say anything appropriate, she simply emitted a contradiction. But "opposite" and "set" tell us little. The important thing was a tendency to say "small" in response to "big," as children say "It is!" in response to "It isn't!"

How big an intraverbal vocabulary of contradictions does one acquire in a lifetime?

The Man from Mars

. . . is not only a badly overworked cliché, it has lost all plausibility. Diderot, in *Le Neveu de Rameau*, borrows from Montaigne the expression *perché sur l'épicycle de Mercure*. He thus describes *Lui* who is engaged in considering "*les differentes pantomimes de l'espèce humaine*." A welcome change in the ultramundane.

The Pleasures of Smoking

In his memoirs Casanova tells of enjoying an after-dinner smoke with a Turk, Yusuf Ali. Casanova "expectorates" while smoking—evidently a common Western custom. The Turk advises him to swallow the "balsam" (now known as "tar"). He then analyzes the "pleasures of smoking," refuting Casanova's claim that he can enjoy only the pleasures of the senses by pointing out that he enjoys filling his pipe and contemplating it after it has been smoked out—i.e., that activities or stimuli associated with smoking become conditioned reinforcers.

Yusuf then "proves" that the chief pleasure in smoking is not the aroma but watching the smoke. He notes that the blind do not smoke and that it is not satisfying to smoke in the dark.

There are aversive elements to be taken into account. A pipe generates a sustained anxiety lest it go out. Preparing the tobacco, packing the pipe carefully, and puffing regularly are in part forms of avoidance. One learns to puff at a rate which maintains a given density of smoke because it is closely correlated with the condition of the fire. This evidence is also missing in the dark.

Symbol

Yesterday morning there was a story in the paper about the gun and bullets that figured in the Sacco and Vanzetti case. Permission has been granted for a test firing, a type-determination of any blood on the bullets, etc. The article was illustrated by a close-up photograph of four slugs. Each contained a band of indentations showing where the cartridge gripped the slug. I noticed the resemblance to the head of a penis. Later, in reading a passage in which a character begged off from engaging in sexual intercourse by confessing that he had just masturbated, I noted that proof might be demanded and immediately thought of the bullets. Is this evidence of an archetypal theme in which pistol and bullet represent penis and sperm? I think not. The evidence of masturbation would have to be, presumably, the emptiness of the gun, not markings on the slug. The slug is the sperm but the physical resemblance is to the penis. Still, one can argue that not only the shape of the slug, but its having been designed for penetration, figured in the recall, as may have the question of testing an assertion regarding the firing of gun or penis.

"Searching One's Memory"

Recalling an episode that occurred in 1946, I could not get the name of the tenor who did not appear because his plane was grounded in Chicago and he was driven by mistake to Bloomington, Illinois, rather than Bloomington, Indiana, and I went through the alphabet. At L, M, I almost got the name; it was clearly very close. I continued and went through again. Again, a strong but unformed response at L, M. A third time, after some miscellaneous recall of related material, I got it—Lauritz Melchior. *Both* L and M, and in that order!

It was not merely the topography of a response. It was a *tact*, a verbal *operant*—i.e., a response under the control of a situation. Is this always the case? Does one ever "search one's memory" (bad metaphor!) for a mere topography of response? After all, I had recalled a situation; was I not "looking for" (correctly put: "trying to emit") a name only? It had to be the name appropriate to (i.e., previously reinforced in the presence of) the situation. The fact that one "instantly knows that such a response is right" means that it is made to a situation. What else is meant by being right?

The same argument holds for recalling the next word in a poem, except that the response is an intraverbal, not a tact. I believe there is a clear difference in what I observe in myself in the two cases. The intraverbal is less subject to a controlling situation.

Odds On

A friend talked about odds as if they were equivalent to *experienced* contingencies. But odds are descriptions of contingencies. If we act on them, it is because we have learned to do so. Odds, like such rules as promises or threats, are among the occasions for action which past contingencies have made salient.

Generalization

"Je l'aime depuis que je la considère comme foutable." (Stendhal, *Journal,* 29 *décembre* 1810.)

What is the process? Can we translate in this way: "She resembles others who have been sexually reinforcing and I therefore react to her as I react to them?" The process is not exclusive to the field of sex. We find ourselves attracted toward other books written by the author of a book we have enjoyed and to other plays in which actors or actresses will appear who have appeared in plays we have enjoyed. If we may not read the same book or see the same play again, it is because much of the reinforcing effect is missing a second time, but the tendency to see a book or play sharing certain properties is not subject to this qualification and may be strengthened by earlier reinforcements.

The Greenspoon Effect

There are many reasons why contrived contingencies in which words of a given class are reinforced may not be effective:

1. The speaker may have learned that isolated verbal responses are seldom reinforced.

2. Stimuli present when a response is reinforced may not recur to evoke later instances. Among such stimuli in normal speech are other parts of sentences.

3. A listener as an audience controls verbal behavior about a particular subject matter or in a particular language. When speaking to X, talk about baseball; when

speaking to *Y*, speak French. When a listener one has met for the first time reinforces a response (about baseball, or in French), a whole repertoire is strengthened; almost none of the responses which compose it have been reinforced upon this occasion.

International

After being stacked up over New York's La Guardia Airport for half an hour, we landed in a fog. To the English traveler sitting next to me I said in my best imitation of British understatement, "Low ceiling." He replied with American enthusiasm: "Yes, and you could see the Empire State Building *sticking up through the clouds!*"

Doing Things for the Loved Object

The effect may be to make the loved object more reinforcing to the lover. Thus, I find myself explaining to skeptics that taking care of the swimming pool is easy (though rather time-consuming) because "I love it." Caring for it is something I do without further reinforcement, positive or negative. I do not have to make myself do it, and I do it "without effort."

But there is an obvious reinforcement: The pool is cleaner, fresher, more beautiful. I "admire" it more, "love" it more for having cared for it. In the case of doing good to a loved *person* this may also be the case:

1. Giving jewels, a car, etc. makes the object more beautifully decorated, fashionable, etc.

2. Being nice may make the object happier, pleasanter, less complaining.

3. The object may be more inclined to do good reciprocally.

Note the different kinds of emotional reactions (and "feelings") in these cases.

Instinct and Reason

In *Daisy Miller*, Winterbourne is at a loss to understand the young American girl. James writes:

"Winterbourne had lost his instinct in this matter, and his reason could not help him."

He has lived abroad for some time. "His behavior had not for some time been contingency-shaped, and he was also unable to analyze the contingencies." I believe that covers the case, but how much easier to put it as James does.

Missing Someone

Lisa, age 21 months, had been away from her parents for two and a half days. She got up in the morning in fine spirits. Eve gave her a sheaf of pictures to play with, mostly pictures of herself. She took them into the living room. Suddenly we heard her crying. She came back into the bedroom and threw down the pictures angrily, then leaned over the bed and wept. Among the pictures we found one of her father and mother. It was painful to be reminded that they were absent, and she threw their picture away as the source of her unhappiness.

Thinking

Behavioral scientists are always competing with self-appointed lay experts. The political scientist must acknowledge the contributions of the success of the politician, the economist of the businessman. Every cattle breeder and animal trainer is an expert on the behavior of organisms. And everyone knows about the everyday behavior of everybody.

There is a special difficulty in talking about intellectual behavior because the people who know are famous as knowers. Mathematicians are likely to describe how mathematicians think. The distinguished chemist is an authority on scientific method.

Granted that such people are favorably placed to see intellect at work, it does not follow that they understand human behavior well enough to spot the relevant facts and formulate a general account of "thinking." The distinction between knowing *how* to behave and knowing *about* behaving is hard to make.

Three Variables

Somewhere I have analyzed the way in which Gilbert Ryle read a lecture. When he wrote it, he presumably asserted it, but in reading it he was *simply* reading, and his textual behavior swamped any assertion. The lecturers on our cruise of the Greek Islands have given their lectures many times before. They have probably memorized much of what they say. Nevertheless, they *assert* their sentences rather than merely emit them as intraverbal behavior. Occasionally they glance at their notes, but presumably not at a complete text even for one sentence. A textual response of a word or two is a sufficient prompt, and they then go on speaking, not reciting.

Afterimage of Size

Last night I briefly watched part of a movie on a small portable television set. The curtains had not been drawn and I glanced out and upward toward a neighbor's lighted window. The window seemed to shrink as if it were receding rapidly. Then I remembered the Jean Gros marionette show with which I spent a day as a volunteer many years ago. At the end of the show Jean Gros himself walked on stage. He seemed gigantic—until one adjusted again to real size. I do not remember that he seemed to shrink.

In watching a small television screen one evidently converts it either to the much commoner larger screen or to life. The movie I watched had few close-ups. It was more like a photographed play, and it must have been a good setting for the marionette effect. When I looked out toward the window, it first seemed unnaturally large—and then retreated to its natural size.

Knowledge, Information, the Facts

I run into an old friend and bring him home with me. I have a few errands to do and so, after taking him into the living room, I say, "There is beer in the refrigerator." Then I leave. Have I:

1. Communicated information?
2. Imparted knowledge?
3. Told a fact?

For purposes of practical discourse there is no harm in saying "Yes," but for either describing what actually happened or specifying an assignment for physiology, something else is needed. Nothing physical has changed places. There is no stuff called information, knowledge, or fact that can be observed in transit or found in place by the physiologist. My friend has not "grasped a meaning."

The effect of my verbal response (similar to past effects which are in part accountable for its strength) is to increase the probability that my friend will go to the refrigerator if a beer is reinforcing in his present state. Whether he goes or not depends upon many things. If we have had a beer or two on the way home, a process of deprivation may need to set in. I can speed it up by offering him potato chips or salted nuts. Salt brings about a redistribution of water in parts of the body leading eventually to urination and increasing the probability of the ingestion of fluids.

My friend has "learned the meaning" of my response when upon hearing similar responses, he has gone to the refrigerator and found beer.

These complexities seem to be avoided when we use expressions like "convey information" or "impart knowledge," but further stipulations need to be made in that case too. Will my friend *"act* upon the knowledge I have conveyed"?

Double Pun

Headline in the morning's *Times:*
 A Trio Glows in Brooklyn

It fails for two reasons. The book *A Tree Grows in Brooklyn* is out of date and largely forgotten, but the main weakness is in making two puns at once. Let us say that a trio has been formed in Brooklyn and is flourishing. Then *A Trio Grows in Brooklyn* would do. Or a fine Christmas tree publicly displayed in Brooklyn might give *A Tree Glows in Brooklyn.* But when a trio gives a fine performance in Brooklyn, it is straining matters to say *A Trio Glows.* The first pun weakens the second and vice versa.

Fear of Bad News

People who will not have tests made because they may discover that they are fatally ill are well known. I have recently failed to act for similar reasons. I have a manila envelope containing several drafts of a contract of some value, but I have not allowed myself to look to see whether the signed draft is among them (if it is not, I have lost it).

It is a complex case. "Fear of a possible future event" does not help. What comparable cases have I experienced in the past? In general, looking for something has one of two effects: Something is found or the possibility that it will

be found is destroyed. Presumably both are equally important: the more reinforcing the found object, the more
punishing the loss of the chance to find it. The number of
places in which one may plausibly look makes a great
difference. When looking in the last possible place, the
chance of loss is much more important than the chance of
gain.

Speaker versus Listener

Cognitive psychologists often make a point of the fact that
when you finally recall a forgotten name, you know it is
right. But this means only that you are a better listener than
speaker. In trying to recall something, you work on
yourself to make yourself a better speaker, but the listener is
already there and would have known that the word was
right if someone else had said it. When psychologists speak
of the meaning of an utterance as common to both speaker
and listener, or of knowledge transmitted from one to the
other, they obscure important details of a speech episode.

The Mystery of Creativity

P. B. Medawar (*New York Review*, reprinted in *Science
News*, May 22, 1976): "It cannot be too widely understood
that there is no such thing as 'a calculus of scientific
discovery.' The generative act in scientific discovery is a
creative act of mind—a process as mysterious and unpredictable in a scientific context as it is in any other exercise of
creativity."

Granted that it is as yet mysterious in most cases and
unpredictable (by definition, since it would otherwise not
be "creative"), still why talk about "the exercise of
creativity" or "an act of mind"? Darwin showed the futility
of that in dealing with the greatest of all "Creations."

And although there is no calculus of truly novel things (if there were, the novelty would be moved back at least one step), there are calculated ways of generating accidents to improve the chances that an important novel combination of events will occur.

Scientists work in the world, even when they are simply behaving verbally. Their behavior is controlled by conditions admittedly too complex for analysis. But we need not then conclude that it must therefore be controlled by mental acts, which, it is agreed, are just as mysterious and unpredictable.

"Eternal Vigilance"

I find myself using mentalistic, purposive terms, and I defend myself by arguing that easy communication demands them. But finding an alternative is almost always reinforced. Just now I wrote "Cultures have permitted individuals to emerge in possession of great power." I saw that "permitted" was wrong. Cultures *make* individuals emerge. I changed it to "In some cultures individuals have emerged because the necessary contingencies have prevailed. . . ."

A great improvement. It "communicates" more. It is not more difficult. I must keep looking.

Fifty Years Later

I have just lettered a notebook using a green felt marker. Because the letters were not very sharp, I edged them with a black ball-point. I drew lines only to the left of vertical or near vertical strokes, giving a three-dimensional effect. Instantly I thought of my show-card lettering days, when lettering was generously reinforced and the three-dimensional effect particularly reinforcing. I have occasionally done similar lettering since then, but the recall leaped over some 53 years.

Double Audience

When someone is speaking to you on the telephone, you may get the impression that there is someone else at the other end. The speaker is not only carrying on a conversation with you, he is composing an intelligible half-conversation for a person near him. Under the control of a double audience, he uses names in lieu of pronouns (so that his companion will know whom he is talking about), paraphrases your statements in the act of agreeing or disagreeing with them, and adds details important to his companion but not needed by you or of interest to you. In a telephone call made by a character in a play, designed to be usefully overheard by the audience, all these features are blemishes. In a detective or spy story they could be used to alert the listener or reader to the presence of another person.

Tact versus Mand

Harlan Lane (*The Wild Boy of Aveyron*) says that Itard taught the boy to name objects but the boy did not "use the words" to ask for them. In other words, tacts do not imply mands. He says Lovaas found the same for autistic children.

There may a hint here as to what went wrong in Kay Estes's experiment at Minnesota. She asked children to describe pictures and then reinforced certain words with toys, but the words did not appear more frequently. For example, reinforcing the response *dog* when a dog appeared in a picture did not increase the likelihood that dogs would be mentioned when they appeared in later pictures. But such responses were already parts of possibly well-established repertoires. No new stimulus control was being established.

She did get a result, as I remember it, with the response *Please*. It is an autoclitic which indicates that an associated, emitted, or implied response is a mand. *Behold, milk!* is a tact. *Please, milk!* is a mand. Reinforcement is specific to the form of the mand, independently of prior stimulation.

Structure

Instinct and habit represent the structure of behavior—what organisms do; they do not explain why they do it. Contingencies of reinforcement or of survival are not mentioned.

That is also true of patterns of development and frequency theories of learning. It is the fallacy of no first time, the belief that things will happen as they have always happened. The sun will rise tomorrow because it rose today. You might as well say that my heart will go on beating because it has done so for many years.

"Giving"

"Why can't my right hand give my left hand money?"

Because giving is the behavior of an organism and properly described only by specifying the contingencies as well as the physical act. It is the mistake of the formalist, the structuralist, to say that giving is the mere transfer of something from one place to another. I do not give the butter to the bread. If we say to a cook, "Give it more butter," we refer to nothing more than the physical transference, but we do so only by induction from a single conspicuous feature of giving. We give by relinquishing something to someone who gains. In other words, giving is described in terms of social contingencies, not the structure of behavior. That the other person may then reinforce our behavior is relevant to why we give, but it need not be mentioned in the definition.

A Behavioral History

Gilbert Seldes in *The Stammering Century:* "The established religion . . . taught obedience; America taught freedom. Calvinism looked backward to the glorious past before the Fall; the eyes of America were toward the future. The great hope offered by Congregationalism was redemption from sin; America had definitely begun to be interested only in Progress."

But is history a succession of philosophies, movements, isms—or of environments? America offered new positive reinforcements. The aversive control exerted by the past was weak, and a new physical environment beckoned.

What historian will write an operant history? We have had thousands of political histories and more recently economic ones. We need a behavioral history—the story of a changing environment and of the changes in human behavior it wrought.

Definitions

"My definitions are straightforward," says W. H. Ferry in an occasional paper from the Center for the Study of Democratic Institutions. " 'Responsibility' means the state of being responsible, that for which one is answerable—a duty or trust." But "answerable," "duty," and "trust" add nothing by way of definition. No statement is made in simpler or more familiar terms.

But if I were to start talking about aversive control—"responsible for doing x" as meaning "punished for not doing x," or likely to be so punished, or "justly" punished —thus insisting upon a reference to behavior, I should be accused of cant, triviality, or—worse—vulgarity. I should be told that we know what responsibility is or what wise men have said it is or felt it to be. Why not let it go at that?

With a little more grace, a little less vulgarity, I might argue that the important thing is to get back to why people show responsibility or behave in responsible ways. Responsibility always has to do with behavior, and some of us look at why people behave. Without mentioning specific variables ("aversive stimuli!") I might emphasize action rather than contemplation, the uses rather than the mere existence of "responsibility." The vulgarity comes down to an interest in doing something besides talking.

"*Motivation*"

A young boy is playing happily until he sees another child eating candy or until someone asks him whether he would like some candy. At once, a repertoire of candy-getting behavior takes over. He no longer plays happily; he teases.

It is easy to say that his hunger for candy has been increased, and he may tell us that he now wants candy, but there has been no change in deprivation. What has happened is that stimuli have appeared in the presence of which he has previously been successful in getting candy. The probability of candy-getting behavior has therefore been greatly increased.

Explanatory Autoclitics

"Did you talk with so-and-so? I'm just curious." Or, "I'd sort of like to know." The second sentence seems to explain the question, but it may mask a more serious reason for asking.

I could have added to *Verbal Behavior* a whole class of explanatory autoclitics. They are more detached from what is said than descriptive autoclitics. "Lest you misjudge me, let me add. . . ." Misjudging is what is prevented by the addition. "I should explain that" implies that a remark will be misunderstood unless the explanation is given. "I should perhaps add . . ." is a shade more specific than "Let me add . . ." or "I hasten to add. . . ."

Spengler

The *Decline of the West* is a psychotic word-salad of delusions of grandeur and assertions of the unique, revolutionary, revelatory position of the author:

"In this book—for the first time. . . .

"Hitherto the possibility . . . never envisaged. . . .

"Our theme broadens into . . . *the* philosophy of the future. . . .

"[My] eye . . . perfectly free from prepossessions. . . .

"[By this *single* idea] one can solve all those separate problems of religion, art-history, epistemology, ethics, politics, economics. . . .

"This idea is . . . indisputable.

"This unphilosophical philosophy—the last that Western Europe will know. . . .

"[I saw] the solution . . . in immense outlines. . . . derived from one single principle . . . never [before] discovered. . . .

"A fact of decisive importance . . . hitherto hidden from the mathematicians themselves. . . .

"An image of history . . . independent of the accident of standpoint. . . .

"What has been missing till now. . . .

"Before my eyes there seems to emerge . . . a hitherto unimagined mode of historical research."

This was taken very seriously by a generation of scholars.

Mind Expansion

In *Daedalus*, Northrop Frye speaks of Spengler's power to expand and exhilarate the mind. Does "mind expansion" mean more than expanding the scope or range of behavior (in this case, verbal behavior)? To exhilarate, to cheer, to encourage, to give hope to—is that any more than to arrange reinforcers or to allude to possible reinforcers and hence strengthen behavior?

Life in the Sixties

I was to be picked up at 7:30 by two students, and one phoned me around six to confirm. My lecture at Brandeis was at 8:30.

No one came, and at 7:50 I called a taxi to be sure of arriving on time, but a car finally came, at 8:00. It was driven by a long-haired boy in a great coat, vaguely military, that dragged on the ground when he walked. His girl was with him.

"Am I late?" "Yes," I said, "half an hour." "We can get there in 15 minutes," he said. "Show me how to get to the Mass. Pike."

He drove erratically. On Storrow Drive, he swerved against the curb and then away and into another lane. As soon as he reached the Pike, he went very fast, swerving from one lane to another. It was spring and the road was covered with winter dirt and not clearly marked. I asked him to slow down. He did, slightly. "I want to get you there on time," he said. "We couldn't find your house," the girl volunteered, as if some explanation were needed. It was clear they were stoned.

We arrived on time, but I told the Program Director that I'd like a different driver back. I got one, but only because the same one was impatient as I stayed on autographing books and papers and talking to students. "One more autograph and we go," he said impolitely at one point. Another student then volunteered to get me home if I stayed awhile longer, and I readily accepted.

The Nonactive Nature of Behavior

It is true that we do not say, "The clock moves its hands," but we do say, "Clocks tell time," "The curfew tolls the knell of parting day," and "The weather promises to be fair." "The rat raised its foot" is merely an idiomatic way of saying "the rat's foot rose." In "The rat ran down the alley" the whole rat is active; in "The rat raised its foot," only a part; but the rat "did" both things. "The baseball broke the window" does not imply an act.

Selection is the clue to a special meaning. Although we say that "the horse as a species developed a hoof because it survived by running more swiftly over hard ground," we do not mean that the species acted. Nor does "The horse walked faster as it neared the barn" mean deliberate action.

Zuriff's examples (*Behaviorism*, 1975) are about push-pull causality. We want a prior act before the execution of the behavior; hence we need an actor or agent. But the nonactive nature of behavior is clear enough. That is the whole point of the operant.

The difference between an instance and a class (cf. especially the abstract tact) explains why one cannot identify an operant with any one instance.

Memory

Putting some new shoelaces in my shoes, I was sharply reminded of the days when I worked in George Harding's shoe store. The order of insertion of the lace, the flip of one lace to get it out of the way of the next, the rhythmic motion and sound.

And all this after almost fifty years.

Developmentalism

An unfortunate by-product of developmentalism: A behaviorist "holds that . . . we all have to pass through a growing-up experience from infant to adult where our minds are shaped and conditioned unconsciously and irresistibly by forces flowing from our environment." To pass *through*? Are we subsequently free, albeit warped by early experience? If the process of growing really explained development, then we should be free of it when we become mature and stop growing. But forces are also working "unconsciously and irresistibly" upon the mature person.

California

The brown hills of the West are not improved by a sparse cover of evergreens. The evidence is all too clear; this is not completed land. The hills are mangy, impoverished, diseased. Nothing thrives. There is no strength. The mountains have thrust themselves up but have never quite made acceptable country. An uncrowned effort, like the half-completed church of a congregation whose funds have run out.

Excelsior

At breakfast I watched men working on the second story of a brick building next door. A moving belt, cleated, inclined at 45 degrees, carried shovels, clods of mortar, bricks, and other things from the ground to the scaffolding. Twenty minutes later I came up out of the subway on a similar device. Halfway up I recalled the bricks and mortar. The moving belt saved labor—the particularly onerous labor of the hod-carrier. The escalator saved the labor that we should otherwise have expended in climbing stairs. The analogy dawned slowly, and I was aware of no emotional accompaniment. I rather doggedly framed a verbal comparison, possibly helped by the inertness of the people ahead of me, who kept me from walking up the moving stairs.

Interference?

When we are trying to recall a name, a wrong response may seem to get in the way. In recalling Clifford Odets, for example, I got *Clifton Fadiman*, presumably because of the common *Clif* and an early *d* in the second name. Nevertheless, in emitting *Clifton Fadiman* I may have been strengthening *Clifford Odets*, since generalization or induction may work in both directions. A familiar technique of recall is to emit similar responses, and wrong responses are examples if they are strong because of induction, even though punitive contingencies may weaken them. Free association to slips or other errors is a standard Freudian technique in getting at the right response held to be responsible for them—what they "really mean." The use of wrong responses as intraverbal stimuli for a right response is a very special kind of verbal self-management. In responding uncritically in order to discover what one has to say, one often generates novel responses.

In What Sense the Truth?

The label on the bottle of 500 mg. vitamin C tablets says "Easy to swallow." They are not. They are very sour, they dissolve quickly and trigger regurgitation as they touch the back of the throat.

If the product is in competition with another which *is* easy to swallow, the label is a lie. If not, it may help. "Hard to swallow" would cause trouble. Silence would be best if honesty were the best policy. But "Easy to swallow" may help, and if it does, it is not a false description but a helpful suggestion.

Freud and Sex

There is little overt sex in Egyptian temple art. The god Min with an erection; a Pharaoh embalmed with an erection; an occasional nonerotic nude, and a nude monkey with possibly emphasized genitalia—that is about it. Nothing compared with Indian, Greek, or Roman art.

But what about symbols? What about the key of life ♀? "Key in lock" is good Freudian symbolism. At Karnak there is a decorative molding which looks like the key of life alternating with a nonsymbolized phallus. It is rather like the Greek egg-and-dart, and when I noticed this I immediately saw the Freudian significance of the egg-and-dart. The egg has the shape of the depositing organ. Mold and casting are reciprocal forms; is the phallus the casting and the vagina the to-be-discarded mold? The dart is the sword of the male symbol ♂, but is it a sword or phallus? And is the female symbol ♀ the mirror of Venus or a slightly modified key of life?

Rambling but passable Freud. In the right mood, one can turn it out indefinitely.

The Age of Reason

"I can allow for the fears of the child, but not of the man. As he became rational, he ought to have roused himself. . . ."—from *Emma*, by Jane Austen.

A curious early example of developmentalism. "As he became rational. . . ." As a faculty grew in him.

The facts can be accounted for in terms of rules versus contingencies or reasons versus causes. When people begin to examine the contingencies to which they have been or are being exposed, they may derive rules which they then obey, or give themselves reasons to which they then submit.

The history of mankind has presumably shown the same "development." Before the advent of verbal behavior, people responded to contingencies, not commands, advice, or laws. It was the *infancy* of humankind in the strict etymological sense of a state without language.

Residual Seeing

For a year or more I have noticed that, after working at my desk, when I look at a darkly illuminated white surface, I see writing or printing very much like the material I have been working with. This is presumably central rather than retinal and appears to be a perseveration of "seeing writing or printing" without the specific control of a current visual stimulus.

This morning I noticed an especially clear case. For about an hour at my desk I read old themes. The typing was rather faint, and I had to "read hard." Then I stopped, went upstairs to read the papers, came down to my study, and lay down for twenty minutes. At the end of the twenty minutes in a fairly dark room, I looked at the off-white ceiling and saw very clear but jumbled typing. I could almost make out whole words. The typing was in more or less horizontal lines, but slightly overlapping.

Is this not a residual strength of "seeing typed material"?

It can scarcely be an afterimage in the sense of a temporary exhaustion of material. It is poorly controlled operant seeing, within the boundaries of a type of stimulus.

Feelings as Causes

In *About Behaviorism* I say that the states of the body which are felt are not the causes of behavior but the collateral products of the causes. This does not mean that private events cannot control behavior—as they do when we describe them (even if necessarily inaccurately). I meant the causal role traditionally assigned to felt states in such expressions as "I struck because I was angry" or "I went because I felt like going." The point of my statements in *About Behaviorism* was that there was no initiating action inside.

Private events are limited not only in the extent to which they control "introspective" accounts but also in the extent to which they are useful in self-management. The injunction "when angry count to ten" can be followed only if there is some evidence of "being angry." The evidence may be introspective, as when one feels activity in the autonomic nervous system or an "inclination to strike," or exteroceptive, as when one observes either an occasion upon which one commonly strikes or behavior associated with striking, both of which may be seen by others.

Contralateral

Julie once said that an injection or a mosquito bite sometimes caused her *other* arm to itch. I have noticed the same thing with my hay fever shots. Of course, I have plenty of scar tissue from injections on both arms, and it is possible that other stimulation from an injection could elicit a conditioned itch, especially since the scar tissue must make itching easy. At the moment I have a strong reaction from a small-pox vaccination on my right arm. My left arm itches.

The Law

A policeman was walking along a snow-drifted street and I stopped to give him a lift. He was heavyset, with the florid face of a heavy drinker. (A block print in two colors—dark blue for the uniform, red for the face—would have done him justice.) I said I was going to Harvard Square and he said, "Are you a professor? What do you think of Kennedy's appointments?" It was no casual time-of-day remark; there was even a touch of panic in his manner. I said I was satisfied. Appointing his brother Attorney General might prove a bit ticklish. That was his cue. "Right. You can't blame a truck driver. Five kids. He can't be a hero. He can't tell Hoffa where to get off. They'd break his legs." He had not bothered to fill in the line of his thought but I caught it in a moment. "It won't be an easy job," I said. "There is a lot of dirty work ahead. Crime, for one thing." He laughed nervously. I had not seen this to be relevant to his uniform. Fortunately I was turning the wrong way for him at the next corner. He got out and as I drove away I saw him flagging down a truck for a further lift.

"Displacement"

Furious at Sophie Brzeska, Henri Gaudier strikes the soft clay bust of her that he has been working on (*Savage Messiah* by H. S. Ede, Knopf, 1931). It must have been very much like striking Sophie herself. Less effective would have been cutting or tearing a painting or photograph and still less so acting aggressively toward a statue, painting, or picture of someone else. Another live person, an animal, or an inanimate object might have served.

Social Contingencies

Luis de Florez could not back the early Project Pigeon because a "couple of other long shots had not paid off." In other words, he was in danger of losing his job or at least the support he needed. Kennedy's advisers are said (by Marcus G. Raskin, reviewing Rapoport's *Strategy and Conscience* in the *Scientific American*) to have thought in terms of conserving "credit points"; it was considered strategically wise not to speak out on every issue "because one's effectiveness would be lessened." This could mean: (a) the more comments, the less the thought inferred behind them, or (b) the more comments, the more often one may be wrong or disagreed with.

Big Horne Tooke

A friend had the chance to name a street in a new housing development in Palisades, N.Y. An admirer of *The Diversions of Purley*, he settled on "Horne Tooke Road." Many families now live on Horne Tooke Road, and the local legend has it that Horne Tooke was an Indian chief.

"Looking For"

When we have been looking for something without success and stop, we exhibit discrimination rather than extinction. That is why the change can be relatively quick. We have already learned not to do again what we have just done unsuccessfully. A place in which we have just looked is a place in which nothing will be found.

Finding a topic of conversation suitable to a new companion is rather similar. Verbal behavior on a particular theme need not extinguish before we stop talking. The new companion quickly acquires discriminative features; he or she is someone upon whom certain kinds of remarks fall without effect.

Act of Love

A common noncontingent "reinforcer" is fair weather. "The sun shone on him and his enterprises." This is particularly important—

　　a. when the weather has been bad or threatening.

　　b. when the weather is important.

I believe something of the sort occurred at an outdoor mass meeting of Nazis; the sun came out just as Hitler appeared. (Had Hitler kept his eye on the sky?)

Eisenhower got fair weather on D-day.

The superstitious conclusion is that God or the gods view the event with favor and will smile on other undertakings. To say "We are destined to succeed in all we do," or "The gods are on our side" is to describe contingencies which may increase a tendency to engage in action under otherwise discouraging circumstances. But the principal effect of the good weather is to strengthen action; the verbal explanation of why the action is undertaken comes later.

The gambler who ends a losing streak by winning is more inclined to extend a later losing streak; the ratio is "stretched." A reinforcer is (or must be) effective on a variable-ratio schedule in restoring strength to an extinguishing response. Accompanying emotional effects are relevant. Is it meaningless to ask whether they add to the effect of a reinforcer? According to earlier interpretations one effect is converting a long run of unreinforced responses into a discriminative stimulus.

"Knowing What to Do"

"Try these, they're delicious" (eating $\longrightarrow$ reinforcing flavor, texture, etc.).

"Don't touch that, it's hot!" (touching $\longrightarrow$ aversive burn).

If the specified behavior (eating, touching) does or does not follow, it is because a prior history has been made relevant to a present occasion by the pointing words "these" or "that."

Replace the pointing words with the description of an occasion, and you have advice or warnings:

"Store a few gallons of drinking water in your basement."

"Don't put electrical appliances near bathtubs."

Extremely valuable to a culture, but not because they "impart knowledge."

Antascetic

"... a Religious [should] err a little by excess [in fasting] ... especially if he finds that his flesh is an enemy that wages war against him." ... .Commentary on the *Rule of Benedict* by Alphonso Orozco.

The "enemy" may have been too much reinforcement from food, aggression, or sex. The suggested mode of attack is obvious in the first, but must have been discovered from experience in the second and third. Someone, while fasting, must have discovered that he was less likely to be aggressive or sexual. Concentration camps and camps for prisoners of war "control" sex and aggression this way; there is a weakening of impulse and interest. This is one physiological solution to the problem of the excessive human susceptibility to reinforcement by sex and aggressive damage—a susceptibility which no longer has much survival value and may prove lethal.

Age

When young we see people of all ages. Old people are not unusual. When we grow old we see old people we once knew as young, and this makes an enormous difference. When I was young I used to imagine the kind of old people my friends would become, but that was not an adequate preparation for what they *have* become.

Never Again!

After Stevenson's defeat in 1956 he said he would never run for president again, and the resolution rose to hinder him in 1960. Why did he say it? What does one get from resolving never to do something again? Obviously, some measure of escape from the aversive consequences of having done it and from aversive stimuli associated with questions about running again. It is a slightly more rational form of wishing one had not done it and a way of creating a less threatening future.

Nixon's "you won't have Nixon to kick around anymore" showed an element of escape—and a clouded crystal ball.

Public Hair

The very attractive young Italian woman with whom we had dinner last night in Florence wore a sleeveless blouse and skirt which would not have attracted attention in America, but, like most Italian and French women, she had luxuriant growths of hair under her arms. This is still evidently an attractive feature, presumably visual (or tactual?) rather than olfactory, as in some explanations of its evolutionary function. Like "public" hair, as I once saw "pubic" misspelled, hair under the arm may have served in the dissemination of sex odors. Insects have hairs with such functions and, of course, special odor glands. But modern human odors are masked with perfumes, which can be made as strong as desired and require no disseminators.

Fear of Control

I have begun to save the letters I receive from psychotics who tell me how they are being controlled by unseen persons. They turn to recent science: brain stimulation, concealed electronic devices, and so on. Fifty years ago it would have been radio waves. A hundred years ago it was animal magnetism or telepathy. Before that, the Devil. It is presumably a matter of explaining oneself to one's self or others who ask the kinds of questions that encourage self-knowledge. People are asked to explain their failure. An accurate analysis of the contingencies—a genuine explanation of failure—might resolve the problem, but reasons are usually invented rather than discovered. The fact that the supposed controller is an enemy should tip us off. How often do psychotics have delusions about benevolent controllers? Gamblers acknowledge the role of Lady Luck and poets of the Muse, but they are not called psychotic when they do so. For a Mary Baker Eddy a bad controller who used malicious animal magnetism could be vanquished by a benevolent one using God's love.

Auras

On a late television show, Steve Allen interviewed a "sensitive." She claimed to see auras, but she failed miserably in reading the personality of a member of the staff. She tried a hesitant "You are musical?" (He was wearing earphones.) He said no. Then she said, "What member of your family likes music?" "My wife." "Of course, I often get confused. Auras get mixed up among members of families."

Need

In a discussion of psychotherapy, *transference* is defined as "unearned" dependence on the therapist or, more generally, any emotional reaction originally evoked by someone else and now evoked by the therapist mainly because of availability. The process is pretty clearly *stimulus generalization*. There is no *logical* reason for loving, fearing, or hating the analyst.

The account goes on to describe the client's *need* to react to someone in a given relation. This may mean simply that one does react, as one *needed* to react to the original object, in which case the term makes a merely gratuitous reference to the presence of activity. Whatever one does, one needs to do—this is a way of speaking of probability or even inevitability.

Or, it may mean that a stimulus enough like the original to evoke a response is reinforcing. The subject *needs to find someone* to whom transference may be made. The behavior of searching for or producing an appropriate object is the sign of the need.

We make the same distinction between *needing to talk* and *needing to find someone to talk to*. Once the behavior has been specified, the superfluity of *need* is evident. We must explain the probability by finding a more substantial variable.

The Near Hit

I suppose I mean the near miss—i.e., a miss but close enough to have some effect or at least to "arouse hope."

How reinforcing is it? The slot machine, the horse race, the Bingo game—all permit the player to come close without actually winning. There is a temporal element. One gets the first two bells, cherries, or bars on the slot machine but misses the third. One's horse is beaten in the stretch. The Bingo card shows four-in-a-row long before someone else gets five. (The slot machine and horse race offer consolation prizes: two cherries win, though much less than three; a horse may show or place.) A lottery ticket may be close to the winning number or may win a lesser prize. A sweepstakes ticket may draw a horse which almost wins the race.

There is undoubtedly something punishing in almost winning. An emotional component is clear: If there is a temporal pattern—if one loses at the very end of a contest— the effect is felt as *disappointment*, a *let down* from the elevation of impending reinforcement. But the net effect must be reinforcing, or the designers of gambling systems are wrong.

Destructive Contingencies

Suppose that the members of an orchestra are friendly with a composer, and that each of them comments on particular features of a work in progress. The trombonist enjoys long chromatic runs, the flutist likes solo cadenzas, and the violinist enjoys passages in pizzacato. Since each reacts to the effect of a detail rather than of the whole, these differential reinforcements could destroy the integrity of a work.

To some extent this may have happened. Music has been written because accomplished players on particular instruments were available, but it would be hard to say whether any damage has been done. The composer may have written more, in fact, because some detail was generously reinforced. But a distortion is to be looked for.

There is clearly an analogy in any cultural design. Congress is always listening to members of the orchestra as it composes its laws. The policies of a business are composed for the benefit of its more vocal owners or employees. Educational innovations are composed for teachers, students, or parents. Strong decisions in all these fields are needed to maintain the integrity of the whole pattern.

Deferred Consequence

Another example of ineffective contingencies from gardening (see the note on raking leaves):

Pulling the *big* weeds is most strongly reinforced when we weed a lawn or garden. Each pull makes a big difference: the area is much freer, the basket much fuller. Yet the little weeds are easier to pull (less deeply rooted) and dispose of, and the net result is greater than waiting for them to grow large before pulling them. But the result is remote; the consequences affect only the experienced gardener who has seen weeds grow or those who have analyzed the contingencies and extracted a useful rule: "Pull *every* weed."

Mother Love

In a discussion about a baby's need for mother love, several students brought up all the old evidence for a need. When orphans are raised in two groups, the group getting lots of personal attention is healthier, but was resistance to disease built up by more mother love or more contact with viruses and bacilli? How much *love* did the experimental group really get? Is it from lack of *love* that monkeys "raised by mechanical mothers" are unable to copulate at maturity? One student suggested that the rocking of the young monkey resembled sexual behavior, but there is not much rocking when monkeys copulate. Is sexual competence the rationale of the rocked cradle, or of the cradle board carried on the mother's back? Or are these things mere pacifiers? Steady movement can be soporific or tranquilizing. I recalled Katherine Mayo's statement in *Mother India* that Indian mothers masturbate their young sons—"to make them virile," but does this cultural practice have survival value in its effect on the birth rate, or is it a means of quieting a baby?

How far are the "mother love" advocates willing to go? Should mothers stimulate their babies sexually, or *almost* sexually, and how often?

Making No Grammar

Lawrence Durrell often strings words together for their own sake. He loves unusual words. He piles up more synonyms than he can use in one assertion. From *Tunc*, p. 198: "sitting like some forlorn collapsing edifice, foundering among its own distresses."

"Forlorn" or "distress"—but not both, please. "Collapsing" or "foundering"—but not both. He has collected too many words, and when put together they are near nonsense.

Unspecified Topography

Creative behavior (behavior having novel consequences) can presumably be encouraged by reinforcing many new responses. Induction to other new responses is then furthered. I have just made a musical toy for Lisa (four months old). She pulls downward on a string and the toy plays music for a few seconds. It appears to reinforce pulling—and what else? Can we say that "doing things in general" is reinforced?

Will she not be more "participating" than if she lived in a world where music plays although you do nothing to make it do so?

Dream

I had a dream several nights ago which is no longer vivid but which went like this:

I was in a house on an island—Monhegan, perhaps. I was looking at an empty Aircrib and I suddenly realized with deep sympathy how sad it must be when Julie looks at it since her child has been stolen from it. I look out the window and see a child walking in rough underbrush and for a second I wonder if it is the missing child, brought back by its nappers, but I see at once that it is not. Then I think, why not inform the police? It suddenly seems very stupid to me, now, that we have accepted the theft and done nothing about it.

I feel now that this last point—action not taken—is the important one in the dream.

Reinforcing Environment

From my hotel window in Aswan on the Nile, I saw children playing in a filthy slum. One ran back and forth, arm straight up, a long white ribbon of cloth or paper streaming gracefully behind. (The next day smaller children were running in the same way with fragments of the same streamer.) One child rolled a hoop, beating it with a stick. One stoned a young goat. One scooped up water from a pool by the community spigot. One pushed a goat ahead of him as if it were a wagon. One climbed over a pile of rubble to what was once the roof of a shed. Some were sitting in the shade, watching others or dozing. One, very small, burrowed into her father's loose robe as he sat in a doorway.

In a few months, I was told, they would all move into a new block of flats. What behavior would survive?

Hearing and Seeing

My discussion with undergraduates in psychology at Cambridge University was, I think, worthwhile. I realized more clearly than before how much needs to be done in analyzing sensory effects. The "motor theory" of consciousness points to the same dimensions as an operant analysis but not to the same variables or contingencies: Only by following the shaping and maintaining of seeing, hearing, etc., can we get at its nature.

Hearing something *as if* it were something else, seeing something *as if* it were something else—these fall between hearing or seeing something which is there and hearing or seeing something which is not there. The point is that you see or hear the same thing in all cases. You hear the phone ring when it is ringing, you can hear it by imagining it, and you can hear it, particularly if you are expecting a call, when you hear some slight noise—say, the triangle in a recorded symphony. *What you hear is the phone, not the triangle.*

Of course we have learned to hear things more or less clearly. We may ask, "Was that the phone?" when a phone is heard at a distance, or in our imagination, or in a recording. But we hear the thing we have learned to respond to, at any intensity level, *as a telephone.*

Off-Spring

"Brainchild" is a common expression for a creative work, but not for behavior that is clearly acquired. A good job of pitching a baseball game is not "having a brainchild." Nor is winning a race or playing the piano well at a concert.

The origin of the brainchild is crucial. Something begins in the mother-brain. It is a "work" of art—an off-spring: something that springs off and away.

Titular Autoclitics

Instead of simply naming the subject in a title, the author adds a response which says to the putative reader, "This is an essay or book *about* such and such a subject." *An Essay on . . .* , *On . . .* , *Concerning . . .* , and *Toward . . .* are examples. So are *A Study of . . .* , *An Investigation into . . .* , provided the essay or book *is* the study or investigation thus identified. The practice may be useful if it makes a useful distinction. Thus, *An Introduction . . .* is different from *A Treatise on . . . .*

A different kind of titular autoclitic has a blunting or softening effect. *The Process of Education*, *The Meaning of Anxiety*, and *The Meaning of Evolution* alert the reader that what follows is not a comprehensive book on education, anxiety, or evolution, respectively. *The Meaning of Meaning* is, on the other hand, more cogent than *Meaning* alone would have been because of its wit. (I chose *About Behaviorism* because *Behaviorism* was preempted by Watson.)

Wait

A simple verb, but what does it mean?

Wait! means *Stop!*

Wait for me! means *Stop doing what you are doing until I get there.*

Waiting for death suggests inaction, but not reinforced inaction.

The superstition of him who waits (Dumas *fils*) refers to behavior that picks up reinforcement by what is being waited for.

To wait is to do nothing *until* something happens.

Learn to labor and to wait (Longfellow)—and we do learn to wait.

I started this note after saying to myself that in demonstrating a discrimination with a pigeon I will reinforce waiting by the key or wait for the pigeon to turn away before presenting the S^D.

By waiting for something we minimize the time that elapses before we get it. Compare the pigeon waiting for the stimulus in the reaction-time experiment. We wait for bad news, to minimize preaversive stimulation.

There is nothing to do but wait almost defines waiting.

Inadequate Aversive Stimulus

I had agreed to give a telelecture to be recorded for broadcast in Illinois at 3:00 P.M. Eastern Standard Time. Three o'clock came and there was no call. I looked at the carbon of the letter I had written: "I will be at home and you can call me there, 864-0848 Area code 212." I decided that they had meant Central Standard Time, and I lay down on the divan to wait. I found myself saying "864-0848 Area code 212." Then I began to wonder. Our area code is 617. Had I written 212?

At four o'clock I was at my desk again, and I saw that I *had* written 212, and I immediately put through a call. For almost an hour I had been vaguely uneasy about a mistake, yet had not decided that I had made it, nor had I made a move to look and see. (212 is the area code of New York City, which I frequently use.)

Strategy of the Linguists

The structuralists (e.g., linguists) argue that one must analyze the forms of behavior (e.g., grammar) before one can relate them to independent variables. The opposite position was, I suppose (though I can never be sure), taken in Dewey's "Reflex Arc Concept." It was the point of my paper on "The Generic Nature of the Concepts of Stimulus and Response." You can't identify the significant features of behavior unless you know the controlling variables. Linguists would find this out sooner if they stopped using their own responses to identify significant features. (In doing so they also confound the accounts of the behavior of speaker and listener.)

Explaining Verbal Behavior

Lenneberg's book *Biological Foundations of Language* shows the archetypal pattern of current linguistics. Given language as utterances (or, more particularly, as acceptable utterances *or* nonutterances or nonsentences) one looks for causes. Ruling out contingencies of reinforcement (all those "impossibles") one turns to (1) the nervous system (very scientific), (2) ethology (only a little less scientific; it is at least biological), and (3) (when all else fails) to cognitive processes (unique to each species). The cognitive processes cannot be inadequate because they are defined as miraculous.

Superego

Elsewhere I have a note pointing out that the superego is a vicarious punisher, not a positive or negative reinforcer. Certainly that is true of the Christian conscience. But it is not standard psychoanalytic doctrine. According to a letter in *Science* (September 6, 1968), the *Glossary of Psychoanalytic Terms and Concepts* lists two kinds of superego functions:

1. the protective and rewarding functions which set up ideals and values grouped under the term ego-ideal.

2. the critical and punitive functions which evoke the sense of guilt and the pangs of conscience.

But certainly much more has been made of the cruel superego. Punishment is the source of the problems which psychoanalysis tries to solve.

Out-of-Date Feature

In *Contingencies of Reinforcement*, Chapter 3, I might have added a set of emotional responses. Many reflexes in the autonomic nervous system are appropriate to survival when certain kinds of intense stimuli are characteristic of danger. A loud noise, a painful wound, a sudden drop must at one time almost invariably have demanded vigorous action, and the autonomic responses which supported action must have had great survival value. They generated conditions felt as fear and anger. These reflexes are now mostly out-of-date, but they may affect a person's health and make it difficult to acquire useful behavior. Loud noises are disturbing even when not dangerous, the pain of medical treatment may interfere with the treatment, and a sudden drop may frighten the child in an elevator or disturb a person learning to fly a plane. The strong emotions generated by these stimuli are commonly said to have psychosomatic effects.

Altruism

Altruism is generally help for the needy—the reduction of aversive conditions or states of deprivation. The literature which made altruism heroic dealt with doing good to the infirm or destitute or troubled, and if there is a decline in that today in America, it may be because there are fewer opportunities. One still helps small children, but only because their lot has not improved; they are still by definition helpless.

Doing good with positive reinforcement is suspect. An interest in making others "feel good"—giving them a good dinner, or a good time, or (particularly) sexual stimulation —suggests either a neurotic, vicarious enjoyment or preparation for return favors (buttering up, seduction).

Both raise the issue of contingency. The unfortunate effects of altruism include the incidental reinforcement of displays of neediness (malingering) and of modes of action producing neediness (prodigality, shiftlessness). The art of doing good consists in the proper timing of satiation or reduction in aversive stimulation so that it will not serve as reinforcement.

An Example of Proustian Recall

I began to write my Page-Barbour lectures in an improvised study at home. On the first day I recalled, seemingly for no reason, the model-builder's supply shop somewhere along the Mississippi, near Fort Snelling, where I tried to buy materials, in short supply because of the war, for the early pigeon-bomb experiments. I first saw the shop when I took up my Guggenheim to work on *Verbal Behavior* in the basement of our house in St. Paul, before going to work for General Mills, Inc.

The following may have contributed to the recollection: (1) At my work table I was once again using a small brown metal filing case that I had used in St. Paul. (2) In the notes spread about the table, I had once again numbered paragraphs decimally (though my handwriting was now italic). (3) Possibly most important of all, since I was once again working at home, I could hear Eve in a distant part of the house talking on the telephone.

Escape Hatch for Teachers

An article in this morning's *Herald-Traveler* says it is unfair to ask teachers to screen their students to find those needing special help. A question is raised of their competence in judging "disability." A much stronger objection (which may have prompted the complaint) is that teachers absolve themselves of failure and get rid of problem students by calling them disabled and passing them along to specialists.

Small Grant Research

"Farewell, my Lovely" was more than a nostalgic sigh. I was unhappy about very long, steady-state experiments done at the expense of more detailed analyses of contingencies. Another "expense" was involved: budgets were being cut. Here are some experiments that could be done with a smaller capital investment:

1. Reaction time. Best possible "ready" behavior. What length of ready signal? What modalities? Off-on or on-off? Or either one? Needed: a very accurate chronometer or oscilloscope display. Also needed: very frequent inspection! No setting up a set of contingencies and having someone run the experiment.

2. Choice reaction as in above.

3. Reaction time and short-term memory. Matching. (We have been doing short-term memory studies since the early 1950s.) (Colored light early in ready period, but with ready period still variable after color goes off.)

4. Same as 3 but coding.

5. The clocks and counters in *Schedules* were quite primitive. The whole thing needs repeating. Daily curves should be significant.

6. Stooge experiments. One organism conditioned to respond to the behavior of another.

7. Cooperative button pushers, as in my cooperation experiment. Is there a generalized tendency to imitate? Condition one member to respond to an adjacent but previously unused key. Does the other bird respond?

(These experiments take time—the experimenter's time—instead of money for long-term apparatus and assistants.)

8. Evidence of afterimages. Pigeon pecks blue-green spot moving on screen. Does not peck red, yellow. Flash of red light. No blue-green on screen. Does pigeon peck?

Easier: Pecks *when* blue-green, not when red. Large red flash. Pecks?

Rate in generalization gradient to locate wavelength of image?

9. Cross-modal generalization. House light: slow, fast. Peck when fast. House light steady, but off-on tone or bobble—slow or fast. Rate different?

10. Paced—single trial. (A) Red key, peck slowly. Green key, peck fast. (B) Fast flicker, press fast. Slow flicker, press slowly. Try: Fast and slow tone—i.e., mediating response.

11. Making stimuli "hot" and "cold."

A. Moving—does O push or pull?
  Going out—covering?
  Going out slowly—covering?
B. Teach pigeon to "peck out" lights (peck turns off light).
Then: O ● O is good; O O O bad. Will pigeon peck middle key out?
C. Change order. Get O ● O discrimination first. Then single key. Peck → "out." Out = food on VI.
  Then O O O again. Which key is pecked?

Early Ethology

I am often surprised by early observations and experiments on animal behavior which anticipate (sometimes by centuries) current ethology. Here are two examples from Donald Frame's biography of Montaigne:

1. "He notes . . . how hens and chickens fear certain animals and birds but not other larger ones: sparrow hawks but not geese." The reference to hawks and geese suggests a recent experiment in which a silhouette resembling a bird

moving above ptarmigan chicks alarmed them when moved in a direction suggesting a short neck and long tail (say, a hawk) but had no effect when moved in the opposite direction suggesting a long neck and a short tail (say, a goose).

2. "He tells of putting out to stud an old horse sated with his own mares but uncontrollable at the scent of others." (Was it Tinklepaugh or Yerkes who showed that a chimpanzee sated with a group of females would instantly copulate with a new female?)

Learned Perception

For more than a year I used a toothbrush with a sharp bend at the neck: ⌢⌢ ———— Then I changed to a straight handle: ⊓⊓⊓ ————When I first used it, I felt the handle bend quickly to this shape: ⌢⌢⌢ ————I had the impression that the handle was rubber or soft plastic, or that it was a practical joker's toothbrush, like the table knife with a jointed handle.

I had learned to "feel" the position of my teeth with the linkage supplied by ⌢⌢ ————. Had I felt something less a part of me than my teeth, I should probably have felt *it* change rather than the brush, since that is the commonest reason why one feels such a change. But I need not have "resisted the inference" that my teeth had moved; with teeth it is always the linkage that accounts for different sets of stimuli.

So Much to Be Done

Everywhere I turn I see people overlooking the enormous contribution a behavioral analysis can make. A paper called "A Prelude to a Phenomenology of Sound" gets nowhere.

Music is not a matter of sense data, not even sense data interpreted by the listener. It is a pattern of stimuli determining action. Much of the time the listener is (to put it crudely) imitating—singing along with the singer, playing along with the player. The listener's behavior is guided, forced, tricked, foiled, confirmed—as in the logopoeia of poetry.

Rhythm is perhaps the best example. Steady, accelerated, retarded, syncopated, duple, triple—all these terms describe modes or manners of action. Melodies go up and down and steady on.

Harmony is harder to analyze. It came late in the history of music, as simple intervals yielded to less familiar, which then became familiar.

All this is evident in the remarkable effect of getting to know a piece of music well.

Music is action. Listening, a form of singing or playing, is much more than phenomenology!

Verbal drh

Aversive stimuli associated with the differential reinforcement of fast responding (*drh*) have little effect on the behavior of public speakers. At conferences, there is often a general insensitivity to speed-up contingencies. Repeatedly, speakers are told "Two minutes" or "One minute" with no effect. Very often the end is merely postponed, either because speakers hurry, express themselves badly, and then take extra time to clear up misunderstandings, or because they respond at greater length because they have been reminded of their audience, where up to that point they may have been talking mainly to themselves.

Idle Hands

I looked in Mencken's *New Dictionary of Quotations* for the expression "The Devil always has something for idle hands to do." (I remember Professor Bowles's joke about the teacher who quoted the line in reproving a student and then said, "Come up here at once, and I'll give you something to do.") I found instead:

[Idleness is] the mother of vices (John Lydgate, 1440),

[Idleness is] the nurse of sin (Spenser, 1589), [Idleness hatches] ten thousand harms (Antony and Cleopatra, 1606), Without business, debauchery (George Herbert, 1640), Idleness is the root of all evil (G. Farquhar, 1707), Satan finds some mischief still/For idle hands to do (Isaac Watts, 1715), If the Devil finds a man idle he'll set him to work (James Kelley, 1721), [He] that is idle [is tempted] by a legion [of Devils] (T. Fuller, 1732), Idle brains are the Devil's workhouses (ibid.), When we do ill the Devil tempteth us; when we do nothing, we tempt him (ibid.), An idle person has the Devil for a playfellow (Arab proverb), Idleness is the Devil's pillow (Danish proverb), Idleness is the cause of all the vices (Latin proverb), and Idleness is the ruin of chastity (Latin proverb).

"Idleness" describes those occasions upon which weak responses get their chance. They are more likely to have evil consequences than the serious business of staying alive. Is that why we love leisure?

"Being Nice"

When a University of Texas student asked me "What is love?" I replied "mutual reinforcement." But I was uneasy about it, because when one does something nice to a person one loves, it is not done to reinforce. Now, however, it seems to me that a superstitious contingency may prevail. I originally felt that when one does something nice to another person, the other person is then emotionally disposed to do something even nicer in return, but adventitious reinforcement should be taken into account. If one is inclined to do something nice because another person has just done something nice, then what the other person has just done may be reinforced. There may be more of this than I had supposed in talking about an emotional disposition to be nice to others.

An emotional disposition to be nice to those who are nice to us is presumably part of a genetic endowment. But what were the contingencies of survival that selected that endowment? Could it not be that this is another example of ontogenic contingencies being taken over by a phylogenic mechanism? A built-in tendency to be nice to those who are nice to one would have survival value in increasing the number of nice things done. (I am assuming, of course, that by nice I mean ultimately biologically good.)

Opposing Self-Control

I went to see Arthur Morgan in Yellow Springs after the publication of *Walden Two*. He picked cherries as we talked. "Not that the cherries are worth my time in picking them," he said. In *My Father's House* Pierpont Noyes has something about picking up the nails dropped during the shingling of a house in the Oneida Community. Even with only partially automated manufacture it was not worth one's time to pick up good nails.

Here is a problem in self-control, masked as a question of value. Apart from social reinforcement, picking something up is a response of near minimal effort and immediately reinforced. Repeated responding generates the reinforcement of an advancing counter: the penny bank fills, the ball of string grows larger.

And social reinforcers are added. Frugality is praised. "See a pin, pick it up; all the day you'll have good luck."

Yet, as times change, this all becomes a waste. Hence the need for opposing self-control. But should a culture lead every child up the same path? Come to think of it, the *children* at Oneida might have collected the nails profitably. But what would that have done to them as adults?

Inherited Susceptibility to Reinforcement

I have seen dogs repeatedly run after pigeons in a park where the behavior is evidently never reinforced by contact or capture. Why? Is the mere flushing of a bird reinforcing?

The question could be answered by arranging an "un-natural" contingency.

In an open field, or even in a large room, confine the dog in a cage containing a lever. A few feet away (not too far if the dog's vision is weak), hold a dozen pigeons in small cages. Each cage, when opened electrically, tosses the pigeon gently into the air. Let pressing the lever eject a pigeon on, say, a variable-interval schedule. What rate will be observed? Can the response be brought under stimulus control?

By making the dog's box transparent, airtight, and to some extent soundproof, the importance of visual components could be estimated; by making it opaque but downwind and sound-conducting, the importance of auditory components could be estimated, and so on.

Closure

When Lisa was a year and a half old, she asked me to print A's. I printed several and then one with a small break in the horizontal line. She looked a little puzzled, and when I completed the letter by filling the gap she smiled. I did it again and she laughed. I did it again. Then I drew a larger A with a big gap, and she said "No!" quite vigorously. When I completed it, she laughed brightly.

How many systems of psychology might one found on such observations?

The Irrational as Amusing

The watchmaker could find nothing wrong with my self-winding wristwatch. When I wore it, it occasionally stopped; when he wore it, it worked well. Then he discovered that the mainspring occasionally slipped, and he tightened its mountings. He explained that he led a more active life than I and that that had probably compensated for the slight slippage. He gave it back with the opinion that it would probably work well for me now. As I left, I said, "Of course, I can always lead a more active life." We were both amused.

I enjoyed the remark as it came out, unrehearsed. It was, in a sense, a logical induction. If the watchmaker had said, "I wound the watch mornings, you wound it evenings," I might well have said, "Of course, I can always wind it mornings, too." But the magnitude of the proposed measure (leading a more active life) in relation to the intended result (keeping an inexpensive watch running) made the remark funny, and I let myself make it in spite of its absurdity.

The Fireman's Hat

Pre-Christmas Fast Relaxed by Pope

VATICAN CITY (UPI) —Pope John XXIII Friday ruled that Catholics who are unable to meet the obligation of abstinence and fasting on Christmas Eve are absolved from the obligation this year. In 1959 the Pope decreed that those unable to meet the obligation on Christmas Eve could observe it on December 23. But because December 23 this year falls on a Sunday, the pontiff granted a dispensation rather than require that these persons observe fasting and abstinence on Sunday.

What does it mean to be "unable to meet the obligation of abstinence and fasting on Christmas Eve"? One can abstain from eating anywhere at any time.

This is rather like Robert Benchley's unwillingness to wear out the magical powers of the fireman's hat which he wore to help Harvard win against Yale. He put the hat away when the cause was hopeless, as the Church wisely refrains from imposing obligations which will not be observed. Better to grant a dispensation than to create a host of little sinners, who may move on to bigger sins.

Placation

"A dentist placating a child with a free lollipop is not very different from a supermarket rewarding a housewife with free trading stamps, a new advertising campaign suggests."
—from an advertisement for a trading stamp company.

Popular usage shows the most careless use of terms referring to contingencies of reinforcement. *Placate* means to mollify, to quiet, as by making concessions. The dentist's lollipop works in that way on Pavlovian principles; it offsets (it is hoped) fear or anxiety aroused by the dentist, the office, and the equipment. (It could also reinforce coming to the office, and future contingencies would be improved as the lollipop conditions new reinforcers.)

But if the supermarket *placates* its customers with stamps, we must suppose that they have been hurt or made angry or resentful, as by high prices, bad service, or the rudeness of employees.

On "Having" a Poem

The comparison with having a baby may be misleading. The poem does not exist inside the poet at any time, as a book is not inside one ("I have a novel in me"). It is the whole process of gestation that must be compared with writing a poem. The baby isn't "in" the mother at conception, either.

What are inside in both cases are the effects of long histories, one phylogenic, one ontogenic. The "having" is a process in which many processes combine to produce a thing—as unique as its multiple sources. The birth is what is called "having," but I should be talking about gestation.

Power of Prediction

Voice teachers often make predictions about the future of their students' voices. Years ago a Longy School teacher undertook to convince me that I could sing, and told me that he was once a tenor but that his teacher discovered he was really a baritone and then changed his range. The other day a student told me he planned to be a singer. "A Wagnerian tenor?" I asked. "Well, my teacher tells me I will have a powerful voice," he said.

Evidently it is possible not to know much about one's own voice, or at least about how it will develop. But his could also be a professional dodge. Some psychoanalysts capitalize on predicting the course of an analysis. Harry Murray admired Hanns Sachs's apparently real success in this. If the reasons for making a prediction are not given, if the statement is not explicitly about *current* facts, then the effect borders on soothsaying, and the accuracy of prediction need be no greater to be effective.

Verbal Atoms

In subvocally describing the fragment of an old ship over our fireplace, I referred to the English system of measurement and said the ribs were *twelve-to-twelve inches* . . . correcting this to *twelve inches center to center*. The *x-to-x* pattern was displaced from *center* to *twelve*. Possibly this was aided by the fact that numbers frequently fall into similar patterns (four by four, three times three, and—with *to*, as in telling time—ten to ten). The *to* gets close to *twelve* in *It's twelve inches from here to here*, referring to the same fact.

Yet in spite of this, there *is* a transfer of a verbal "atom" from one component to another. It is like putting the possessive *'s* on the wrong word or capitalizing the wrong word, but the example is not syntactical or orthographical.

It would be very hard to prove much of this (especially statistically) and very hard to generate much of it experimentally, though a comparable case might turn up, like rubbing your stomach with one hand while patting your head with the other. Fortunately, it doesn't matter in the present state of our knowledge.

A Curious Incentive Wage

According to C. C. Gillespie (*A Diderot Pictorial Encyclopedia*) the eighteenth-century slate cutter was paid at piece rate for usable slabs hacked from a block of slate minus the cost of the block. He says this resembles "the peculiarly nerve-wracking way in which diamond cutters are recompensed" (today). Presumably not all slabs hacked from a block were usable. The cutters' wages depended upon skill and luck as much as upon work expended. It was a curious combination of an unpredictable (variable-ratio) schedule of reinforcement ("It's a gamble") and a quite predictable cost.

Whether it is "nerve-wracking" depends upon the cost. We are all under essentially the same contingencies if we paint pictures, compose music, write poems or stories, invent things, explore the world, do scientific experiments, or simply *think*—where the block of slate or the uncut diamond is represented simply by the time we give to our work. How nerve-wracking it is depends upon how much we value time.

Curtain-Raiser

When plays were longer and possibly duller, it was customary to begin with a one-act play. This protected the major play from the damage done to the first act by latecomers. It was probably more reinforcing than a comparable part of a first act and may have helped get people into their seats early.

This is related to the point about "good" versus meretricious literature. One learns to like "good" literature as one continues to respond on a stretching ratio. One listens to more preparation—often dull in itself—because the effect of the reinforcement is heightened when it comes. The curtain-raiser is designed on a short mean ratio. It pulls people in who can then be exposed to a schedule with a longer mean ratio.

Perception

I had placed my coffee cup on a small slip of paper to protect my desk. Busy with other things, I reached for the cup and put it to my lips. Something fell on my other hand. *I felt it as a drop of water* and reached to wipe my hand after putting down the cup. Then I saw that what had fallen was the slip of paper, which had gone past my hand and was on the floor. The procedure of picking up a cup and putting it to one's mouth has preceded drops of fluid on various parts of one's body and clothing thousands of times. In each case some effort is made to wipe up.

In addition to acting to wipe my hand, it is quite correct to say that I felt the stimulus *as* a drop of liquid.

Multiple Sources of Verbal Strength

About twenty minutes ago, listening to the news, I heard a singing commercial: *Schaefer is the one beer to have, when you're having more than one.* I speculated briefly, as I have done before, whether that is really good advertising, with its suggestion of heavier drinking, and I wondered what the sales of Schaefer beer might show.

Just now I was reading the Evanses' *Dictionary of Contemporary Usage: In the United States the plural term* tons *is preferred in any other construction, when speaking of more than one.*

The last three words "hit" me. My textual behavior had a special strength. I read with some of the tempo and possibly the melody of the commercial.

I have often commented on the extra strength of, say, reading a word just as someone else is saying it, but in this instance a good deal of time elapsed between the variables which joined forces. (At least ten minutes must have elapsed between my last query about the advertising and my reading the line, and during those minutes I had read at least two pages of the book.)

When I Write

I avoid telling the reader that I am saying what I am saying, that what I put down is my belief or opinion, that what I write I find interesting.

That is, I avoid autoclitics like:

It is interesting to note
In my opinion
I should say that
As far as I am concerned

I assume that the reader knows that I have written what is on the page and that I should not have written it if I did not believe it or find it interesting. Is this arrogance or lack of deference to the reader? I think not.

ESP

Suppose I teach a pigeon to match the Rhine cards. When a square appears in the sample space, the pigeon pecks the square among the choices. It should be easy to get 100% accuracy. Now suppose I enclose the sample card in a light-tight box, and suppose the pigeon still matches better than chance. How does the stimulus from the sample card get to the pigeon? That is a question for a *physicist*.

It is only because we assume that the pigeon must have a visual image of the sample ("in its mind") in order to choose a match that we talk of extrasensory *perception*. What is "in" the pigeon is an appropriate set of responses under the control of *physical* stimuli, not mental images.

Extinction

Someone has found a drug which spoils the effect of alcohol. Antabuse produces an aversive effect; the new drug simply cancels the reinforcing effect. It is said to be successful in combating alcoholism.

Something of the same sort is possible in heroin addiction. I believe methadone relieves withdrawal symptoms without producing a great high.

Nature takes care of the matter in sex. Frank Beach has found that a drug (or was it old age?) reduces "sex drive" (= the power of sexual reinforcement) through the atrophy of sense organs in the penis. Sexual activity declines when it is no longer reinforced.

Defined by the Consequences

In preparing my lecture to the Oxford Scientific Society I suddenly saw how evolutionary theory simplified the task of the ethologist. Instead of describing instinctive behavior in detail, specifying topography, it is enough to analyze its role in furthering survival. This is quite analogous to defining operant behavior in terms of the production of reinforcing consequences. I should have seen this in writing "The Phylogeny and Ontogeny of Behavior." I did quote Huxley on the ethological unit of response, but this is more than that.

Phenomenal

The problem of knowledge is not solved by locating apparent discrepancies between reality and experience in the body. The Greeks could not understand how a person could perceive an object at a distance and hence invented an inner copy to be perceived. The science of optics now brings the object to the retina (somewhat changed), and physiological psychologists and neurologists take it from there. It is only "what is left to be accounted for" that attracts attention.

We can see what has happened in the way the meaning of certain critical words has changed. *Phenomenal* once meant anything cognizable by the senses. Later it meant "things which seemed so to the senses but of the reality of which there was a question," and then something "perceived but [not to be] accounted for." *Perceptual* is going the same way. Gestalt psychology attacked the older introspective psychology by pointing to *phenomena* it could not explain. (Köhler tried to find explanations in terms of physical transforms in the brain.) *Cognitive* is on its way. It specializes in behavioral processes not yet satisfactorily traced to contingencies of reinforcement.

The curious thing is that almost all those who study the transformation of the real world into the perceived world still feel it necessary to maintain a dualistic position. At the very last moment, when the brain fields are all arranged, perception is said to occur. For some reason it cannot be the external physical world which is perceived. Some sort of physical intimacy is required.

Desultory

Lying in bed, thinking in a desultory way about what young people do, I said to myself: *If chess is just another way of avoiding the draft* . . . and immediately thought of draughts or checkers. It would be impossible to trace reliably the sources of the remark, but were *chess, draughts, young people* all part of a pool of primordial responses from which I cooked up a desultory sentence? I heard checkers called draughts in my childhood, though possibly not later.

I suppose we shall never be able to discover all relevant variables in an episode of that kind or create a comparable set to produce such an effect.

Consequences

The Ten Commandments are followed by a long list of Thou shalt's and Thou shalt not's, many of which we should at once reject today. For example, if a man strikes his servant and kills him at once, he shall be punished; if the servant lives a little while, he shall not. An immediate consequence is accepted as the effect of an action; a delay not only destroys that evidence, it opens the door to other possible causes.

Immediacy is also important when the effects are positive. Striking a rock with a staff clearly causes a flow of water if it begins immediately but is less clearly related to a delayed flow. The speech of a political leader followed by an immediate rise in morale leaves no doubt of its effectiveness. A change in policy a decade after a proposal is published could be due to many other things.

Verbal Miscellany II

In writing about forming a letter by following a stencil, I tried to find a word that described the act of guiding a scriber along a wax groove. *Draw* seemed right, and for the first time I saw its significance. A *draft* is not far from a *dray*. (In writing this I "stammered" on the word *describe* and then saw the significance of *de-scribe*.)

I wrote a note about *situation*, suggesting *setting* as a casual synonym. I had just used it in a sentence and was delighted with it as an alternative to a hackneyed term. Then I went back to the sentence and discovered it to be this: *Setting problems usually solved by observing different parts of a current setting*, where the second *setting* is clearly prompted by the first and may have seemed particularly *juste* for that reason. I had found a useful synonym for *situation* by echoing a word which had been used with a different meaning.

After taking up italic handwriting, I noticed a great increase in solecisms and malaprops. They appeared to be errors in taking dictation, such as *the* for *there*, *or* for *are*, and so on. Evidently my old handwriting was primordial verbal behavior; in italic, I was taking dictation from myself.

I have known the word *sedulous* almost exclusively through Stevenson's expression, *the sedulous ape.* I knew it meant *diligent*, but it also suggested (erroneously) *emulative* or even *sycophantic.* Simple association in time and place had an effect.

Literary Theory

Helen Vendler said that in my contribution to the Richard's *Festschrift* I seemed to be taking a communicative position rather than a mimetic or expressionistic one. I had almost forgotten theories of that sort—or how *Verbal Behavior* bears on them. Off hand, I should say that the literacy critic is vaguely aware of the three-term operant contingency. Writers are controlled by three things:

1. *the situation*—and if that is mainly responsible, their writing could be called "mimetic," the best example being detailed description,

2. *their own states (and histories)*—in which case they "express themselves," and

3. *the effect they have on their readers*—when they "communicate."

But all three must be taken into account in every case. *Why* do writers describe scenes? Because of past experiences —including past settings *and* consequences *and* their effects on *them.* What do they express and *why?* The answers: Personal histories and their probable effects upon writers and readers.

Knock on Wood

A practice is passed on by the culture, but that does not explain its origin, or why it is easily passed on, or what effect it has. The Greek gods were thought to be jealous of the success of mortals and the jealousy was something to fear. To be successful was to run a risk. To boast of success was particularly dangerous.

We "knock on wood" to offset bad luck when we have reported good luck. "A perfect day for our excursion." "Yes, but knock on wood." Question: Do we believe in jealous gods? If not, why or whom do we appease?

A change to bad weather may be particularly aversive just because we have called the weather good; we may be criticized for a false prophecy; but there is something more. It was once customary for radio and TV sports commentators not to mention the fact that a pitcher was pitching a no-hit game. If a hit then followed, the announcer might be charged with spoiling the record.

Is it possible that the behavior of keeping still when good luck prompts a lot of action is reinforced in some special way? Certainly it is acquired slowly if at all, and that may suggest deferred consequences. It may be something like savoring good news before telling it.

"*Relations*"

I am more and more convinced that this is a mischievous word. The interpersonal relation of the psychotherapist and patient is only one example. "Social relations" as an academic discipline is a more comprehensive one.

The word suggests a *functional* relation—as between the pressure and volume of a gas. Change one, and the other changes. But what is changed in one person that changes his "relations" to others?

I think a much better analysis is to be found in *Science and Human Behavior.* One person is a discriminative stimulus or a source of reinforcers to another. It is the contingencies that establish the "relation."

drh

I have used chess to illustrate a kind of generalization. In many situations we act quickly to get something that someone else may otherwise get first. In chess there is no differential reinforcement of a high rate ("drh"). (Time clocks may make players move fast but not to gain an advantage by being first.) Nevertheless the chess player, especially the beginner, tends to play quickly. Because of generalization of the drh contingency? Possibly not.

A threatening move by an opponent is aversive. One is in danger. An answering move reduces the threat, and the sooner the better.

A quick move is still a tendency to be resisted, because deferred reinforcing consequences are contingent upon considered action—on "sophrosyne."

Creativity

It was not until the eighteenth century that one spoke of creating original things without giving some of the credit to God (see Raymond Williams, *Keywords*, Glasgow, 1976). The seemingly miraculous nature of the *original*, the *innovative* (but not so seriously the *novel*) came from the absence of any conceivable anterior cause. This was not true of all acts of will because intention, expectation, or purpose suggested relevant *ends*. The creative work, not having a predictable end, could not be intended, expected, or purposed.

Operant Prepotent over Respondent

"Napoleon III sat absolutely calm at dinner while a footman emptied a siphon of soda down his neck. The father of George Moore's friend, Lewis Seymour, continued to play a tricky passage on the flute while a fly crawled all over his face: 'Pray, do not remove it, I happen to like the sensation.' " (*London Diary*, by Maurice Richardson, quoted in the *New Statesman*, March 8, 1958.)

Presumably Napoleon III did not "like the sensation" of the soda. He "maintained his dignity" in the sense that he continued to behave according to certain social contingencies in spite of strong stimuli which in most of us would elicit behavior incompatible with sitting absolutely still. Are princes and princesses trained to control themselves in that way or is simply "maintaining a dignified mean in spite of small annoyances" enough to set up the heroic example?

Pencil

Early this summer, to improve working conditions in my study, I bought a good mechanical pencil—with a rich red barrel and a blue eraser. For some reason it was in my letter case this morning, though I usually leave it on my study table. Because I have enjoyed the work I have done with it, I was aware of a warm response as I came upon it.

It has become a beautiful mistress, on Stendhal's principle in *De l'Amour*.

A Stretched Ratio

Jigsaw puzzles are solved with a variety of behaviors: classifying similar pieces, moving pieces about to discover congruence, coding shapes in some kind of verbal system, and so on.

By turning to bigger and bigger puzzles a devotee stretches the ratio. Reinforcement is presumably the result of a single fit, the appearance of completed areas, and eventually the whole picture, and these depend upon the size of the puzzle. Apart from clues from patterns, the time required to find a fit must be some function of the number of remaining pieces. A child begins with perhaps a dozen pieces, but the aficionado may do a puzzle of 2000 pieces. Patterns begin in helpful ways, but eventually a 2000-piece puzzle may have no pattern at all.

There is a progressive simplification, of course, as the remaining pieces grow fewer, and an increase in reinforcing effect as the picture nears completion.

What Is Natural?

We need a better way to distinguish between natural and social. The social environment is perfectly natural. Natural scientists study nature and social scientists study society, but society is a part of nature. "Scientists create molecules which, so far as we know, would never occur in nature," but nature produced the scientists who do so. Silkworms produce silk and scientists produce nylon. The fibers are put together in different ways, but they *are* put together and hence are both synthetic.

Winning

In general an audience cheers when it is told that rival teams are being defeated, in part because one sometimes advances to a championship as a rival loses. And the defeat of the team one is playing is reinforcing. The marks of defeat are the lower score, signs of unhappiness, being called "beaten," and so on, and these may be reinforcing even when a future competitor is defeated by another team.

At the University of Minnesota, however, the crowd at a football game would cheer when it was announced that another Big Ten team was *winning* against an outsider. I remember that this surprised me, and it still seems rather remarkable. But, after all, it is always good practice to praise your opponents. If they beat you, you have prepared your alibi; if you win, it is all the more to your credit.

The Superego Goes Public

It must have been a great step in the evolution of a society when aversive control became "internalized" in the sense that an external aversive overseer was no longer needed. People behaved as they ought when a punisher was not around. As societies grow, however, this device may be strained until it no longer works. Personal understandings become contracts once again. Two signs of this have turned up recently.

A London paper reports a rise in bankruptcy in the United States. As an alternative to a debtors' prison, bankruptcy was a humane practice. Let someone start all over again. The suppression of misuse was left to ethical sanctions. A bankrupt was in some sense guilty, at least a failure, which in the culture of my childhood came to the same thing. A current increase in bankruptcy may mean, not that more people are going into debt, but that they no longer respond to ethical sanctions (do not "feel guilty") and are taking bankruptcy as a way out of trouble.

A second example is tipping. This is a way of paying for personal services, but when people start chiseling, as is likely to be the case with travelers who never come back to face the consequences of tipping too little, it becomes necessary to add a service charge.

The trend is toward explicit enforcement of what were once useful conventions.

Money as Reinforcer

I have commented on the need for an aversive supplement to a weekly wage and on the fact that a prior contract kills some of the reinforcing effect of wages. The workman described by the Ménagier of Paris (writing in 1392–94; see Eileen Power, *Medieval People*, Chapter IV) uses an appeal to simple contingencies in lieu of a contract to good effect.

The workman says, "Milord, it is nothing—there is no need [to agree on a price]—you will pay me well and I shall be content with what you think fit." But when the work is done: "'Sir, there was more than I thought—' and they will not take what is given them and will break out into shouting and angry words."

The Ménagier recommends a contract: a specified sum to be paid *only when work of a specified kind is completed.*

It is not a matter of using money as a reinforcer to induce the workman to behave in the same way again. If a contract is not fulfilled, further contracts will not be accepted. That is an aversive contingency, similar to the weekly wage—something that will be lost if the employee is fired by a supervisor during the week.

Conditions of Recall

A friend once pointed to a plant in his apartment and said, "Someone was thoughtful enough to give my wife a bonsai olive tree." Since the apartment was full of plants, I was puzzled by his singling out one of them with a special comment. Later that evening I learned that his wife managed a large olive ranch, but I did not tie that in with his earlier remark. About 90 hours later, I drove past a florist shop with bonsai trees in the window, and I immediately recalled the remark and saw its significance. If I had heard about the ranch before seeing the bonsai olive tree, I should have understood the remark at once. The window display of bonsai trees presumably revived my puzzlement, and by then I had what I needed to get the point.

Multiple Sources of Strength

Much evidence of verbal processes is very tenuous, but it should not be neglected. In London, driving in a taxicab with Eve, I mentioned a friend named Harry just as I saw a neon sign in a window reading "Harry's Bar," and I was vaguely startled. I can't be sure of the exact temporal order (an occasional field observation is almost always inferior to a planned laboratory analysis in that respect), nor can I be sure of the precise effect. Did I say "Harry" with a probability which was unusual enough to attract my attention, or did I read the sign with unusual strength? It is especially easy to say a word while seeing it and to see a word while saying it, but what I noted was an unusual strength due to two sources.

Cognitive Dissonance

Bem's explanation of Festinger's data has a curious resemblance to my argument about dignity in *Beyond Freedom and Dignity*. A person who is paid $20 to say something about a given situation is less likely to be said to *believe* it than someone who is paid $2. "Belief" refers to the control exerted by the "something said." A person who says it for no visible "reason" (i.e., is paid nothing) says it because an invisible something is in control. A person who says it for $20 says it "for $20," with negligible control exercised by the "something." (Individual strengthening suggests origination. Not the despot, *you*, the citizen. Not the owner of tools, *you*, the worker. But what are the sources of the revolt or the strike?)

Ideas

The other day someone mentioned fiesta time in Brazil, and I asked if he had seen the movie *Black Narcissus*, which I knew was not quite right and changed immediately to *Black Orchid*. (The movie was actually called *Black Orpheus*.) He said something about cognitive search.

Just now "looking for" the word *vocation* (as of a priest) I kept getting *call*, *recall*, and *calling*, the last of which is, of course, what the word means.

This is the kind of thing that seems to suggest a preverbal cognition. Did I not get the "notion" or the "meaning" before the word? But cognitions, notions, and meanings are simply substitutes for contingencies. A given set of circumstances (Brazil and fiesta) evoked a response. The response originally evoked by the movie was similar to responses evoked by flowers. (I believe that there is a story called "Black Narcissus"; certainly there is Conrad's *Nigger of the Narcissus.*) To some extent any flower evokes other flower names as "mistakes." The common features of flowers (*not* "the concept of flowers") are tied to flower words.

Much more needs to be done in analyzing this kind of thing. But it is less than needs to be done to account for concepts, cognitions, and the search for stored memories.

Liberal Wedding

The meeting house (not "church") had a beautiful exterior, and much of the interior may have been beautiful, too, but we did not see it. In the vestibule we passed a table displaying stacks of pamphlets—social, political, anti-clerical—and went down a few steps into a drab, badly lighted room. Plain chairs had been pushed against the walls out of the way. Shelves and wall cabinets held doggedly non-Christian art. Scrolls and paintings of a universal religion covered some of the grimy walls. We waited about for the rest of our party while a typewriter clacked in an adjoining office. Eventually, as the last friends arrived, the typewriter grew silent, and a man emerged from the office carrying a plain book. He took his place in front of a polar map of the earth (no political divisions indicated) framed by a flat gilt ring. He read from the Psalms and the Sonnets of Shakespeare. The repeated vows were modest and contained no reference to gods of any kind. Bride and groom followed the man to a paper to be signed, as did selected witnesses (there was no best man or bridesmaid). After a few awkward moments, we walked to a restaurant for a wedding lunch.

None of us knew just what to do and, in fact, were unable to do what we wanted to do—express our pleasure, offer congratulations, wish the couple the best of luck. What was done was awkward, unsatisfying.

Ritual is the monopoly of the practitioners of the supernatural and hence rejected by the naturalistic, who are thus deprived of its usefulness. It can become meaningless or, worse, a mockery, but in its proper place it serves as a script to be followed in negotiating social behavior.

Causality

In Book 3 of *The Iliad* Menelaus has overcome Paris in single combat and is dragging him along the ground by his helmet when the strap breaks and Paris escapes, possibly by losing himself in a fog, and immediately goes to bed with Helen. In a rage Menelaus flings the helmet all the way to the Grecian lines.

We need not debate the fact. The strap broke; there were witnesses. But why? We can only speculate—and only then according to our histories.

The practically minded (a scientist today): "The strap was being pulled at an unusual angle; possibly it was cut by the edge of the helmet."

The statistician: "That kind of strap breaks in such cases 10 percent of the time."

The psychologist: "The strap was old and weak, possibly because Paris believed the helmet brought him luck and would not change it."

The superstitious soul: "It broke because Paris's luck held."

Menelaus: "It broke because I pulled too hard. I was overanxious."

Paris: "I planned it that way. I deliberately used a weak strap." (A few years ago he would have been the football player who wore a tear-away shirt.)

Homer (and he should know): "Aphrodite broke the strap so that her favorite could escape and go back to bed with Helen."

Saying Something While Not Saying It

According to Christopher Isherwood, Ramakrishna was fond of saying that you could get the central message of the Gita by repeating the word several times: "Gita, Gita, Gita." You then found yourself saying "ta-Gi, ta-Gi, ta-Gi," "Tagi"meaning one who has renounced everything for God. In *Verbal Behavior* (p. 282), I note the children's trick of repeating "bell-lie-mud-um," only to find themselves saying "I'm a dumbbell."

Nervousness

A baseball pitcher who is "under pressure" is under aversive control. He must throw, but the behavior is likely to be punished (the ball may come straight back at him at great speed, or the batter may get a hit, possibly winning the game). Under these conditions, he is likely to show "nervous habits"—wiping his hands, adjusting his hat, tugging at his belt, and so on. Some of these are "superstitious"; any gesture adventitiously followed by a successful throw will acquire a slightly higher probability of emission. But many are simply ways of postponing a possibly punished act; a pitcher who stood stock still for a comparable period of time might be booed.

Mathematical Models

The absolutely certain can be absolutely useless, as the Barsuk-Ulam theorem illustrates. At any given moment there are two points on the earth precisely at the antipodes which have exactly the same temperature and pressure. I used to prove to my students in Natural Sciences 114 the simpler case of one continuous variable on a plane: at any given moment there are two points a hundred miles away from a point (I established the moment and point by striking the lectern with a piece of chalk) in exactly opposite directions having the same temperature. I asked my students to consider the weather map in the morning paper, with cold air masses moving down from Canada, and imagine how it would be possible to make such a statement. Yet you "prove" it this way: imagine a circular wall with a 100-mile radius, the height of which is proportional to the temperature. A vertical pole stands at the center, and a rigid bar slightly more than 200 miles long, with a hole in the middle, is laid across the wall with the hole around the pole and free to slide up and down on it. If when you first put the bar on the wall, it is horizontal, it marks the points in question. But suppose the end A is lower than the end B. Rotate the bar, its ends resting on the wall, until A and B have changed places. B will then be lower than A, and at some point the two ends must have been at exactly the same height. Perfectly true. And perfectly useless. Such points can be found only empirically. It is not even a question of temperature; any variable—pressure, humidity, anti-Communist sentiment—will work provided it is free of sharp breaks.

Logicians are fond of similar apparent statements of fact: "There must therefore be at least one case in which . . . "

But which case?

The Cop on Sparks and Brattle

Two or three years ago a new traffic cop took over at the intersection of Brattle, Sparks, and Craigie. He works entirely through aversive control. Sarcastic, vicious, a martinet—he began by deciding that the lane farther from the curb was for Craigie and forcing all who arrived at the intersection in that lane to go that way. A favorite trick was to wait for a polite protest, "I was going down Brattle" and then to shout, "You're going down Craigie!" Within a month or two he had the traffic hugging the curb a block away in order to get to Brattle Street. Only an occasional stranger caused trouble.

Musical Patterns of Strength

Arrangements of popular songs—though usually not the published versions—often used to end with this kind of pattern: If the last line was, say, *Nice and easy does it every time*, the singer repeated the first part about three times:

Nice and easy does it
   "   "   "   "   "
   "   "   "   "   "
—every time

The orchestra and singer built up the volume during the repetitions and retarded slightly before the final phrase, which was loud, slow, and clearly enunciated in the most winning and ingratiating way.

This is a crude example of building up the strength of the listener's tendency to join in with the singer on the last phrase. The intraverbal stimulus *Nice and easy does it* is given three times, overpreparing for *every time*. Something comparable must happen to one who is merely humming or actively listening. Someone playing an instrument in an orchestra must get the same effect.

Personal Attention

At a cocktail party a young woman who "felt I had been misunderstood" but obviously misunderstood me said she had heard of a project in which retarded children were to be confronted for many hours each day with machines! "But *they* above all need personal attention!"

She had never, I'm sure, seen the personal attention they get or are likely to get. Nor had she ever seen the excitement and sustained interest generated by a machine.

This is the fallacy of personal attention. It is part of the theme of the Freudian nursery, the good teacher, the excited classroom. How can I make the point that all the admirable features of good teaching spring from the contingencies of reinforcement, not from the nature of the reinforcers? Is it our "need for personal attention" that misdirects us?

The Reinforcement of Perorations

A friend of mine takes advantage of the fact that he gets closer attention from an audience if he appears to be approaching the end of his remarks. He acts as if he were approaching an end when he is not. He launches into a few sentences at high speed, pitch, and volume, which then slowly fall. At what one expects to be the end, he jumps to a new set of high values and repeats the pattern. Listeners who know him have extinguished and stop reinforcing his speech with special attention. New listeners, however, maintain his behavior in strength.

Glimpses

I have just been watching "The Ascent of Man" on Einstein and Newton. Bronowski spoke of the problem of light as the problem of communication between two people, and I suddenly got a glimpse of the future, when we shall have an adequate theory of knowledge and can talk about all these things sensibly. But I also felt that I shall never return to my first love and resolve all these difficulties. An article about nonstandard mathematics asked the question whether certain properties were matters of how we think or really properties of nature, as if we could ever tell the difference. I still believe that physicists could get out of a lot of their traps with even a crude theory of knowledge based on my *Verbal Behavior*. And a refined theory? It could make all the difference.

Fields to Conquer

Almost every day I run across something to which I could give a year of my life. Just now, reading Clark's *Life of Bertrand Russell*, the passage on Russell's first contact with Peano reminds me of my old project—a behavioral analysis of logical concepts closely related to my analysis of autoclitics.

> *If, then*
> *Either, or*
> *All*
> *Some*
> *Is contained in*
> *There exists* (assertion as autoclitic!)

We need to examine the contingencies from which the rules governing these expressions are "extracted." (Dangerous word!)

Verbal Distortion I

In silently spelling the name *Jaqueth*, I said *q, u, e, eth, t*, as if lisping on an *s*. I had some vague feeling of a single letter like the runic þ (thorn) for *th*. But I was pronouncing the end of the name. Note, too, a probable contribution from *q* [*r*] *s t*. I was aware of a spatial alphabet in the region of *t* as I said it.

What Is a Reinforcer When It Isn't Reinforcing?

Sitting in a taxi in very slow traffic, when late for an important appointment, what does any forward movement reinforce? Unless I look for openings, for example, and ask the driver to change lanes, the movement doesn't reinforce any of my behavior. Every stop increases the likelihood of missing my appointment, and if I could do something to reduce these aversive stimuli, the change would be reinforcing. But what shall we call it when I do nothing? We need a word for reinforcers when they are not reinforcing. Aversive does well enough for negative reinforcers, but "appetitive" will clearly not do for the positive case.

Chained Operants

Lenneberg (*Biological Foundations of Language*) criticizes the simple-minded notion of the link-by-link chaining of verbal responses—a straw man commonly set up in attacks on behavioral learning theory. I suppose it goes back to Watson. In running a maze, playing a melody, or reciting a poem, the travestied account is that response A evokes response B, which then evokes response C, and so on. I don't know whether anyone ever said that, but it doesn't matter. Surely there is some linkage, and we make use of it to get a running start when we forget. But response B doesn't erase the stimulus effect of response A, and response C is no doubt controlled by both, with some weakening as the distance increases.

It may also be a question of the size of the unit. Maybe a series of turns, or a run of many notes, or a group of words functions as one response—even though learned bit by bit. There is nothing mysterious about any of this, and there is still a functional chaining, a temporal order useful in interpreting cases and getting results.

Lenneberg argues against an analysis which he assumes requires chaining. The pronunciation of a letter (*e* in *the*) depends upon what *follows* (vowel or consonant). We can't appeal to "larger units," he says, because novel instances of speech show it. But in what sense does one word follow another? Primordial behavior is all around us as we speak. We edit it in advance—or too late. We make anticipatory slips—or recurrent ones.

Lenneberg also raises the question of the integration of speech-sound production. Some nerves are long, others short, and timing is therefore critical (hence stuttering?). But a dog leaps and catches a ball, although its hind leg nerves are long and the jaw-snap nerves short. The ball is caught.

Written Blend

In writing dates, I have frequently made a mistake like this: "7/11/7" for "7/11/67"—a blend of the stroke /and the figure to follow. It is a written example of a process usually analyzed only in vocal verbal behavior and a good illustration of a common effect in speaking and writing.

Excessive Reinforcement

A cultural design that restricts the range of reinforcers solves the problem raised by the excesses of a gourmet or Don Juan, but it also solves the problem of those who feel they have missed something. It was the ecstatic accounts of sexually happy wives which sent Colette's *ingenue libertine* in search of sexual happiness, with a happier than usual dénoument. In a world in which sex was never discussed (or, or course, witnessed), the condition would not have arisen. The tone-deaf, the color-blind, the deficient speaker of the language of a poem—all may have evidence that they are "missing something," but the ecstasy of the devotee may seem merely silly. Even so, enthusiastic reports may create the same *dévot manqué*.

Infant

The root of the word means "unable to speak." How important can that be? We deal with babies as we deal with animals, without verbal "communication." Does that fact override all the other distinctive features of a small child?

Function of Secrecy

When I was a boy, we used *Cucumber* and *Tobacco* to mean *Come on in* and *Go back*, respectively, in playing hide-and-seek. The terms were known to the seeker as well as to the hidden, and nothing was therefore concealed. What function was served? Might the literal words have been subject to punishment as unfair help? Or as words apparently spoken to no one? But was it not just as unfair or foolish to say *Cucumber* as *Come on in*?

Saying *Gol darned* for *God damned* or *Jeepers* for *Jesus* serves a similar function. Punishable expletives are displaced. Once the replacements lose any connection with the past they become harmlessly nonblasphemous. Is it any longer a secret language?

Autoclitic Placement

Follett (*Modern American Usage*) misses the autoclitic function of *presumably*, *certainly*, and *unfortunately* (in the sense of *I feel safe in saying*, *I strongly say*, and *I am sorry to say*, respectively). He discusses where to place these adverbs without noting that they "refer" to whole responses. "One may put the adverb in a place where it will enforce a pause and heighten a feeling, but then it must be set off by commas: The Communists, presumably, are making headway with their propaganda." It is set off because it does not "modify" any one term.

Aversive Control in the Classroom

Behavior is strengthened when it reduces aversive stimulation, but the reduction may mean less behavior (at least until the aversive stimulation is restored). Perhaps this is why teachers who use aversive control do not want their students to be right too often. Students who are right cannot be accused of being wrong and have no reason to do anything right again.

Personal Contingencies

Why did Freud emphasize *personal* successes and failures?

1. He was interested in himself and his patients and the interpersonal relations between him and them.

2. Confined to his office, he could manipulate only personal stimuli, particularly his effects as a reinforcer, positive and negative.

Is it by any chance true that the difference between clinical and experimental psychology is not in the experimental design so much as in the freedom of the experimenter to manipulate *non*personal contingencies? Is that why experimentalists are accused of failing to treat persons as persons?

Animal Experiments Using a Stooge

I planned a series of experiments on innate social behavior in which one participant would be conditioned to play a role as the stooge of the experimenter. Two rats would be placed in cages divided by a common wire screen. When the experimental rat (ER) approached the screen, the role-playing rat (RP) would immediately go into an enclosure where it could not be seen. As soon as ER went to another part of its cage, RP would again appear. (All this could easily be done with switches under sections of the floors and a food dispenser in the enclosure.) The net result would be that whenever ER approached RP, RP would go away. What would be the effect on ER? Would it begin to show aggression? (Compare the case of the ugly man who may begin to exaggerate his ugliness to frighten children if at first they simply avoid him.) In other words, would ER begin to act "to drive RP away"?

Some early results were not promising. Rats may not be appropriate subjects. The experiment should be done with monkeys.

Active Perceiving

The "motor" side of visualizing (a nineteenth-century term for seeing in the absence of the thing seen) is clear when one sees a pattern "concealed" in another pattern. It is easiest, perhaps, in listening to music. I have been listening to a harpsichord recording of Buxtehude and noting how simply one of the voices was being played—as if the harpsichordist were not at the same time playing many other things. In listening to the voice I was "hearing it along with the player"; in silence I should be said to be imagining it ("image" is an inept term for a copy of music). Can I not do so more easily because I have played keyboard instruments and thus acquired external behavior which produces auditory stimuli? And is that not why active hearing is so much more readily identified as such than active seeing? Could an artist "see" more easily than a layman? Yes, if Whistler's method (described in *The Technology of Teaching*) were apropos.

Long-Term Effects

During the night, reaching for the flashlight on the table beside my bed, I thought I heard some small thing fall off the table. I shone the flash on the floor but saw nothing, and that was that.

This morning I saw my plastic shoehorn on the floor and instantly knew it was what had fallen. But why the connection? Why not simply notice the shoehorn and pick it up?

There was something unresolved about the sound of a falling object. But what does "unresolved" mean? Unsolved? The unanswered question?

The long-term effect is like recalling a name you once searched for when you now see it in a newspaper.

How active we are as thinkers may be a matter of how many unresolved problems we are carrying at any moment.

Survival Value

Attacking a sexual rival should have survival value simply because, of two otherwise equally endowed males, the one that fights harder for a mate (because of some variation, such as sensitivity to sexual reinforcement) should be more likely to breed. The trait is directly and "purely" related to successful copulation. It need have no connection with general strength or vitality. But once males begin to struggle, other traits are selected which presumably relate to other aspects of existence than copulation: The stronger, the more skillful, the quicker to learn are selected. Jealousy "purely" related to sex may have survival value.

Attacks on possessions, verbal attacks on prestige, etc., may seem equally silly but entail useful competition.

A Nonverbal Autoclitic

In a discussion with some graduate students yesterday, the question of the temporal order of an autoclitic and its related response came up. Must you emit the response as inchoate or incipient behavior before it triggers the auto-clitic which in the final version precedes it? I said I thought not and gave as an example opening a door by turning a rather stiff knob but pausing first to dry your hands because you cannot open the door easily with wet hands. Do you "think of opening the door" before you dry your hands? No. *The contingencies are there*, and they are enough. A natural sequence takes place; the first steps make the later steps possible. An autoclitic makes a response more likely to be successful, as drying one's hands does before opening a door.

Don't Stop with Feelings!

No doubt as the effect of a very long verbal history, I myself describe and explain human behavior by talking about feelings. I was thinking about a particular set of social contingencies and said to myself, "It induces people to do things they don't want to do, things they feel guilty do-ing." I caught myself and "translated": "things they have been punished for doing." (I might have added the rule-following parallel: "or things they have been told they will be punished for doing.") There is an immediate gain. We begin to ask questions. Is there an important difference if the behavior is contingency-shaped rather than evoked by a warning? What kind of punishment, by what or whom?

The "feeling" serves as a simple but deceptive summary of punitive contingencies.

Incidentally, this is not a real translation unless the feeling *is* merely a summary. It is going back to relevant causes, rather than stopping with a collateral effect.

Amount Remembered

Ebbinghaus set the pattern. He would have preferred to know how we learn, but he settled for how fast we forget. His method continues to be used for the same reason. Graphs showing amount recalled are common in current literature, and possibly some psychologists are genuinely interested in retention, but the facts are most often used to infer something about learning—about acquisition or storage. What is needed is a measure of increasing probability of response—a measure which is still left almost exclusively to the operant conditioners.

Arrighi

I have just written a note in the best italic hand of which I am capable. I am sure I did so because yesterday I spent some time looking through a reproduction of three sixteenth-century textbooks on chancery cursive. What can the effect be? Did I, in looking at a text by Arrighi, attend to it with covert behavior sharing some topographical properties with what I have just done? Not executing actual letters, perhaps, but sighting the slope, margins, spacing, and so on? Or did I, in admiring the text, set higher standards of reinforcement of a special subrepertoire of careful writing?

(A year after writing this note I looked at some material from the Society for Italic Handwriting and my hand immediately improved. *This must be taken very seriously.* If one creates one's own models, they may suffer a progressive deterioration.)

Paraleipsis

Meeting a friend in an unlikely place, you say, "I won't exclaim 'What a coincidence!'" But you have exclaimed it. One arrests a cliché before emission if clichés have been punished, but one is still aware of the tendency to emit them. *I won't exclaim* does not quite make the remark unpunishable, at least by a listener who knows something about verbal behavior.

Indirect Self-Prompting

One may use a partially recalled verbal response to prompt a complete response in the listener. To the chauffeur from the Merck Company who was driving me from Philadelphia to West Point, I said I preferred going through a section called something like Mishocken. "Conshohocken," he said at once. I could have done the same thing by working on myself to get an eventually complete response. Since I recognized his response as correct, I could have recognized my own recollection as soon as the prompt worked.

Terms

We lack a word to describe the taking of action with respect to a subject, and the lack is particularly conspicuous when the subject is human behavior. How should we complete the sentence: "Why are we not more effective . . . ?"
1. . . . in dealing with human behavior
2. . . . in treating human behavior (therapy only?)
3. . . . in having to do with human behavior
4. . . . in concerning ourselves with human behavior
5. . . . in attending to human behavior
6. . . . in doing something about human behavior
7. . . . in manipulating human behavior
8. . . . in changing, modifying, or altering human behavior

Physicists and chemists deal with, treat, have to do with, and so on, and nobody suspects their motives. Do we need a better word in psychology just to "deal with" the problem of control?

A Vestige of Stimulus Control

There is a great deal of stimulus-response psychology in everyday usage. "The carrot rather than the stick" does not mean reward rather than punishment. A carrot may be reinforcing to a horse, but when used to attract or draw forward, it is a discriminative stimulus, which has acquired its power because moving forward and seizing a visible carrot has been reinforced by a carrot in the mouth.

"Distracting" a student who is beginning to misbehave is also using a discriminative stimulus, creating an occasion upon which behavior incompatible with misbehaving is often reinforced but not actually reinforced in the act of distracting.

"Making something more interesting" is likely to involve arranging more reinforcers, but what *interests* a person is an occasion upon which some behavior will be reinforced. Reinforcing is more than making interesting.

In all these practices a stimulus is used because of an immediate effect rather than as a reinforcer (with possibly longer deferred results).

Social Aversion

I have noted that I walk around a fallen branch quite coolly but around a thoughtless group of people blocking the sidewalk only with a touch of anger. Stendhal has something like it (*Journal,* 13 *juillet* 1810) roughly as follows: How does it happen that, caring nothing about 25 louis, my heart is filled with anger if someone pulls a trick to get out of paying me them?

Presence

In making a list of the songs my mother used to sing, I tried to make myself receptive to other recollections. I got fragments, and a strange sense of something hovering near. Something of the sort is exploited in witchcraft, in the belief in poltergeists, in the belief in a divine afflatus, and in religious mysticism.

Practices which suggest a "presence"—animate or inanimate—build belief in the sense of disposing people to act in various ways. They frighten believers in the sense of disposing them to escape or submit, and create sensitivity in the sense of making normally trivial stimuli unusually effective. The good teller of ghost stories knows the technique. There is a distant noise, and the teller starts. "Listen! What was that?" acting as if afraid. The slightest sound then evokes in others a response characteristic of a more conspicuous stimulus, the presence of which is then inferred or asserted.

Word Square

In *Verbal Behavior* (p. 292), I cited *Sator arepo teret opera rotas* as an example of word play. Martin Gardner, in the *Scientific American*, says, "The most beguiling riddle is that of the Latin word square written

```
R  O  T  A  S
O  P  E  R  A
T  E  N  E  T
A  R  E  P  O
S  A  T  O  R
```

Long prized as a charm against death during childbirth, this formula has been found all over Europe and Asia Minor since the fourth or fifth century. It will also put out fires and guard against mad dogs. The five Latin words have meaning, if not clarity; *sator* is 'a sower'; *rotas*, 'wheels,' and so on. The cross-word *tenet*—'he holds'—and the ingenious discovery that the square can be built up from PATERNOSTER crossed on itself, plus two A's and two O's (the alpha and the omega), strongly suggest that it was a cryptic sign of the early Christians, like the fish. But the dates seem uncertain, and even these notions are not the only ones. SATOR is still a puzzle, as it has been for a millenium."

From a newsweekly: "This square appears on a column in Pompeii, and supernatural powers were attributed to it during the Middle Ages."

The meaning of the Latin is, I gather, controversial. According to Marcel Brion in "Pompeii and Herculaneum," one scholar interprets these "occult" words to mean: "God is the creator of all things." Another thinks they mean: "God has held the works of man in His hands since the beginning of the existence of things."

I used TERET in place of TENET, which works as well. AREPO may be a proper name: "The sower Arepo holds (or wears away, *teret*) the wheels with his work."

Saving Labor

In Green Park, London, an area of perhaps 1000 square feet was covered during the winter by a great pile of leaves. The leaves have been taken away, and the area is being prepared for grass or flowers. Three young men spent the day spading the evidently very hard soil.

A gasoline rototiller would have done the job in one or two hours in the hands of one man. Would it be a better solution? The tiller would have added a small amount of pollution to the London air. It would have cost money, and a fair amount of labor and material would have been needed to make and maintain it, but the wages of three men, even at going British rates, would quickly cover the investment.

But what would happen to the men? By "saving

labor"the rototiller would dispense with these laborers. Would they then go on relief, in which case should we include the cost of the relief in the charge for the tiller?

And how would the men on relief fare? They would be less strong, probably less healthy, and more likely to cause trouble.

When is labor really to be saved?

Audio-Analgesia

My dentist has been involved in the design of a device which is said to relieve pain. The patient wears earphones, listens to pleasant stereo music, and can add "white noise"—rather like the sound of steam escaping under high pressure—by turning a knob. The white noise can be made quite intense and is said to offset dental pain. Whatever the explanation, I discovered an important fact this morning. The dentist filled my mouth with cotton pads and an aspirator, and then lectured me on four types of people classified according to their pain reactions. When I could talk, I expressed my reservations about typologies and said I thought one important effect was that the apparatus gave the patient something to do about pain. I meant simply turning up the white noise, but I quickly learned something more definite. The dentist admitted that he eased off on his drilling when his patient turned up the noise.

The device makes it possible for the patient to do something about pain, reducing it by turning a knob. It is a simple operant—*with no emotional counterpart*—and has the advantage over crying or pulling away of being free of criticism for cowardice.

By scheduling pain reduction, very much as in stretching a ratio, a dentist may build up strong knob-turning behavior, as a replacement for, or substitute for, emotional reactions. And it may be these reactions, rather than the pain itself, which are troublesome to patient and dentist alike.

Sublimation

"Archytas made a rattle which, as Aristotle says, 'was useful to give to children to occupy them from breaking things about the house (for the young are incapable of keeping still).'" (H. W. Turnbull, "The Great Mathematicians," in *The World of Mathematics*)

What is the behavioral process? *While* playing with the rattle, a child is not breaking things, but if, *after* playing with it, a child is less likely to play with, and hence break, other things, it is a matter of satiation or fatigue.

A Curious Autoclitic

As if this were not enough, there are further possible difficulties.

What does *As if this were not enough* mean? It alerts the reader to the fact that there is more to follow with something of a previously sampled effect. In that sense, it is like *Moreover*, but it has a touch of drama, as if the reader were inclined to say *Hold, enough!*

Intelligence versus Superstition

Far from being due to a lack of "intelligence," superstition is closely associated with it. If an organism happens to respond just before a reinforcing event occurs, and if the reinforcement significantly increases the responding, then further coincidences become more likely. An organism which is not substantially changed by less than, say, ten reinforcements is practically invulnerable to such fortuitous contingencies. If to be intelligent is in part to learn quickly, then intelligence makes superstition more probable.

However, it also predisposes the individual to use various sorts of special methods which have been invented to offset the vulnerability. Coincidences are less likely under "controlled conditions"; repeating an observation is a further check. Statistical techniques of collecting observations and determining degrees of association are quite explicit correctives.

Verbal Donnybrook

Yesterday I agreed, as my editor at Jonathan Cape requested, to write a letter to the *Observer* answering my critics, particularly the *Observer's*. I had not then read the *Observer* review. I read it last night and realized at once that I could not answer it, very much as I realized I could not go on Zero Mostel's television show. It was "beneath my dignity," I would "demean myself" by replying, I could not "stoop to answer," it would be "beneath me" to reply, the *Observer* was "not worthy of my steel," etc. What does all this mean?

To reply would have shown control by rather trivial matters. Answering a critic who has taken a book seriously is making a possibly significant contribution, like carrying on a conversation with someone who speaks one's language and is talking about worthwhile things. Answering someone who is ignorant and aggressive is like spending time talking to a gossipy chambermaid or a drunk one meets in the street. One makes a distinction between what is worthwhile (a significant expression) and what is not. It may be as straightforward as the money one gets for doing something. A singer performs either for the full fee or for nothing (as for a charity) but never for a small fee.

(Not a very good analysis. It is a point about social behavior that does not seem to be well analyzed. Why is a verbal donnybook "beneath the dignity" of intelligent people? The means are too conspicuous? Too much unnecessary effort to get an effect?)

Stimulus Control

How little *thinking* one does on a cruise. Fresh stimuli take over, wholly prepotent over the self-stimulation of reflective behavior.

Dangerous Nonsense

ANNOUNCING
A SPECIAL JOURNAL FOR—
. . . those searching for new direction and deeper
meaning, for personal growth and inner harmony,
for greater understanding, for the realization
of their real nature, of their deepest potential for
emotional, mental and transpersonal unfoldment.

New, deep, real, growth, harmony, understanding potential, unfoldment—an opiate soothing syrup for humanistic psychologists, hashish for the searchers for identity.

The Selection of Synonyms II

Headline in the *Boston Sunday Globe* for May 14, 1972: CHINA: A GIANT PEEKING CAUTIOUSLY AT THE WORLD. Was peeking chosen from a set of synonyms because of *Peking?* Was a giant Panda playing a part?

From an article in *The New York Times* about massage parlors:

The resident-manager and eight toga-clad masseuses of Caesar's Retreat were arrested on prostitution charges. But the manager had, just a week earlier, paid a $250 fine for permitting prostitution and had been back in business the same day. The rub, suggests Assistant District Attorney John Tully, is court leniency.

If the article had been about burglary, for example, would court leniency have been *the rub?*

From the *New York Review:*

They allege that the genetic basis of this language was established when our hominid ancestors became male hunters and female gatherers. But it is worth noting that for evidence they point to the research of primatologists and other ethologists, particularly on baboons, and to some work in physiology. Their use of their own knowledge of the variegated forms of human society is restricted to a few selected examples, is savagely reduced when they deal with hunting societies, and is reduced to absurdity when they deal with complex societies of an ancient world, of medieval periods, or of the industrial era.

Would *savagely* be the word if the authors were not writing about primitive societies?

From an article in *The New York Times:*

She was quick to point to more palatable semimoist and canned foods that are also complete and balanced foods, according to the guidelines laid down by the National Research Council publication, Nutrient Requirements of the Dog. . . . Neither Dr. Jonas nor Dr. Wasserman was dogmatically opposed to nondry foods.

Dogmatically is certainly not an apt synonym, but dog has its day.

Operant Belching

In gastric distress a belch is often reinforced by the reduction of pressure in the stomach. The mere escape of gas under pressure is not "behavior," and it would be meaningless to speak of its reinforcement. Reflex responses of the cardiac sphincter to the stimulus of pressure are not operant behavior and probably not reinforced as an operant by the reduction, but movements of the diaphragm or of other muscles of the abdomen may generate stimuli to which the cardiac sphincter responds, and this behavior may be reinforced by the resulting change in pressure.

The same musculature may be used to draw air into the esophagus, as in a well-executed theatrical belch. The relief from such "swallowed air" may reinforce the behavior as an operant. There may be no connection with the release of gas from the stomach, but stimuli are generated which normally precede or accompany that release, and those who are suffering from pressure may produce false belches for that reason. It is a curious example of the operant simulation of a reflex response. If a true belch follows, it is an example of the operant mediation of an autonomic reflex.

Proofreading

When I was teaching Deborah to read, I noticed a few examples of mirror-reading. (Incidentally, she is left-handed.) She occasionally read *and* as *the*—a pretty fair mirror image. Here is the proofreader of the *Times Literary Supplement* doing the same thing: "Rousseau's view that such groups prevent the formation of a general will and promote and [*sic*] growth of factions was, according to Hegel, responsible for much of the despotism and fanaticism of the French Revolution."

From the Modern Library Edition of Henry James's *Portrait of a Lady* (p. I 408): "Isabel in truth needed no urgjng. . . . " The book had been carefully proofread. I have found no other mistakes. Is it relevant that the *g* is pronounced *j*? Or that *i* was once often used in place of *j*? Or that *i* and *j* are side by side in the alphabet? Or that both are dotted?

Superstition

During an eclipse "Roman soldiers believed that by beating drums and cymbals they could cause the moon's disk to regain its brightness." —Lecky, *History of European Morals*, I, p. 366.

But how often is there an eclipse of the moon when soldiers have drums and cymbals at hand? Much more plausible is noise-making in general. Superstitious contingencies could then easily take over. A soldier with a drum or cymbal would use it, but only as a convenience.

Once such a practice has arisen, it is easily sustained and cannot be proved false. Even if one soldier or group of soldiers stops beating to test the theory, others are presumably still beating somewhere else and hence the bright moon returns.

Secret Language

Karl Lashley was impressed—and puzzled—by the speed with which children learn to speak Pig Latin. The product of a fairly simple transformation, it is usually intelligible only to the initiated. The Goncourt brothers report a form of secret language in Parisian brothels: "All these girls from time to time speak *javanais*. Each syllable is separated by a *va*. Prisons have their *argot*, and the brothels have their *javanais*. They speak it very rapidly, and it is unintelligible to the men." Apparently, it, too, was easily learned. A study of the acquisition of Pig Latin by children might yield surprising results.

Astrology

In 1964 at Abu Simbel I kept searching the skies for a satellite. I wanted to see both ends of a period of 3200 years. The next night, as we were sailing back toward Aswan, there was a disturbance outside the cocktail lounge, and someone said "Satellite." I dashed out on deck, and there it was, almost directly overhead. It was moving fairly slowly in a southwest-northeast course. No one knew whose it was—Russia's or America's—but it might have been "Echo." It was very bright.

What would the Egyptian Astronomer Royal have done with it? How many offerings to the gods would have been made upon its appearance?

Feeling Sorry for Oneself

. . . is not one of the seven deadly sins, yet it is of the same magnitude. Occasionally one has insight and nevertheless continues to practice it. More often it goes unanalyzed.

But what is it? What is felt? And what conditions breed what is felt? What does one who is sorry for oneself do?

We feel "wronged" when an aversive situation is due mainly to others. We tend to protest or attack as a means of righting the wrong. But we may feel sorry for ourselves simply after misfortune from any source, and in that case we can only protest to or attack nature, chance, or God. If we do no more than feel a tendency to act, feeling sorry for ourselves is wholly unproductive, since it falls short of changing any condition.

Rather than protest a wrong, whether due to others or to chance, we may seek the consolation of having others feel sorry. But simply to court a feeling on the part of others is again unproductive. We should induce action to correct the wrong.

Approval and Disapproval

The effects are remote. We gain from approving and disapproving what people do when they behave in a different way—but only at a later date. Hence the practices are likely to deteriorate. As children we are taught to say "Thank you," but we usually continue to say it only if we are censured when we forget. We stop expressing disapproval because *we* are likely to be censured when we do so.

Social or ethical control grows weak, and a culture cannot easily support it by indicating the remote consequences. Nothing much follows from pointing out that if we say "Thank you" or risk expressing our disapproval, people will behave in ways that please us in the future.

The Borrowed Dream

Let a psychoanalyst collect ten dreams from ten different patients and redistribute them among the patients. Each is told, "Imagine you have dreamed this dream. What can you say about its relevance to your problem?" The analysis then proceeds. How much difference would it make?

Would the analyst know that it was not the patient's dream? An experiment is needed. Different patients would dissimulate more or less successfully. A man receiving a woman's dream might have a problem. Barring some unmistakable clue, however, I suspect that a great deal of depth-probing would go on, much of it indistinguishable from the real thing.

A possible rejoinder: "Might it not be as good as the real thing?" What would be more revealing than a patient's interpretation of a dream as applying to him- or herself? It would be a kind of thematic apperception test. And is that not what is done in suggesting that one shares a problem with Ivan Karamazov or Leonardo or Oedipus? The archetypal patterns are borrowed dreams. So are myths and the exploits of heroic figures. They illuminate aspects of one's behavior as the analysis of one's own dreams may do.

But then what is the significance of the dream one has had, apart from the significance one finds in discussing it with an analyst? Is the value of the interpretation of dreams simply in the interpretation, not in the dream itself?

Practical Eisegesis

Joshua Rann, in *Adam Bede:* "I . . . could say the Psalms right through in my sleep if you was to pinch me; but I know better nor to take 'em to say my own say wi'." He was referring to the Methodists who spoke largely with borrowed biblical phrases and hence with borrowed authority. If you could say something with God's words, God must agree with you.

Something of the same sort could be said of prose which is full of literary allusions. "Classical quotation," said Samuel Johnson, "is the *parole* of literary men all over the world." It also has much of the effect of name dropping. One borrows some of the prestige of the original speaker.

How much distortion comes from a ready-make repertoire of sentences? It is easy to fall back upon quotations in lieu of composition, but also easy to use the nearest available quotation although it is inaccurate. Quotation, as Bertrand Russell said of hypotheses, has the advantage of thievery over honest toil.

Irritability

How strange that the first observed response of nerve tissue was attributed to "irritability," as if our most conspicuous reaction to the world was to be annoyed. Why could it not have been wakability, alertability, liveliness? Eventually, "excitability" took over, which is fairly neutral, but no term was ever used to suggest the pleasurable side of stimulation. Stimulus itself, of course, meant goad.

Stalking

In "The Phylogeny and Ontogeny of Behavior" (*Contingencies of Reinforcement*, Chapter 7) I used *imitation, aggression, territoriality,* and *communication* as phylogenic repertoires for which there were ontogenic parallels—or, in other words, repertories shaped either by natural selection or, independently, by operant conditioning.

I might have added stalking. Predators stalk their prey in the sense of moving toward it in ways which avoid detection—slowly, upwind, crouching, under cover, and so on. The behavior could be due to contingencies of survival, because individuals who were more likely to behave in these ways were more likely to capture prey and survive and contribute the increased likelihood to the species. But similar behavior is shaped by contingencies of reinforcement. Approaching rapidly, downwind, conspicuously, or in the open leads to premature flight of the prey, but stalking is reinforced by successful approach to the point at which an open attack is successful.

The two sets of contingencies are similar, but one involves survival and the other operant conditioning. The difficulty is that the topography of the behavior suggests a single explanation (with which a structuralist might be satisfied).

The 88-Lever Box

A student at Hamilton College insisted that you must use punishment in raising children. He described an instance in which a mother and her small son came to call, and the boy immediately went to the piano and began to pound the keys. The mother frequently told him to stop but to no avail. The student insisted that he would have spanked a son of his, and justly, under such circumstances. I agreed that the mother should have backed up her first request, possibly by punishing or by separating the boy and the piano, or should not have made the request.

A piano is *designed* to make such behavior likely. Two centuries of skill and thought have gone into devising an instrument which provides reinforcing consequences when white and black keys are struck. Beautiful tones are ideally contingent upon striking. A piano is an 88-lever box.

Having provided such an instrument, it is foolish to allow a child to come into contact with it unless you wish to shape and sustain a great deal of behavior. Pianos can be locked; children can be left elsewhere; those are the simple solutions. The objectionable solution is to offset the reinforcement with punishment. It is objectionable because it has unwanted by-products.

Good Luck and Good News

The claim to be able to mediate good and bad fortune—from witches to priests—can be analyzed a little further. (1) *If you submit to me*, or pay me, or buy my charms or services, you will have good luck. (2) *If you do as I tell you*, you will be rewarded by success or good fortune.

The first claim plays on intermittent and fortuitous contingencies. The "consequence" is not contingent on the required act.

The second claim could be genuine. The advisor could be describing actual contingencies.

Angels appear to be in still another class. They *bring* good fortune, contingent on no act of the recipient. If they do not magically produce physical benefits, they bring good news; they are *herald* angels.

Incentive

I have often pointed out that bonuses could be used to add a gambling (variable-ratio) element to the pay of employees—instead of a standard bonus at Christmas, an unpredictable $5 or $10 in the pay envelope from time to time, or a ticket in every envelope and a weekly or monthly drawing, in an outright lottery.

Another possibility is to make ticket or money contingent on *quality*. A given amount for every so many items which survive inspection—a fixed ratio—would be a form of piece-rate pay with quality contingencies included. A graded scale of bonuses for runs of perfect items: $5 for x items in a row; $10 for $2x$; $25 for $3x$; and so on, a little like the winning streaks of teams.

One ticket for every day at work should cut down absenteeism.

Control by a Worsening Schedule

The Collier brothers, found dead in a house completely filled with rubbish, show the effect of a "stretched" schedule of saving or collecting, ending with contingencies in which reinforcement must have been very rare. It is not hard to imagine the "stretching."

1. Saving string, newspapers, and boxes is occasionally reinforced when they prove useful, but adding one more item to a stock is less powerfully reinforced as items accumulate. The more string you have, the less useful an additional piece, but the attenuated reinforcing effect may still sustain behavior.

2. The collection slowly becomes aversive. "Throwing it all out" is a form of escape, but it may not be triggered by any one addition. The Colliers' massive collection was not made noticeably more aversive by the addition of any one new item. And escape eventually becomes aversive in itself. It required Herculean labor to clean up the Collier house, and the brothers could have done it only by calling in outsiders who would have ridiculed the whole thing.

Three Sources of Strength of One Verbal Response

I took part in a centennial celebration at Boston College. His Eminence was there, and President Kennedy, who referred to the Pope's Encyclical, and many nuns and priests—in short, it was a Catholic occasion. I came home to find Rowland Sturgis giving Deborah a piano lesson. Later

I talked with him about music instruction in schools. In the discussion, he mentioned a man named Mooney, and the name of Mary Mooney instantly struck me with great force. The whole afternoon had built up its strength. Mrs. Mooney played the organ in the Catholic church and taught singing in the early grades of my school. She would put up great charts in front of our class and point to note after note as we dutifully solfèged. Two thematic groups— Catholicism and school music—had one verbal response in common: *Mrs. Mooney*, and a third stimulus—a formal prompt—made the response inevitable.

Freud's Data

I was struck by Ernest Jones's report that for many years Freud had very few patients. During the war he was once down to one. Yet he was giving and publishing papers on many cases—Dora, Little Hans, the Man with the Rats, the Wolfman, a Case of Female Homosexuality, children's theories of sex, a Special Type of Choice of Object made by Men, sexual anesthesia among women, the erotic fantasy in *A Child Is Being Beaten.*

Evidently a large percentage of his cases contributed to his theories. He was strongly disposed to see significances (Freud has monopolized "significances," after all). Of course, he discussed other cases with his coterie, but you have the impression that he could make something significant out of almost every case he saw. This testifies to a lively imagination, even to profound insights, but does it not testify, as well, to universality or a passion for systematizing —a passion which, to be successful, must make sacrifices in rigor and respect for all the facts?

Le Mot Juste

The Evanses say that *share*, as compared with *part*, *portion*, etc., suggests a *fair* or due portion "possibly for no better reason than the rhyme involved." What is the mechanism?

1. Because of echoic tendencies, as in *fair share*, *share* takes precedence when *fair* occurs. (A formal explanation.)

2. *Air* in *fair* is under the control of the stimulus as a separable unit. In situations involving justice, etc., *air* is strong. *Share* is thus a blend, or includes a blended "atom." (A thematic explanation.)

3. Either effect in a few speakers might lead to an effect on the community. *Share* becomes the preferred word in speaking of a just division of property. It is then acquired under circumstances involving a sort of audience variable— an appropriate supraordinate stimulus. In the speaker, the processes of (1) and (2) are then no longer necessary, though they would "support" the usage.

More on Rules

It used to be said that a pilot might fly a plane "by the seat of his pants" rather than by following the rules and that people might behave well because they were good rather than because they were obeying the law. In admiring such people, we are not really admiring personal traits or virtues; we are admiring contingency-shaped rather than rule-governed behavior. The former is preferred because it is more sensitive to the contingencies and freer to change as contingencies change. The pilot begins by following rules, as citizens begin by obeying laws. The pilot comes more quickly under the control of the actual contingencies because they are more immediate; it is only in face-to-face contact with other people that we discover the contingencies maintained by a social environment which have been encoded in laws.

The mathematician who seems to skip over pages of proof to reach valid conclusions (sometimes thereby setting problems to be solved by other mathematicians) is probably another example; we attribute the behavior to intuition because the actual contingencies are hard to identify.

Swatting a Fly

The first rule is to get your extended hand close. When the fly crouches (mostly with its forelegs), you are as close as you can get. The second rule is "Slap *downward* only." Drawing back the hand adds nothing to the downward stroke except a speed and terminal force which are not needed, and it gives the fly a signal and plenty of time to get away.

I have just discovered a third rule. A slap can hurt the slapper, and to the extent that this is so, slapping may be uncoordinated. The hand should be shaped to come comfortably to rest—flat on a table, cupped over the knee. It improves the slapping motion to imagine the position of the hand at the completion of the slap. It would be even better to *place* the hand in the completed position if you would not then lose the fly. But imagining *is* a kind of placing.

Delayed Prompt

In Harvard Square one noon I glanced down Dunster Street toward a little sidewalk café to see whether it was crowded, saw that it was, and went on to another restaurant. I stopped at a drug store for a moment and as I came out, I found myself silently singing *Auprès de ma blonde*. But I noticed that I was continuing *il fait bon*, instead of *il fait beau*. This puzzled me until I recalled the name of the sidewalk café: *C'est si bon*. I could not have *seen* the name of the café when I looked down the street and am quite sure I did not say it to myself. Yet the episode must have led me to sing the song and to sing it incorrectly.

Ritual

Rituals are superstitious; they are adventitiously reinforced. The more conspicuous and stereotyped the behavior upon which the reinforcer is accidentally contingent, the greater the effect. In my original experiment the pigeons seemed to develop more and more complex and energetic responses for this reason. Some contribution may have come from the fact that since some responses were not reinforced, extinction may have produced slight differences in topography and more vigorous responses. But the contingencies would also have been improved; the pigeon "would have known what it had done." (It is hard to shape behavior where the reinforcer is made contingent on a response, such as intersecting an invisible beam of light, which supplies little feedback.)

"Just Growing"

If a language just grows, matures, develops—like an embryo—why are there something of the order of 5000 languages? It does seem as if an inner process should have done more to shape semantic and syntactic structures. The "universals" of grammar are not the answer. They are the effects of the standard contingencies maintained by verbal communities—without which verbal behavior would be useless.

History or Thinking?

In the old delayed-reaction experiment, an organism went to that one of several covers under which it had seen food placed a short time before. The experiment was interesting because no stimulus was acting as the response was made. What, then, controlled the response? A symbolic process?

But why should an earlier stimulus not exert control? What the animal "uses" is a combination of stimuli in the form of instructions (see *Verbal Behavior*, p. 362). The behavior of "going toward" is transferred from food to a particular cover. Why should the transfer not last?

The actual performance is a kind of rule-governed behavior. Exploratory, cover-opening behavior is shaped by its consequences as food is found. Time is saved by following instructions: "Look under *this* cover." If the food could be seen, it would be simply a controlling stimulus. The instruction takes its place when it cannot be seen.

Short-term memory experiments appear to proceed with similar material.

Instruction involves both respondent and operant behavior. In a reflex the stimulus is an obvious "cause." In a conditioned reflex the past contingencies are part of the "cause." In an operant past consequences are also part of the "cause." They have worked changes, which do not need to be represented by an inner entity such as intention, purpose, act of will, or symbolic process. Only a description of past contingencies tells us what we actually know.

Exploitation

"The oppressive and despotic exploitation of the workmen" (Pope Pius XII, *Optatissima Pace*) suggests oppressive, despotic control but complains, as Marx complained, of the diversion of proceeds. Yet the contented schoolmaster, dying just as he consumes the last penny of his retirement fund, could in that sense be said to have been "exploited" by those he taught. True, he may have taken joy in the achievements of his pupils, but why do exploited workers not take joy in the pleasures of their exploiters—as, indeed, in some cultures family retainers once did?

Rules

The Golden Rule directs people to look at the effect of similar behavior upon themselves in order to manage their behavior with respect to others. Were the Puritans applying rules derived from self-observation when they attempted to suppress all things which gave them pleasure? Did they conclude that since the deferred consequences of some pleasurable activities were aversive, all pleasurable activities were to be suppressed?

But no rule was needed. Reinforcers become conditioned aversive stimuli when followed by punishment. "Anxiety" is frequently associated with sexual pleasure although we apply no rule, such as that "whatever gives pleasure is wrong." The contingencies may, of course, be analyzed and rules extracted from them.

Fractional Verbal Operant

To some extent vocal verbal behavior affects the listener visually. We are less intelligible in the dark or on the telephone, given the same level of articulation. When auditory conditions are difficult, we amplify the visual properties of our speech. If there is no chance of being heard—if we are speaking above a loud noise, through thick windows, seen from a distance through binoculars, or to a friend at a distance when we must remain quiet, we may speak silently, with exaggerated movements of lips, jaw, and tongue. The exaggeration greatly exceeds any level previously established by differential reinforcement, but this is not surprising, since we also strike with a wholly unique force when weaker blows are ineffective, provided some differential reinforcement of more powerful blows has occurred. I reported the effect in *The Behavior of Organisms* (Chapter 8).

Praise and Blame

We praise or blame as if people were responsible for their actions. They are right or wrong, admirable or despicable. But any resulting change is due to the praise or blame, which is outside the individual.

Praising and blaming recognize the individual "as doer," but there is no reason to say "originator."

Flight from Behavior

I don't believe many of those who study proactive and retroactive inhibition, reminiscence, obliviscence, and so on, are actually interested in behavior. If they were, they would look more closely at the behavior. They set up experiments in which subjects are, indeed, behaving, but they are looking for, and trying to study, inner processes. An apparent analogy in the physical sciences reassures them. But concepts come much later in the evolution of a science, when more has been done to clarify the facts the concepts are useful in talking about.

The "processes" studied in verbal learning are incomplete formulations rather than heuristic devices justified because they encourage research.

C. N. S.

If sleep is a kind of behavior—or even the absence of behavior—then has "physiology" told us something we didn't know? Only by amplification. REM is observed behavior. So are reports of dreaming. Electroencephalograms are "physiology." Do they throw any light on the behavior? Not on any explanatory mechanism. Not on any bridging of past experience with current action.

The Wrong Word Written III

In my notebook I wrote: *He is getting to to talk to an executive club* . . . where the first *to* is an egregious error for *me*. But note that the next word was *to*, as was the third word following. I did not see the mistake until today, two months after writing it, though I may not have looked at it since.

Changing a sentence, I struck out *by no means* and inserted *not*, but I actually wrote *note*. The following word was *rote*, and an early part of the passage referred to playing the piano and understanding music. *Not* with the *o* pronounced as in *no* sounds like *note*.

I dictated *but most* and corrected it to *but both must*. Did *but* preempt *both* and hurry me along to *must*, producing the blend *most?*

I wrote *is well demonstrated* and reviewed it several times before getting what I wanted: *is illustrated.* Note the formal overlap:

And is the fact that *ill* and *well* are antonyms significant?

Gross mistakes keep turning up. I wrote "The more the *student* teaches the less the student learns," where, following Comenius, I meant *teacher.*

I started to write *pleo* for *people*. The *l* looks like an early appearance of the later *l*, but I was going to write *were bland*, and the *bl* is more likely to have produced *pl*.

Fiction as History

In most of the uses we make of history, fiction will serve as well. We demand consistency and plausibility in lieu of truth and thus preserve what really matters, a bit of vicarious experience.

This is equally true of the case history in pyschotherapy. As early as 1906 Freud was analyzing a fictional character (Norbert Hanold in *Delusion and Dream*), and he argued that he could do so because fictionalized early experiences (imagined rape, for example) could be treated as if real. The materials which went into the fantasy had real sources somewhere and may have retained useful properties.

The case history also illustrates another point about history: it is obviously selective. Freud built a picture out of historical or fantasied fragments; he had no interest in reconstructing a complete account. To disagree with Freud one has only to select contradictory cases.

Looking as Action

Yesterday I went to the ball game with Debs. We had Roof Box seats, front row. I could look over the edge straight down to seats perhaps 75 feet below. At first I was pretty acrophobic, but as the game went on I relaxed. The only surviving twinges came as I looked at someone on the field or, better still, all the way across it, and then suddenly "fantasied walking toward him," whereupon I was aware of the drop below me. The fear seemed to accompany an incipient movement associated with looking. ("Fantasied walking toward him" is not accurate.)

People interested in perception often criticize a behavioristic analysis on the grounds that it doesn't cover simple looking without doing. Contemplation, the enjoyment of "perception"—how can these be treated as behavior? But the shortcoming is on the other side. What *is* looking? What does one *do* in contemplating something?

The answer is to be found in the discriminative contingencies. What is differentially reinforced as one learns to see? The development of "eye-hand" coordination and of spatial relations is one example. One sees *where* a thing is by acquiring the behavior of reaching for it. One sees *what* a thing is by acquiring all the behavior under its control as a stimulus. These survive in contemplation. The man I see across the field is someone I can reach by moving in a given direction; he is someone I can or cannot speak to in a normal tone of voice; etc. Hence all these behaviors are part of seeing him. If one bit of behavior is moving out of my box in a straight line toward him, and if part of that is looking for immediate footing, then the acrophobic reaction is reasonably well accounted for.

The Status Quo

There is a natural inclination to believe that survival testifies to usefulness, but things survive for the wrong reasons (or, without competition, for no reason at all) when judged against anticipated uses. Thus Mary Wollner can argue that children's classics must have satisfied some basic need or they would not have had such a long history. The need may now go unfulfilled if they are to be replaced by something else. But there is another possible explanation. Perhaps "Jack the Giant Killer" (in the version in which the giant really dies) is reassuring to the small child in a world of towering grownups—but perhaps it is simply a story adults have found effective in holding the attention of children because they fear giants. (No one has more reason, since all adults are giants.) In the latter case, it is the story *teller* who perpetuates a story, whose "need" is satisfied. The gripping concern which keeps the child motionless and reinforces story telling may be injurious rather than remedial.

Awareness Blunted

My "French personality" has rather maudlin and certainly undisciplined or careless characteristics. I can assert myself —or some part of myself—in French, but the editing is deficient. I allow things to stand, in part because they are not aversive enough to delete. I "know" that something shouldn't be said, but I say it. My ultimate escape is into English, where I am on guard.

There is some evidence of a deferred critical editing. I have found myself coming up with an isolated correction 24 hours after making a mistake—and when I have not gone over what was said.

I became aware of another hidden repertoire when I wrote the "poem" in *Verbal Behavior* in which quite unrelated words were used as a kind of phonetic alphabet or syllabary. I was not translating a theme already stated in standard terms, and I was surprised by the Germanic flavor of the poem as it unfolded.

Using Behavioral Tendencies

In making up a general outline sheet with seventeen entries, I divided the page into seventeen parts and then started to put in numbered topics. *But I put all the numbers in first.*

I did it because I have found that if I add a new item, after finishing an earlier one, I tend to write the same number as the preceding. I have recently done that several times. I was also aware that I was opposing that tendency by resorting to the intraverbal sequence in simple counting.

This is a subtle, but possibly typical, example of the use one may make of a behavioral process.

Control

Gregory Bateson: "Malinowski . . . gives us a dramatic description of the almost physiological extremes of rage which the Trobriand black-magician practices in his incantations."

Acting to make something happen which then doesn't happen may evoke extreme forms of behavior—like pulling violently at a stuck door. This is true of behavior affecting other people—commanding, threatening, and so on. There are many autonomic components in the rage evoked when people do not respond, but they are by-products of failure (extinction), not operant behaviors. Simulation of rage may be reinforced as an operant and may be an important part of black magic.

Therapy?

I have been writing about my grandparents and my father and mother. I have become absorbed in a world now more than fifty years past. It has flowered anew. I remember names, incidents, comments as if it were yesterday. There is a feeling of discovery. There are "things inside me" I had thought had long ago vanished. And I now see them in two ways—more or less as I saw them then and as I see them now. I could not then have seen their eventual significance, of course.

How much of this occurs in analysis? Have I been releasing repressed memories? No. I have been reconstructing (or simply constructing) a setting in which I remember things. How much of what occurs in analysis is not a sign of therapy but merely facilitated recollection? And what is therapeutic "insight" but seeing an earlier event in the light of subsequent history? Did Freud simply discover the value of getting his patients to write or speak their autobiographies?

Russell on Knowledge

Russell: "Is there any knowledge in the world so certain that no reasonable man could doubt it?" Such a question presupposes some kind of knowing and doubting quite different from acting upon. Are there any statements about facts to which one may respond with a probability of 1? What contingencies could lead to such behavior?

Russell distinguishes between Knowledge by Acquaintance and Knowledge by Description. Knowledge by Description is exemplified by "the tallest man in the United States." "Probably no one knows who he is, but there no doubt is a definite man to whom this description is applicable." But is that "knowledge"? Russell has fallen prey again to the mechanical arrangement of words.

"There is one great question. Can human beings *know* anything, and if so what and how?" But that is precisely what an operant analysis of the behavior said to "show knowledge" is all about.

And it is not a question that cannot be answered until we understand how it can be asked. We can analyze behavior (given the repertoires supplied by our culture) and *then* look at what we are doing as we analyze it.

The Function of Grammar

Some parts of the Loeb Library edition of Suetonius are left untranslated—for example, in reporting Tiberius's diversions while swimming with young boys. A Latin-English dictionary gives the meanings of the words, but without a knowledge of grammar it is impossible to discover "who does what with which to whom."

Knowledge of What Is Stored

Several years ago at a friend's, I picked up a C-melody saxophone. I had not had one in my hands for perhaps 25 years. I started to play, and my fingers reached out and found relevant keys with surprising accuracy. I am sure I could not have *described* the arrangement of the keys.

Perhaps I could have done so by playing in fantasy (and may have so played, of course, during the 25 years), but without behaving I could not have *seen* that I remembered. There was no "stored image." (Of course, it is only a bad metaphor to say that my *fingers* remembered.)

The Importance of Knowing about Learning

In *Contingencies of Reinforcement*, Note 7.1, I pointed out that what we have discovered about how pigeons learn has made it quite clear that they do not learn to make nests. It is the study of learning, not of innate behavior, that has clarified the point.

The same thing may be said about the importance of cultures. What can a person do in a single lifetime in acquiring the skills which seem so characteristic of the human species? Not much, as I point out in *Beyond Freedom and Dignity*. It is the study of learning, not of cultural practices, which clarifies how much is due to culture.

History of Rules

Members of a group live according to the social contingencies maintained by the group. The strong take, and the weak permit. A lie, found out, brings a beating from the deceived. Conditioned reinforcers take over; escape becomes avoidance. Beating yields to *tut-tut*. In a homogeneous group the contingencies become quite stable. Then they begin to be described. Someone defines "property" and "lying." Taking property and lying have been punished and are now called wrong. The *code* must now be *obeyed*. One then lives, not in the light of one's experience with the group, but by rule. Is something lost?

Reinforcement of Verbal Behavior

Bill Verplanck once introduced me to an audience at the University of Maryland by recalling some of his first contacts with me at Indiana. It was a rather difficult introduction to acknowledge, and I said something like this:

"Professor Verplanck must realize how dangerous it is to indulge in reminiscences. When I first met him, I was just starting as chairman at Indiana University. He was the first psychologist I ever hired. He has told you that I used to trap pigeons for my experiments. It wasn't always necessary to set traps. Once when I was making a telephone call, a pigeon came in the window, landed on my desk, and began to walk about. I reached out slowly and caught it by the feet. I finished the call, took the pigeon upstairs to the laboratory, and eventually taught it to play a kind of piano. Now I realize that that is very much the kind of thing that happened when I hired Professor Verplanck."

There was great laughter and applause, and I was off to a good start—a big reinforcement rather cheaply purchased, partly at Bill's expense. Four hours later, alone for the first time and waiting for sleep, I found myself retelling the story, casting the last line in various forms, perhaps searching for the most effective form but mainly just repeating the remark. I would drop to the last line, and then return to the whole passage again. Before going to sleep, I must have said it 25 or 30 times.

Long-Term Recall

Waiting for a stoplight on a fairly quiet Saturday morning, I turned on the direction indicator. Its tick-tock immediately reminded me of a clock of my Grandmother Burrhus's. I remembered the dimly lighted kitchen on Broad Street, the silence of the night, the ticking. It was either a green and black marble clock with ormolu fittings, or a wooden Seth Thomas, with a painted glass front.

I heard that clock, in that setting, about 40 years ago. What has survived all these years? A few cells? A pattern of molecules—patched and repatched until nothing of the original remains?

It does not matter. The important thing is the distinctive character of the stimulus—the timing and stress, tick-TOCK, tick-TOCK, plus a pitch and vowel quality. These are enough to generate thousands of distinguishable stimuli, any one of which might have found no confusing counterpart during 40 years.

"Unconscious" Slip

In *The Shaping of a Behaviorist* I tell the story of a young woman, living apart from her husband, who asked me to come over one evening to play piano four-hands. It was a rainy night, and as I took off my wet coat, she said, "A good night for seamen—*sailors!*"

She saw the relevance of the sound of the response *seamen* to another variable but saw it a fraction of a second too late. If we had been planning to go to bed together, her remark could have been taken by both of us as wit. Even so, it might have been "unconscious" at the moment of emission. Instead of correcting herself, she would have laughed and taken credit for the double meaning.

Play

The brush-tailed porcupines, according to Gerald M. Durrell in *The Overloaded Ark*, apparently play on slides. They go to the top of a slide, place their backs or bottoms on the slide, and let go of the ground; and this behavior seems to be reinforced by the movement, acceleration, and abrupt stop.

A fairly long program of contingencies is presumably needed to shape so complex an act. How long would it take a young animal to discover the trick by itself? A short slide first, perhaps? Then the discovery of a particularly good spot? If others are already playing, is the behavior acquired through imitation? Being near other porcupines at play would mean being near a prepared slide, and a prepared slide would speed individual discovery, but imitative contingencies are presumably at work, phylogenic or ontogenic.

Future French

When an editor objected that a word was not French, the Goncourt brothers wrote: *"Le mot de Hugo me brûle la langue: ≪il le sera!≫"* Was Gertrude Stein thinking of Hugo when, upon being told that her works could not be translated into French, she replied, "Try it and see what happens to French!"?

Group Goals

The confusion which arises from using goal to represent reinforcer is clear when it is said that a given culture puts group goals ahead of individual goals. This could mean simply that ethical sanctions and the sanctions imposed by organized governments, religions, economic systems, or educational establishments are so powerful that people spend most of their time working "for the good of others." The good of others could be called a group goal in the sense of a miscellaneous collection of reinforcers affecting those who compose the group. But group behavior itself is not reinforced as a collective entity. Its "good" is presumably its survival, and a culture which emphasizes behaving for the good of others may or may not have any great survival value. Individual goals and group goals are different kinds of things.

Golden Rule

Long before the Golden Rule was formulated, certain social contingencies must have prevailed; certain social actions generated responses which positively or negatively reinforced the action. It was useful to be able to predict such consequences. If one could observe or predict effects upon oneself, one could reach a general principle. Aversive consequences could be avoided by treating others only in ways which one would oneself find reinforcing. The contingencies could have controlled behavior before they were ever formulated; the Golden Rule was derived from them. It enjoined people to examine in themselves the effects of measures they proposed to use with others. To follow the rule, a person needed both self-knowledge and self-control.

"Bad Habit"

"Habit" as a customary way of behaving is a useful word. Etymologically it is akin to "be-having." But I object to the "habits" which physiologists implant in animals to use as explanations. "He does that from habit" means nothing more than "He does that frequently." "He acquired the habit" means nothing more than "He began to do that frequently."

Watson used "habit" appropriately, because he believed that organisms behaved simply in ways in which they had frequently behaved. Frequency, as an explanation, was worth investigating. But habits, like instincts, crept inside as things possessed.

Ethology

An ethologist once seemed particularly excited when a colleague said that he could probably not produce some of a dove's nest-building behavior through operant reinforcement. Why is that any more surprising than the converse point that heredity cannot produce an extensive verbal repertoire?

My colleague was clearly right. If it were somehow possible to wipe out all traces of instinctive behavior in a pair of doves, leaving modifiability intact, it would be extremely difficult, if not impossible, to shape and maintain comparable behavior through reinforcement. The contingencies needed to program building a nest would be fabulous. (One might take birds that do not build nests, or that are not in their nest-building period, and try it.)

Cooperation and Competition

These are not true alternatives. Two organisms *cooperate* when joint action is reinforced. They *compete* when the behavior of only one can be reinforced in a given episode. (Does game theory *really* analyze such contingencies?)

The roles of cooperation and competition in society are not closely related either. Roughly speaking, cooperative arrangements are productive. Things are done which would not be done otherwise. New ways of doing things may be discovered as contingencies interlock and are mutually altered. Competition simply supplies aversive consequences which add strength to behavior, particularly under *drh* (the differential reinforcement of high rates of responding). Discovery, invention, and enterprise appear when competition makes behavior strong; but they would follow as well from other means of increasing strength.

Memory Shaken

Waiting near the Post Office for a bus, I remembered meeting a man there a year or so before whose name I could not recall.

A few days later, writing about feelings and states of mind, I looked at an old note about "Culture Shock." I said to myself a few words like *shock* and *shaken*, and then remembered "Schenkman," the name I had tried to recall.

More of My Lost Future

Ronald W. Clark (*The Life of Bertrand Russell*, p. 11) says that Russell struggled for years with certain contradictions. Points under consideration:

1. ". . . denoting phrases, in contrast to proper names, could describe non-existent objects, such as the round square." Clearly, "described" does not mean "to be evoked by." No nonexistent object can evoke the response "round square"; such a phrase is simply put together word by word, not emitted as a verbal response.

2. ". . . specific objects such as 'the president of the United States,' or unidentifiable and therefore ambiguous objects such as 'a man.'" (Clark's quotation marks are wrong; these are the things described, not the denoting phrases.) "The president" is a proper tact if the President is present, or an intraverbal in talking about an absent president. "A man" is an abstract verbal operant; the properties of a controlling stimulus are not all present upon any one occasion; they can be discovered only by examining a number of instances.

Later: "every denoting word or phrase referred either to a thing or concept." The abstract tact problem again.

Later: "whatever may be an object of thought . . . has being, i.e., *is* in some sense." If "thought" is an act of denoting (a tact), this is true. But phrases generated by putting words together, repeating something heard, or reading nonsense are not thinking in that sense. The analysis in *Verbal Behavior* is crucial.

Later: "the logical subject of a proposition [can be] 'the golden mountain' even though no golden mountain exists." But only if propositions are accepted when generated by (when they are the result of) moving words about as independent objects.

Russell comes to the same conclusion: "The problem of granting *is*-ness to round squares and golden mountains was merely a pseudo-problem solved by analyzing and then redefining what one was talking about," says Clark.

Later, paraphrasing Ryle:

The self-subverting statements were of this sort, neither true nor false [i.e., not tacts], but nonsensical simulacra of statements. Notice that it is only of such things as complex verbal expressions that we can ask whether they are significant or nonsensical [complex because containing autoclitics of assertion; significant as being tacts rather than mechanical assemblages of words]. The question could not be asked of mental processes [Why not?]; or of Platonic entities [What question? Why not askable?]. So logic is from the start concerned, not with these [these what?] but rather with what can be significantly said [i.e., with tacts].

Russell's paper "On Denoting" seems to get to the point: Don't spend time on paradoxes constructed by moving words around.

Psychotherapy

Exercise in translation:

"Types of therapy [which] rely primarily on the healer's *ability to mobilize healing forces* in the sufferer by psychological means . . . may be generically termed psychotherapy."

Step one: Omit "ability," yielding "the therapist's mobilizing of healing forces."

Step two: Omit "healing forces" (compare the *vis medicatrix*), yielding "the therapist healing the sufferer."

In other words, types of therapy which rely primarily on the therapist healing the sufferer by psychological means may be generically termed psychotherapy or, better, psychotherapy is psychological healing—as the etymology makes clear.

Applause as Assertion

In his *Journal*, Stendhal reports many instances in which French and Italian audiences applauded lines which could be taken to refer critically to Napoleon. Applauding is close to asserting. It has the effect of *Amen!* or *So be it!* It is a way of making it more likely that the same thing will be said again. And it successfully avoids punishment because, like hissing, booing, or murmuring disapproval, the assertion has a form difficult to trace to one "speaker." It is not clear which of those applauding are applauding for that particular reason and therefore responsible for the significantly greater volume. As in wit or allegory, the "speakers" can always claim a harmless reason for their applause.

Stages

When we have been punished we may start to act and then stop. Have we suddenly "realized it is the wrong thing to do"? No, preaversive stimuli have built up.

If, as we stop, we say, "This is the thing I have been punished for," we describe the contingencies to which we have been exposed.

If we say, "This is wrong," we state a rule about the behavior—a law: "This is punishable behavior."

Adventitious Contingencies

In my demonstration lecture at the Royal Institution, the superstitious contingencies worked very quickly. When the food dispenser began to operate every twenty seconds, the pigeon first picked up a response I had reinforced earlier (turning to the left) but quickly went on to striking its head against the left wall of the apparatus, swinging back and forth with its breast pressing against the wall. Reinforcements consistently followed good instances.

To what extent was it true that the reinforcement was then fortuitous? Given a clock which operated the dispenser at fixed intervals and a process of operant conditioning, future instances of responses which were at first fortuitously related to the operation of the food dispenser were no longer so. There was no *mechanical* connection between response and consequence, but there was a behavioral connection, and a perfectly lawful one.

This reminds me of L. J. Henderson's *Fitness of the Environment.* If organisms have adapted to a given environment, the environment must be adapted to the organisms. *Of course,* the pigeon could stop throwing itself against the wall and still receive just as much food, but if it were to do so, it would be as likely to stop responding in other ways. Up to a given point in evolution, the risk of useless behavior must be run.

"Taking In" the World

The internalization of contingencies by cognitive psychologists is memorialized in certain idioms. "Do you take my meaning?" was once a common expression. The tourist "takes in" Paris. Someone on the edge of a conversation "sits there taking it all in."

No Stimulus?

A paper by Suedfelt (in *American Scientist*) argues essentially that if we go on behaving—especially perceptually—when stimuli are at a minimum, there must be spontaneous, creative activity. Hence, cognition.

But it is only in a crude S-R formulation that stimuli are demanded for all responses. The concept of probability of response takes care of both "spontaneity" and "creativity." Past reinforcements have made behavior—including seeing and hearing things—likely, and when particularly likely, no relevant current stimuli are needed.

In trying to figure out what dreams mean (compared with what daydreams are "about"), we tend to overlook the fact that dreams have no *currently* reinforcing consequences. The meaning of behavior is in the controlling variables. Daydreams are controlled by consequences. Night dreams are not.

Experimenter

Humans and other primates can be kept active with trivial reinforcements. Children play with electric typewriters, monkeys operate locks. Is this a question of a susceptibility to reinforcement by trivial environmental events? Or a matter of scheduling?

Try a young, healthy rat, fully fed. An easily moved lever produces a variety of effects: steady light, flashing light, steady noise, intermittent noise, etc., in random order. Then go over slowly to a variable-ratio schedule. Can you thus construct a "dedicated investigator"?

Gold Epaulets

Someone asked me how I would get able-bodied men on relief to clean streets without protesting the "indignity." I suggested some mechanizing of equipment. (Gasoline motors would increase pollution, but what about storage batteries?) I also suggested a distinctive uniform. Not distinctive in the sense of setting apart; on the contrary, something close to the police, firemen, doormen, or chauffeurs (or Nixon's palace guards). "Whitewings," with gold epaulets!

Currently prestigious terms in psychology show how effective this can be. "Mathematical models," "cybernetics," "algorithm," "stochastic," "matrices," "logistics"—these are the gold epaulets which sustain young psychologists engaged in laborious thinking. The only difference is that epaulets on the street cleaners would get the streets *clean.*

Differential Reinforcement of Short Response Times

The English allow phones to ring longer before answering. An American is advised to let a phone ring longer than in America when making a call. At first blush this looks like a temperamental difference. The English are less hurried, more casual. But note that the contingencies are different. In England you *can* answer at a more leisurely pace because your caller will let the phone ring longer before giving up. For possibly inscrutable reasons a different set of times has become established. In America you answer quickly because your caller will stop the call if you wait, and you do not let the phone ring very long when making a call because if there is no answer at once, no one is at home. In England both behaviors—calling and answering—have different temporal properties.

Alerting Stimulus

An expanding object in the visual field often elicits dodging or other evasive action. There are reasons for such behaviors in both natural selection and operant conditioning.

Television advertisements often use an expanding stimulus. The name or picture of a product comes out of nothing at a distance and swells as it appears to approach the viewer, until it fills the screen. It is difficult to look away from such a threatening stimulus, but is the name or object when viewed thus aversively likely to be favored?

And if a surfeit of such instances extinguishes avoidance behavior, including careful observation, are we more likely to be hit by real approaching objects?

Proverbs

"If you want fire, do not fear the smoke."
"A knife that cuts never fails to get nicks."

These are metaphorical descriptions of contingencies. More literal paraphrases: "Do not draw away from the aversive features of behavior that will be reinforced." "The most effective behavior is most likely to run into trouble."

The concrete object in the metaphor helps in (1) memorizing, and (2) seeing ("knowing") the contingency.

Can we say that, in general, mental expressions serve as metaphors for behavioral contingencies? Is "fear paralyzing will" another way of saying "punishment suppressing behavior"?

The Cost of Confidence

Psychiatrists assigned by a court to say whether a person was legally insane when a crime was committed presumably get all available facts in the case, but psychiatrists who are consulted for help confine themselves to small selections of facts. To maintain the confidence of their patients, they do not consult close associates in private. They solve their cases like Nero Wolfe, sitting in a chair. But Wolfe had investigators, and the psychiatrists have none. They do not go into their patients' homes, the places where they work, the clubs they belong to, or any of the places where they spend a good deal of time.

Do they not want to know as much as possible about their patients? Of course they do, but they must respect confidence. They must not appear to know much more about their patients than the patients themselves have revealed. But is this principle not merely a justification of limitations imposed by the psychiatric situation? Sitting across desks or behind couches, psychiatrists can let their patients talk out their problems, possibly directing the lines they take, but in doing so they work changes primarily in verbal behavior. They may suggest that their patients make changes in the circumstances of their lives but are in no position to make such changes for them. Since respecting confidence is highly honorific, there is a real danger that it is a rationalization of professional shortcomings.

Identification

The echoic or imitative repertoire should be investigated as a clue to Freud's concept of identification.

Does "identifying with" mean more than "acting like"?

Does the boy learn that he is like his father as he begins to behave like him? What other evidence of similarity has he? Reported feelings? But how often does one learn the similarity of feelings compared with the similarity of action?

Rights

To say that the state "finds its ultimate justification in war" is to make a possession (justification) out of an act (making war successfully). A personal or civil right is made of the same stuff. A person has a right in the sense of the power to prevent harm of one sort or another. My right to liberty is my genetic and personal capacity to keep myself free of physical restraint or aversive stimulation, by prevailing against would-be controllers.

To associate personal rights and the justification of a state with aversive power seems to put one on the side of violence, but that is true only if we limit ourselves to aversive measures—in the control of people by people, people by government, government by people, and government by government.

"Justification" and "rights" are no more than terms used to discuss aversive countercontrol. A different kind of personal or governmental control is possible, with respect to which they have little meaning.

Innate Behavior

An old note reads as follows: "What can an inherited 'musical ability' actually be? How could nature have foreseen its usefulness?"

Pretty obviously the "ability" must have been selected by practical consequences. But what phylogenic contingencies would have produced the behavior and the susceptibility to reinforcement which, together, yield musical behavior, particularly in its extreme forms? Here is a chance to uncover some basic features of the human genetic endowment.

A similar question may be raised about "thinking mathematically" or speaking grammatically. What conditions of selection could have produced the behavior and the susceptibility to reinforcement which lead to mathematical and grammatical behavior? (As I have pointed out, there is no special essence of verbal behavior—or of mathematical behavior, for that matter.)

Implied Consequences

In discussing some examples of advice, warning, orders, and maxims, I have found myself saying things like, "The contingent reinforcement is implied rather than mentioned." But there is danger in that *implied*. In "Go West and you will make your fortune" the consequences (making a fortune) are specified. In "Go West, young man," the consequences are only implied. If the advice is effective, it is not because of an "implication." We take advice only if taking it has been reinforced in the past. To say that advice works because of implied consequences is a convenient shortcut, but there is quicksand waiting.

A Remote "Association"

Reading J. B. Bury's *The Idea of Progress*, I suddenly "saw" a village street, possibly at an intersection marked by some sort of stop sign, with a concrete pavement leading off to the right, along which I should have expected to find—about a mile away and on the left—a tourist home or possibly a stand where something was sold. This seemed to go back to my early motoring history. I located it vaguely in New York State, and then as a late stage in the route from Scranton to Hamilton College. I might have driven it as late as 1928, possibly in the late 1930's passing through Colgate, just possibly in the late 1940's. But why think of it when reading Bury?

A very brief search revealed the stimulus: five or six lines earlier the name Seneca—one of a whole group of classical place names in New York State near Hamilton College, including Rome, Ithaca, Utica, Troy, and Syracuse.

"Sociologese"

Under this title in *Encounter* (December 1968), W. G. Runciman tries to show that sociologists write badly because those who write well on the same subjects are not called sociologists.

He blames "jargon." But is that really it? It is not so much the secrecy of the language as the way it works that causes trouble.

The great fault is the invention of nouns—finding, or seeming to find, things when there are only actions. The result is not only a stylistic bog into which the reader sinks immobilized, it is misdirection. The fault is in looking for things behind behavior rather than at behavior itself—at supposed causes rather than the variables of which behavior is a function. It is not a matter of elegance, or of being comprehensible to laymen, but of clarity of *thought*.

"Those Who Gamble Punish Themselves"

Some schedules of reinforcement are aversive, and organisms escape from them when they can. Gamblers "know" that they are losing their fortunes, and accidents that interrupt their gambling may be looked back upon as good luck; yet if there is no interruption, they do not stop. A pigeon will peck a special key that turns off the whole experiment when comparable conditions prevail, although it will not stop responding if the experiment cannot be turned off.

Is it begging the question to say that the variable-ratio schedule is so powerful that it forces players to continue to play in spite of growing aversive stimuli? Certainly they continue to play, and certainly their condition becomes more and more painful. Escape should be strongly reinforced, yet they do not escape by stopping, evidently because playing is stronger.

An analysis of the contingencies, resulting in a rule (stop gambling if you do not want to lose), will have an effect only if (like all rules) there are special contingencies to maintain the rule-governed behavior.

Bedside

The argument that operant conditioning was "the best that nature could do," even though it made such things as superstition likely, can be extended to sexual behavior.

Heterosexual behavior is closely related to contingencies of survival, but nature could not be too specific. Strong personal affection, various forms of sexual stimulation, and possibly some built-in susceptibilities to particular visual forms and particular modes of stimulation—these are about the closest nature could come. But they produce homosexual and autosexual behavior, which are not otherwise related to survival.

For an anatomical parallel, compare the male breast. No great harm done and possibly safer in preserving the genes responsible for the female breast.

Translation

From a review in *Scientific American:*

There is a tendency to think of a probability as being inherent in the event rather than in something the individual who is trying to predict the event has done. As Rapoport observes: "In this light, probabilities which we assign to events become reflections of our preferences rather than of our knowledge."

Is a probability "inherent" in anything? The word shows the uneasiness with which probability is discussed.

If we assume that a response is strong because upon similar occasions it has been reinforced on a given schedule, then the probability is:

a. "inherent in the event" in the sense of due to the scheduled contingencies,

b. "something the individual . . . has done" in the sense of the exposure to these contingencies, and

c. a matter of "trying to predict the event" in the sense of the strength of the behavior itself (strong if the event is "confidently predicted") or in the sense of formulating the contingencies in a rule for future action.

The statement that "probabilities we assign . . . become reflections of our preferences" means that the probabilities *are* the preferences.

Sensory Invention

A stimulus is sensed, or perceived, *as* something. A banging on a door is dreamt of, before waking, as a series of shots. A smile is seen by the paranoid as a sneer. Two adjacent spots appearing briefly in a certain temporal relation are seen as a moving spot.

Two stimuli are sensed as causally related if they have the temporal and spatial relations of causally related events. This is particularly true of action-followed-by-stimulus. The sound of something striking the floor when one is carrying an awkward armful of objects is heard as something dropped.

That all of this is "sensing what is expected to be sensed" is only another way of saying that these are common reactions in their appropriate spheres. We tend to sense what we have already sensed. Part of a common stimulus complex evokes a response appropriate to all of it. (Compare the analysis of metonymy in *Verbal Behavior*.) This may be something like conditioning, or it may be a form of generalization. The response *seeing-red* may be evoked by orange or even yellow. The response "seeing-red-hearts-on-a-playing-card" may, evidently, be evoked by black hearts.

It is curious (or is it?) that many examples are taken to require invention. Elaborate paranoid delusions seem *ingenious*. But no process of imagining is needed, though something of the sort is not ruled out. Of interest are the facts that paranoid reactions are original or idiosyncratic, that they are exaggerated, and that they hang together. The last requires explanation by way of the importance for the individual. The former suggest ranges of generalization as functions of deprivation or aversive stimulation.

All this should be studied in connection with active invention as self-management.

In rearranging an equation to get it into factorable form a strong tendency to *see* a factorable form is obviously useful (even though it may also set off false—i.e., unproductive—responses).

Creator

Yesterday, in answering questions after a talk, I reported my belief that I myself had not written *Beyond Freedom and Dignity*, but rather that it was the product of my genetic endowment and my personal history working *through* me. In my lecture I had discussed Socrates and maieutics and perhaps that is why I was reminded later of my point that a mother could say the same thing about a baby. The mother participates in the production of her child, as I participated in the production of my book, but what else has she done? She has not designed the baby. It is as much a surprise to her as to anyone else.

Before writing this note I had a flash of anxiety. Was I not being inconsistent about maieutics? But I was not. Neither the midwife nor the mother is accountable for the child. (Non-Socratic) teachers contribute to a student's history, as future geneticists may contribute to the genetic sources of a baby. They are responsible simply in the sense that they now bring new genetic endowments and personal histories to bear upon the product.

Tired of Feelings

I was slightly resentful when I read that some psychoanalyst had said that early risers are egotists. They get up early because they feel the world needs them, is waiting for them. The analyst was presumably a slug-a-bed. It is the kind of remark one can make with no evidence whatsoever. It would be just as easy to say that "early risers are very humble people who feel they must apply all their energies to make up for what others have given them." Both explanations are quite meaningless. People don't get up early because of what they *feel*. They may feel something *as* they get up, and from it they, or we, may infer something about the causes of early rising. But feeling is not among the causes.

The Creative Mind

An article in the *Heritage Dictionary* on transformational grammar takes the Chomsky line. It is a useful statement. I should try writing a parallel in transformational botany, using phylogenic rather than ontogenic contingencies. "An essentially infinite number of different plants," "non-plants," etc., proving the need for a creative Mind which follows rules.

Effort, Energy, and Fatigue

Many efforts have been made to use work output as a basic dimension of behavior in place of probability, rate, or "strength." There is a relation. A fair estimate of probability might be made from the amount of work an organism will do to get something, like the amount of shock it will "take," because effort usually means aversive stimulation. We say that behavior must be strong if the organism is not deterred by punishing consequences, possibly generated by the behavior itself. But the relation between probability and effort is complex. An operation may change probability or rate though effort remains constant. (There is an especially confusing relation when rate is taken as a measure of probability, since if each response requires a constant expenditure of work, the rate of responding and rate of expenditure vary together.)

A related issue is whether the saving of effort is reinforcing. If we can find the product of 10×6 either by adding ten 6's or by adding a zero to 6, we shall probably do the latter. In what sense do we do so because it saves time and energy? The reinforcement in either case is the safe arrival at 60 as the product. *This* reinforcement occurs sooner in adding a zero, but apart from the delay, the net positive reinforcement is less because of the time and effort in adding ten 6's.

The search for labor-saving methods and machines includes (a) self-controlling procedures for minimizing the aversive effects of labor, (b) a readiness to abandon current methods or devices, and (c) various inventive, searching behaviors.

Encounter

"People who fear free interaction with others preserve an 'inner world' of emotion which is disconnected from external reality, a world of fantasy. They may not be willing to admit this to themselves, let alone others." To help them, a psychiatrist must spend a good deal of time "penetrating their defenses" and making contact with the buried "true self." The "transference relation" in psychoanalysis may help them form fruitful relations with others. The patient must come to "experience a real relationship." A prolonged encounter with a highly skilled "other" is needed.

The implication in all this is that an encounter is not at the level of behavior. But how does one self enter into a fruitful relation with another? Almost always by behaving verbally—by describing feelings, reporting fantasies, asking and answering questions about feelings and fantasies, and so on. And what is the effect? Better social *behavior*, which is what was at fault in the first place.

The inner life is simply those parts of a person's behavior, or relevant bodily conditions, which are not visible to others and hence known to others only when described by the person whose inner life it is.

The Joke Shop

What is a practical joke? Some of the gadgets for sale in a joke shop may be classified as follows:

1. Deceptive stimuli leading to vigorous behavior found to be unnecessary: harmless imitations of spilled ink, dog's droppings, or cigarette burns to be placed on valuable possessions, or snakes and spiders where one might touch them. When the fake is exposed, the occasion for vigorous behavior vanishes. The effort has been unnecessary. Is there any compensating relief? If so, it resembles the consequences of effective action—when the mess is cleaned up or the spider or snake killed. A forgivable joke if the behavior was not too costly. The gold brick of the confidence man is no joke.

2. Occasion for behavior lacking the usual consequences: the thread hanging from a buttonhole which, when picked off by a thoughtful friend, turns out to be many yards long; the pencil with the rubber point; the glass with no accessible water; the book of matches that do not light or light and go out instantly; the cake candles that relight after being blown out. Mild enough to be tolerated.

3. Aversive consequences added to standard behavior: the palmed vibrator that operates during a handshake; the lapel bouquet that spouts water when smelled; the cigar that explodes; the proffered stick of gum that snaps back into the pack as the victim reaches. Funny if not too aversive.

4. Aversive social consequences: the dribble glass; the "uncouth" squawker to be placed under the cushion in a seat; the cigarette lighter that breaks into pieces when the borrower operates it; the book with a sexy cover that fires a cap when one peeks into it.

5. Novel, inexplicable stimuli: the tube and bulb which slowly raise and lower the plate a person is eating from.

Déjà Dit

To examples of descriptions which precede the event described (*Speak-of-the-Devil!*), add the scriptural device: *That it might be fulfilled which was spoken by the Prophets.* Precept and practice.

"Misperception"

I have on my work table a round plastic tray which was once the cover of a dish of ice cream. I use it as a coaster for my coffee cup. Semi-transparent, it shows some black letters in reverse. Recently I have started to collect some small white plastic caps from soft-pointed pen refills, and I put two of them in the plastic tray. This morning, in a quick glimpse, I saw the thing as a dirty ashtray. The black letters were ashes; the white caps were butts. I made, but then interrupted, a move to throw it out.

Cross-Sections

I am more and more impressed by the value of sticking with "historical" variables until genuine alternatives are available. In the first sentences of Chapter 1 of *Beyond Freedom and Dignity*, I said that the problem is to change *attitudes* about the size of families. It is no such thing. It is to induce people to have fewer children and to refrain from criticizing or laughing at those who have none or applauding those who have many. "Attitude" oversimplifies (how long an inventory would one need to evaluate properly an "attitude toward family size"!) and points in the wrong direction when it comes to taking action. We don't change attitudes, even if you define "attitude" as a tendency to behave; we change environments, in this case mainly social and verbal.

Yet why do *I*, of all people, still try to get at the cross-sectional present instead of the useful past (and future!)?

"Visual Imagery"

In "Drug-Induced Hallucinations in Animals and Men" by Ronald K. Siegel and Murray E. Jarvich (in *Hallucinations: Behavior, Experiences and Theory*, Wiley, 1975), Dement is quoted as follows:

"In other words, both monkeys [treated with PCPA] appeared to be experiencing and responding to internally generated visual imagery projected into the outer world."

Why not say simply "appeared to be seeing things in the outer world"? Why make the monkeys do two things: (1) create imagery and then (2) respond to it?

The drug could be said simply to induce the monkeys to behave as they behave in response to real objects. The monkeys must *see* things in both interpretations; that is all they do in a behavioral account. So far as we know, there are no images inside the monkey (or in a person) either (1) when seeing real things, (2) when recalling real things, (3) when imagining real things, or (4) when seeing real things as the effect of drugs.

Philosophy

"Verification" is too close to "knowledge" and "truth" (*veritas*) to have any place in an analysis of verbal behavior. Confirmation, in the sense of "making firm by providing other stimuli for a verbal response," has a place, for both tacts and intraverbals.

Providing definitions ("all the philosopher can do," says Ayer) is setting up controlling stimuli, verbal and nonverbal, which lead one to say or not to say a given word.

On the linguistic side of philosophy I, too, "take an interest in how words are used." But a discussion in "ordinary language" will not suffice.

Several "Memories"

Some bridge players note and remember only until the hand is finished; others remember some hands for a long time. The distinction is not between forgetting and remembering, but between noting and *noting in order to remember.* Why should we not note for short-term use?

Ebbinghaus's forgetting curves have misled us. They do not show how "memory traces survive," not even the memory trace of a series of responses learned to a criterion. Lists of words or nonsense syllables have a special nature.

1. After exposure to a pair of printed words, can we speak the second when we see the first again?

2. Can we improve our chances of doing so by "studying"—i.e., by observing the pair in such a way that we can recall?

3. What change comes from a second presentation, as in either (1) or (2)?

4. What change comes from a second exposure of the second word after failure to speak it as a response to the first?

5. What change comes from a second exposure of the second word after speaking it in response to the first?

6. What change comes from speaking the second in response to the first a given number of times?

Then—and only then—what effect has the passage of time on *all of these*—severally! The "number of pairs successfully recalled" is a hodge-podge, a quantifiable datum of almost meaningless dimensions.

If we can "learn to observe in order to recall," why can we not learn to "observe for short-term recall only"? Does not the nonprofessional bridge player do just that?

A request to "remember to tell x to call his wife before he leaves the office" is forgotten the next day because it will have no effect after x has left his office. A confusing day might lead a person to ask, "Was it this morning or yesterday morning that your wife asked me. . . ?" but a "confusing day" is precisely a day when such time-bound assignments tear loose.

Ego Ideal

When I once pointed out that the Superego, as the vicar of Society, is wholly aversive and that Freud evidently had no interest in the "internalizing" of positive reinforcement, an analyst insisted that the Ego Ideal served that function. Even so, it ranks below the triumvirate. And is it adequate?

A person wants to be a doctor, a poet, a successful broker, a saint. What is the connection with a history of reinforcement? When I was young I wanted to be a writer—to *have written* but not to write. Now I want to write, but being a writer or having written means little, at least in inducing me to write further.

Educators try to lift their students' sights, to give them a better picture of the advantages they will gain from an education. Programmed instruction, on the contrary, contrives reinforcers which are like the natural reinforcers of writing. The ego-ideal, the self-image, as part of a long-term career plan, is a feeble conditioned reinforcer.

Self-Understanding

Freud was unable to stop smoking cigars, up to 25 a day, though smoking must have been obviously related to the heavy "catarrh" he suffered from most of his life, as well as to the protracted cancer of the jaw in his last years. (*Did* he stop toward the end?) An astonishing lack of self-understanding or self-control. Was he not bothered by it, or did much of his theory spring from the need to acknowledge that the habit was "bigger than he was"—that contingency-shaped behavior (the "unconscious") prevailed against rule-governed ("the rational conscious mind")?

Key to Cognition

Verbal Behavior is the key to the cognitive scriptures. An adequate analysis of how a subject follows instruction ("visualize a cube, paint all six sides red, cut into 27 equal cubes") requires an analysis of a verbal history. So does the subject's report of what he or she does.

A common misunderstanding is that the behaviorist replaces "image" with "verbal report." That is as wrong as saying that discrimination is the same as sensation. The verbal report "I see a red cube" may be a basic datum for psychology, but it is not to be identified with "seeing a red cube." Only the physiologists can tell us what that *is* as a bodily function. (This is true of all behavior.) A behavioral analysis can tell us about the contingencies of reinforcement under which a person forms the discriminations involved in seeing a red cube.

Cognitive psychologists are confined to verbal reports and verbal instructions. A behavioral analysis of verbal behavior is a prerequisite for putting the facts they collect in order in a science that will make contact with physiology and supply the principles needed in the technological extension of a science of human behavior.

"*What a shame this is not a sin*"

Stendhal, in the introduction to *Les Cenis* in *Chroniques Italiennes*, attributes the comment to a princess tasting an ice on a warm evening. There are other versions, such as that plain water would be delicious if one were forbidden to drink it. Is this simply the principle of forbidden fruit? Punished behavior is so often behavior that is strongly reinforced that the threat of punishment becomes reinforcing. Eating an ice *would* be more delightful if it somehow aroused the emotion associated, say, with punishable sexual behavior.

But there is another point. People are more likely to engage in punishable behavior when extremely deprived. Hence punished behavior is often particularly susceptible to reinforcement. If you want a passionate mistress, find one who feels guilty about what she is doing. The imminence of punishment gauges the extremity of her passion. This appears to be Stendhal's argument with respect to the Don Juan type.

Feeling Good

In writing "Humanism and Behaviorism" I said, "Sex is not reinforcing because it feels good; it feels good because it is reinforcing." After I had sent the paper off, I realized that I had made the mistake of which I had accused William James, and I sent the editor a note: Change it to read ". . . it is reinforcing *and* feels good for a common phylogenic reason."

But even that omits something. We call things good when they are reinforcing because that is, in part, a way of getting more of them. We describe reinforcers as good, and good things feel good, as we say. It is important not to overlook the phylogeny, but being reinforcing and feeling good are not exactly cognate.

Verbal Summator

In *Verbal Behavior* I gave examples of "echoic probes" from Tolstoi and Arnold Bennett. Here is another from Henry James's *The American:* Valentin, at a performance of *Don Giovanni*, is considering whether to go to America. "And then a certain fiddle in the orchestra—I could not distinguish it—began to say as it scraped away: 'Why not, why not, why not?' and then in that rapid movement all the fiddles took it up and the conductor's stick seemed to beat it in the air: 'Why not, why not, why not?'"

The Ways of the Linguist

One generation of linguists specializes in phonetics. Subtle differences in phonemes, intonation, and accent are detected by the skilled as the real Mysteries—the hidden significance of speech.

Another generation goes in for syntax. Another set of mysteries, important because "this is the way the mind works." Yet treated just as formally as in phonetics.

(The element of mystery is important. All the linguists I have known have enjoyed using their technical vocabularies in part because they impressed nonlinguists.)

There has been some gain. The sheer topography of verbal behavior has been clarified; possibly only because all this activity has made people look at it closely. The descriptive terms are not optimal, mainly because the linguists have sneaked in references to independent variables. The phoneme is not a merely formal unit. A purely formal grammar has been tried again and again and abandoned just as often.

The Case of the Missing P

We no longer defend the snake it, or punish the psychotic—
I discovered that *p* was missing from the word *pit* several days after I wrote this. Was my subvocal behavior outstrip-

ping my writing so that I was transcribing late and caught only the echo of *pit?* Did the *p*'s to come—in *punish* and *psychotic*—preempt the letter? Was the silent *p* in *psychotic* "written silently" as well as *pit?*

Pavlov's Roots

According to Horsley Gantt (*Journal of the Experimental Analysis of Behavior*, 1973, *20*, 131), Pavlov, who had enrolled in a seminary to study for the priesthood, read a copy of George Henry Lewes's "Physiology of Common Life" and decided to study medicine at the University of St. Petersburg. (Gantt calls Lewes the "spouse" of George Eliot, but they were merely cohabiting.) According to Gordon Haight (*George Eliot: A Biography*), Pavlov's copy of the German translation is at Yale.

What would Lewes have thought if he could have known the effect of his book!

Attention as Behavior

A student at my colloquium yesterday thought I was neglecting attention. One had to attend in order to behave successfully. I tried to show how the contingencies that explained the successful behavior could explain the attending also, but he remained convinced that one first looked a situation over before acting and that if one did not, the behavior failed. There are no doubt novel or complex situations in which that is true, but "looking something over" is behaving, not attending.

As to the span of attention, I cited the mongoloid in Ellen Reese's film *Born to Succeed* whose "span" was stretched almost without limit when the task-behavior was skillfully reinforced.

Gestures

Gesturing may be a kind of modeling. It may also resemble normally effective behavior which in the present instance lacks physical consequences. A gestured "Come here" is a kind of pulling, "Go away" a kind of pushing. Pointing to something to be looked at or in a direction to be followed could conceivably be regarded as the position of the arm after throwing something, but responding to a point is probably learned without help from the generalization of practical action. All these gestures are verbal, though not vocal, because they are effective only through the mediation of a second person (the "listener").

"Building Courage"

A swimming pool offers many opportunities to see how unwisely parents use their approval to "build courage." A four-year-old reacts aversively to cold water. His father watches him constantly, exclaiming "Oh!" or "Well!" whenever any progress is made toward immersion. "Oh, down on the second step! Good!" What is wrong with that? Some possibilities:

1. It may make parental approval aversive by pairing it with aversive stimuli.

2. Nothing about going in deeper is really admirable. The child is being misled.

3. As soon as a response (say, going down one more step) is acquired, the approval ceases, being withheld for further use. The extinction may evoke slight aggression toward the father.

4. The father is reinforcing skeletal behavior, but the main change to be brought about is an emotional adaptation to an aversive stimulus.

5. The comments make it clear that the child is being watched, at a time when he is already being viewed

critically, possibly by others. This is particularly important if the father also shames the child—and this is very easy to do without knowing it: "Come, now, it isn't *that* bad!"

Better to let the child alone. Water is, in time, very reinforcing by itself, and others who are enjoying it serve as useful models.

Avoidance

A handbook on usage points out that one *avoids* what already exists and *prevents* what has not yet happened. A rat may *avoid* electrified grids by not stepping on them, but it *prevents* a shocking current by pressing a lever. The word *avoid* may have come into use in obstruction boxes or T-mazes where an area was already electrified, then extended to shuttle boxes where the organism might be shocked after changing sides, and finally to the Sidman experiment, in which a shock is clearly *prevented*. The dictionaries also give a second meaning of *avoid* as "to prevent the occurrence or effectiveness of" something.

A Vulnerable Concept

"By six years of age, males perceive themselves to be less vulnerable or susceptible than females of the same age."

Boys are less deterred by small injuries. They climb jungle gyms in ways which are more likely to produce cuts and bruises. They run faster over rough ground even if they fall more often. These are the kinds of facts available.

But do they do these things because they perceive they are less vulnerable? Isn't it simply because the social contingencies differ? Boys are less likely to be "nurtured" for small wounds and more likely to be shamed for crying.

"Boys behave as if they thought they were less likely to be hurt" is not a satisfactory translation because "thought" is too close to "perceive." They are less inclined to avoid small hurts, under contingencies which are, if not biological, social.

Sticking to the Observed

Saying that "A rat is required to lick a milky surface 50 times in order to get a bit of food" does not describe the situation accurately. The apparatus establishes contingencies under which the last of 50 licks is followed by the presentation of food. All the things thus referred to have clear dimensions. But what are the dimensions of a "requirement"?

To say that "licking a milky surface is reinforced by running" omits even more, nor is "giving the rat the opportunity to run" much better. Licking is followed by the opening of a door to a running wheel and if the rat runs, a greater probability of licking may subsequently be observed. Nothing is lost by sticking to the actual dimensions of the event; misunderstanding is far less likely.

Some Progress Has Been Made

Even cognitive psychologists have refined their terms. Few would go so far back as to use the following definitions (from *The New World of Words, or, Universal English Dictionary.* London, 1706):

Action: "Among Physicians and Naturalists, Action is distinguished into *Voluntary* and *Spontaneous,* the former being that which is directed by the Will; as Walking, Running, Handling, etc., whereas the other does not depend upon the Will; as the Circulation of the Blood, the Beating of the Arteries, etc."

Will: "A particular Faculty of the Soul, or the Act of that Faculty."

Intention: "The End proposed in any Action."

Stoicism

In the narrow sense of the concealment of pain, what is the value of stoicism?

Phylogenically, there is presumably value in showing pain when it leads to succor. The child cries, and the mother takes care of it. In combat with a rival or predator, however, a conspicuous response to pain shapes and maintains damaging behavior in the opponent. Contingencies of survival will therefore favor the "stoic," and animals in combat will minimize cries of pain and other conspicuous effects of successful attack (not to be confused with cries which make the crier more frightening). The ontogenic contingencies work in a similar way. The boxer must not show that he has been hurt; to do so will strengthen similar behavior on the part of his opponent. (Is this contingency described in a rule to be used in instructing fighters?)

It may be said that a fighter loses respect when he shows he has been hurt, and crying for one's mother is eventually punished by one's peers. These are different contingencies, though possibly connected. Stoicism may have phylo- or ontogenic significance if, by suppressing pleas for help, the species or the culture builds self-help and independence. The schoolboy refusing to show pain when he is being caned is:

a. Counterattacking the teacher by reducing the teacher's reinforcement. (A sadistic teacher may then cane all the harder, abandon caning and turn to other practices, or cane less stoical boys.)

b. Gaining the respect of his fellows by not responding to a conspicuously powerful stimulus (and hence suggesting inner control).

Not showing the pain of a toothache seems to be a matter of (b) alone, since crying will not teach the tooth to ache less or less aggressively, but is there possibly a reduction in pain through some kind of self-management? Or simply through a reduction of bodily activities felt as pain? Fred Keller knew a psychologist who claimed he could reduce the pain caused by a dentist's drill by "letting the pain pass through his nervous system" rather than trying to stop it. That is a metaphor, but possibly a supportive myth for the stoic.

Loyalty

A lawyer friend has been defending a teacher who refused to sign a loyalty oath. I suggested that he argue that the man who is forced to swear that he will behave loyally is robbed of the credit he would otherwise receive for behaving loyally when not forced to do so. My friend argued the point but got nowhere with it.

The marriage ceremony is composed of two loyalty oaths, as young people today are discovering.

Soul-Searching

Much more needs to be done in analyzing what one does when doing nothing. My analysis of leisure is a start. But what is achieved when one practices meditation? I don't know the technique well enough to make a good analysis, but I can see something of what happens as I sit listening to music. If I do not read or look at pictures, I am thinking under very weak control of external variables. I fantasy easily, and often intensively. I observe myself doing so. Notes come to mind and I write them down, as I am doing now. If I control some of this, keeping myself from thinking about problems, I limit myself to—what? Exactly! "To *what?*"

What does one do when there is nothing to do?

Things turn up which would otherwise be displaced and concealed. One discovers unfamiliar parts of oneself.

As I have noted elsewhere, the absence of conspicuous control may suggest that this is *me*, the inner *me*.

It is often worth looking at.

Paradoxes

1. The proof of the theorem that there are no uninteresting numbers runs like this. You proceed to point to something interesting about each number so long as possible. The first number for which nothing interesting can be found is therefore of special interest. Hence it is an interesting number, and if there is no first uninteresting number, there can be no second, and so on. But to be interesting because uninteresting raises the same issue as the heterological paradox. You have jumped to a second language for a criterion which ought to be found in the first.

2. In opening the first session of a symposium on generalization, Norman Guttman noted that those who use the term automatically illustrate its use by applying it to a great variety of cases. A verbal response can exemplify itself in the sense that a response of similar form could be made—necessarily at some other time, by the same speaker or someone else—to describe the occasion upon which it is emitted. This is not to say, as in the heterological paradox, that "a word describes itself." The essential point is that a word does not describe anything. It is a form of response which, under some circumstances, can be controlled by the stimuli it is said to describe. The response *generalization* can be evoked by a response of the same form acting as a stimulus. There is no paradox.

"I Wonder"

I wonder is often used to soften a question (a species of mand). *I wonder when, what,* or *why* are softened forms of *When, What,* or *Why. I wonder when he will return,* though apparently a statement, mands a reply. It is, however, weaker than the blunt *When will he return?* The softening effect is a little like that of *I'd like* prefacing the direct mand *a glass of water!* *I'd like* is not an autoclitic, because it refers to nonverbal behavior. *I wonder*, like the dubious *I think* or *I guess*, qualifies the effect of a verbal response on the listener.

Imitative Behavior

Lisa is almost five months old. Two or three days ago I was playing with her and I held my left hand up with my palm toward her, my fingers spread-eagled. She quickly held up her right hand in the same relative position and I put my palm against hers and interlocked our fingers as much as possible. We repeated the trick several times during the next two days. Yesterday Julie did the same thing with her left hand and then with her right. Julie then put both hands up with fingers spread, and Lisa did the same instantly. There is no question that this is imitative behavior, especially the wide spreading of the fingers. (When contact was made, Lisa smiled and sometimes laughed; it was by then a reinforced trick, but not when it first occurred.)

"Turning Stimuli On and Off"

Broadbent makes a lot of this. I believe it is he whom I quote in *About Behaviorism* to the effect that the brain can turn on one ear or the other. I have just been listening to two dictated passages, one on my Sony cassette recorder, one on my Norelco. If I hold the speakers near my two ears, I find it quite easy to attend to the one rather than the other, and the other is then little more than noise. But it is clear that I am not turning an ear on or off. Both are equally loud. I am "attending" to one. That seems to mean speaking along with the voice. This is the active side of understanding, as I present it in *Verbal Behavior*. There is no "gating" of stimuli; there is active supplementation and "understanding" of one source and not of the other.

Perception and Misperception

Current research in perception is in large part an effort to maintain the preeminence of the stimulus in theories of knowledge. For Plato, as for the British Empiricists, knowledge of the world was a kind of copy—though necessarily distorted and incomplete. It stopped with an inner comprehension. Introspective psychology followed this line by making the sensations derived from stimuli the elements of mind. How stimuli might initiate *action* was less important than how they corresponded with experience.

When it became clear that other variables were important—such as past and present contingencies of reinforcement, deprivation, and emotional conditions—it was said to be because they affected the way things looked. Knowledge still stopped with the Inner Man.

Policy making in the conduct of war is another example. Policy is said to be made with respect to a current "situation"—a variable having the status of a stimulus, although its effects depend upon many other things, among them what followed when similar policies were made and acted upon in the past. Other relevant consequences determining policy are the effects on employment, the availability of goods, the reelection of officials, and reactions to what the enemy has done or threatened to do. If all this is said to be important because it determines how the situation "looks" to the policy maker, an unfortunate policy can be traced to "misperception." Yet it is the behavior of the policy maker that counts, and the variables just mentioned have a direct bearing on that behavior. How the situation is "perceived" is secondary.

Oedipal Contingencies

Is it possible that the so-called Oedipal relations to mother and father are simply mythical representations of positive and negative reinforcement? The boy longs, not to sleep with his mother, but to be close to one who positively reinforces his behavior. He longs, not to kill his father, but to escape from or destroy one who punishes. The myth merely represents these effects of consequences with concrete figures. Were the practices in Freud's strong-father Jewish-German culture particularly likely to suggest the myth?

Consciousness and the Autoclitic

When I spoke recently to the staff at McClean Hospital, someone asked me how I would handle the unconscious. I said that behavior, its controlling variables, and the relations among them, do not include or presuppose a conscious state. Behavior comes about for specifiable reasons. In Freud's term it *is* unconscious. Freud himself showed that behavior did not demand consciousness. Conscious behavior is built on unconscious behavior when verbal communities induce people to talk about themselves.

I then saw that you could not be conscious without having something to be conscious of, and I suddenly realized that autoclitic behavior is a special case of consciousness. There must be first-order verbal behavior before one can emit an autoclitic as a second-order response. The verbal community induces a person to say both *I say* and *I see* or *I feel.*

Misplaced "Atom"

I was turning off the hot water faucet on the bowl in the bathroom with my right hand while closing the cabinet door just below the bowl with my left. The door snaps into place with a spring catch. I suddenly found myself pressing the door lightly against the catch with my left hand while with my right I was tightening the closed faucet forcefully to make it click into place. I was surprised when it failed to click, getting a very clear feedback from the tight faucet.

Two relevant points:

1. It was early in the morning (6:15) and others were asleep; the door is noisy as it clicks shut, and I was "avoiding noise." I was avoiding snapping the door into place.

2. A moment before, I had snapped off a portable transistorized radio, using my thumb in an awkward position and making the switch snap with difficulty. The switch is a small disk, one edge accessible, which also functions as a volume control. The faucet was perhaps five or six times as large and operated with a different grasp and motion; nevertheless, I turn both faucet and switch to control volume and, beyond low volume, to turn something "off." The door was shut by pushing it almost straight against the snap.

Stendhal's Principle

It is a common remark of old men that a greater percentage of young women are prettier now than when the men were young. Stendhal's principle in *De l'Amour* is relevant. A relatively unattractive woman who "gives sexual favors" becomes attractive (as a conditioned stimulus), and presumably so do those who resemble her. It should follow that a man whose sexual behavior has been reinforced by women of many different appearances will find many more women attractive, since in the population at large an increasingly larger proportion will resemble women who have reinforced his sexual behavior.

Stock Verbal Responses

I often slightly miss the point of a question asked after a talk, and after I answer it the question is patiently restated. It usually happens when I am lecturing on a subject I have already discussed many times.

Yesterday I spoke on teaching, a field in which I must have answered a thousand questions during the past fifteen years. Naturally, the questions fell into categories and my answers were similarly compartmentalized. Fifty standard answers have taken a prominent place in my "teaching" repertoire. A given question triggers one of them—the one that is nearest but still not quite apt. I can no longer, without great effort, *tailor* an appropriate answer. I take my answers ready-made off the shelf.

Trap

Bird-lime, the sticky stuff used to catch birds, was made of mistletoe (*L. viscus, viscosity*). Is this the origin of the use of a sprig of mistletoe to get permission to kiss someone? The "bird," could hardly be caught *on* the sprig, but she is vulnerable to capture beneath it. If so, a good example of a nonverbal trope or figure of speech, like metonymy.

Geography

During my life as an Easterner, driving along the coast with the ocean on my left is going south. It was hard for me to place La Jolla north of San Diego because I drove to it with the ocean on my left. But what is the *behavior* when I "think north and south"?

The Whole Man

One of the psychiatrists whom I met at a local hospital kept bringing up the complexity of man compared with pigeons. He could not see (because I was not taking the time to point out) how operant principles could be applied. In a way he tried to be helpful. He referred to lobotomy and shock therapy (not aversion therapy) as ways of making man less complex and hence amenable to therapy. I added that severe tranquilizers have a similar effect. I did not know whether he was proposing to simplify the psychotic in order to apply behavioral principles, but I summed up my position by calling all such measures "fractional euthanasia."

Censored and Censured

A nice distinction. *Censor* is to control by physical removal of a stimulus which generates unwanted behavior. *Censure* is to punish the behavior in question.

Both evidently come from the Latin for value or tax. One must evaluate before either removing stimuli or punishing behavior.

Taxing was originally, I assume, a way of raising money. When did it begin to be used to manipulate the behavior of the taxed?

Two Roles

All members of a culture control people by commending, censuring, and so on. Those members of a culture called behavior modifiers also arrange new contingencies, including new social practices in which members control each other, but *they* are not controlling when they do so. In the same sense, teachers and therapists differ from governors and employers. Only the latter continue to "modify behavior" by the direct control of positive or negative reinforcers.

"A Reflex"

By mistake I turned off the coffee maker as I put in a second cupful of water. My action would typically be called "automatic," "a reflex," "thoughtless," "careless."

But what was it really?

It was a response normally evoked under rather similar circumstances, with reinforcing results. Here the result was mildly aversive; it was "wrong" behavior under the circumstances, but it was not automatic or reflex. The behavior was evoked by a stimulus that was simply not very appropriate to the occasion.

Self-Control

How far can an analysis go? In *Verbal Behavior* I noted that writing the first part of a paragraph or article may be difficult because the writer lacks a clear-cut audience. Once something has been written, it serves as a discriminative stimulus evoking the easier writing that follows. There is another explanation. Writing tends to be reinforced on a ratio schedule, and a "pause after reinforcement" may be due to conditions under which reinforcements are not obtained. We might solve the "difficult start" problem by making some special reinforcement contingent upon early steps. Thus, we might write or type the first pages of an article on paper of a special color. The completion of a colored page should become reinforcing because writing then becomes easier. In effect, this reduces the size of the ratio and shortens the pause.

Acceptance of Life

The noble quiet sufferer is a common literary theme— accepting "what will be" with simple resignation, without kicking against the pricks. The Indian film *Pather Panchali* documents the tragedy of this fine art of the acceptance of life. Somewhere, ages ago, a saint discovered a way of avoiding the ravages of protest: Submit and save your soul. There was a good deal of this in early Christianity—and left to itself it produced the same result: the poverty, disease, famine, and ugliness of the Dark Ages. In India there has been no renaissance—the acceptance has continued.

There are circumstances under which that solution may be recommended. If one cannot bathe, accept the stink. If one must labor, do not grumble. If one must suffer, suffer in silence. If one must die, die without fear. But it should not be accepted as a universal principle. One *can* usually escape filthy odors, exhausting labor, and an early and painful death.

The behavior generated by aversive control may be as aversive as the stimuli used; it may be often irrationally compulsive; it may be disturbed; and to *accept* the aversive event is one way of avoiding these aspects of avoidance. But there are better ways: we can minimize aversive features of our world; we can make escape and avoidance a trifling part of our lives.

The people in the film suffered—steadily. They suffered at last because they could no longer accept, and they tried to escape. (I doubt whether the full surrender of the last scene—the ox-cart emigration, against the pleas of the elders—can be understood by many Western viewers.)

And all this came about because somewhere, generations ago, it seemed better not to repair a house, or build a better plow, or sew a pocket on a sari, or build a chair to sit in or a spoon to eat with, but rather to accept one's lot with quiet dignity.

Snowballs in the Sun

Waiting for friends near a small Vermont village school at lunchtime, I watched boys throwing snowballs. My first impression was that the scene would have interested Peter Brueghel and might once have turned up on the cover of the *Saturday Evening Post* in a painting by Norman Rockwell. Healthy, out-of-doors boys, boys who will be boys, the backbone of America. But as I watched, the scene became clearer. There was bullying. Not all the boys wanted to throw snowballs or be thrown at. A small boy, too small and weak to arouse retaliation, had a good time with the bigger boys, but his time would come. One boy was happy enough when things were going well, but when he got a ball unexpectedly in the ear, he viciously attacked the thrower, rubbing snow in his face and threatening him with "his father's gun" if he tried that again.

I began to ask myself: why are they throwing snowballs at each other anyway? There are some pretty obvious *natural* answers—as there is a *natural* answer to why a nervous boy wets his pants. Throwing snowballs is fun. Hitting another boy is more fun than hitting a target because there is a livelier result. Boys and some wet snow are the perfect contingencies for creating bullies and cowards and for nursing aggressive and craven behavior. We take action about the boy wetting his pants; we try to arrange a better situation. But we do nothing about snowballs. They will produce *men*—as the public schools in nineteenth-century England with their hazings, canings, ostracism, and "silence" produced "bottom."

What is the answer? Set aside an area in which those who want to throw snowballs at each other may do so?

Supervised play? Something more productive is possible. Targets could be designed to shape skillful behavior, targets which do something interesting when hit. If desirable, they could be competitive. A horizontal paddle wheel could rotate in either direction according to the hits made by two teams. With cooperative targets a group could work together to get some special reinforcing result. A Utopian dream?

Myself and My Subjects

I used to represent the behaviorist's attitude toward himself by describing a lecturer who explains human behavior, including the behavior of other lecturers, and leaves the stage. Then he sticks his head out from the wings and says, "And I'm like that too!"

Brief Glossary

AUTOCLITIC: a verbal response added to other verbal behavior that indicates something about the variables affecting the speaker. *I see by the papers*, for example, tells the listener the source of what is reported. More subtle autoclitic processes are involved in grammar.

INTRAVERBAL: verbal behavior under the control of other verbal behavior. *Dog* and *cat*, for example, are intraverbally related, which is to say that one is likely to occasion the other.

MAND: verbal behavior that specifies its reinforcer. For example, *Milk!* is maintained by the presentation of milk.

OPERANT BEHAVIOR: behavior that is modifiable by its consequences. Most human behavior (walking, talking, driving, etc.) is operant.

REINFORCER: an event that strengthens the behavior that produces it. The presentation of food will normally "reinforce" the behavior of a hungry organism, and almost any stimulus can serve as a reinforcer under appropriate conditions.

SCHEDULES OF REINFORCEMENT: a specification of the way in which reinforcers occur in time. Some simple schedules include fixed-ratio (the last of a certain number of responses is reinforced), variable-ratio (the required number varies from one reinforcer to the next), fixed-interval (the first response after a certain period of time has elapsed is reinforced), and variable-interval (the interval varies from one reinforcer to the next). A schedule is "stretched" when the ratio or interval is increased.

TACT: verbal behavior under the control of a specific stimulus. *Milk*, for example, is an appropriate reply to *What's that?* in the presence of milk.

Index

Editor's note: The index includes major subject headings; names of publications, works of art, and people mentioned in the notes; and the complete titles of all the notes. Beside each note title in parentheses appears the date upon which a note was originally written (in some cases, estimated or missing). If a note was substantially revised since that date (see the introduction for details), the date is followed by the letter *r*. Some members of Skinner's family are listed in the index by their first names: Eve (his wife), Julie (his elder child), Deborah (his younger child), and Lisa (Julie's elder child). The notes contain references to a number of other works Skinner has published, as follows: "The Generic Nature of the Concepts of Stimulus and Response" (1935), *The Behavior of Organisms* (1938), *Walden Two* (1948), *Science and Human Behavior* (1953), *Schedules of Reinforcement* (1957, with C. B. Ferster), *Verbal Behavior* (1957), "The Phylogeny and Ontogeny of Behavior" (1966), *The Technology of Teaching* (1968), *Contingencies of Reinforcement: A Theoretical Analysis* (1969), "Creating the Creative Artist" (1970), *Beyond Freedom and Dignity* (1971), *About Behaviorism* (1974), "Farewell, My Lovely" (1976), *Particulars of My Life* (1976), and *The Shaping of a Behaviorist: Part Two of an Autobiography* (1979).

interest, 285
*Interest (10/25/61), 51
*Interference? (6/11/58), 224
internalization of contingencies, 323
*International (12/1/56), 210
interpersonal relations, 26, 262, 279
intraverbals, 44, 91–92, 94, 130, 206, 208, 212, 225, 273, 311, 320–321, 339
*The Invention of Myths and Rituals (9/25/60), 171
invention, sensory, 332–333
investigator, 324
*In What Sense the Truth? (7/28/70), 225
*The Irrational as Amusing (6/12/60), 251
irrelevancies, 198
*Irritability (6/10/73, r), 297
Isherwood, Christopher, 271
*Is "Need" Needed? (5/2/75), 203
italic handwriting, 110, 283
Itard, J.-M.-G., 217
*I Told You So (10/15/60), 59
*"I Wonder" (2/2/73), 350

J

jackdaw, 81
James, Henry, 206, 211, 293, 343
James, William, 342
jargon, 330, 343
Jarvich, Murray E., 338
*Jean Renoir (9/19/61), 160
Jesuit, 56–57
Jesus, 117
Jews, 57
jigsaw puzzles, 264
*Joachim in the Yard (6/14/59), 84
Joan of Arc, 72
Johnson, Samuel, 95, 297
joke, 88
*The Joke Shop (11/10/56), 336
Jones, Ernest, 6, 204, 301
Journal, 285, 322
Joyce, James, 109
Julie, 54, 131, 228, 238, 351
Jung, C., 38
*"Just Growing" (10/19/75, r), 304

K

Kalamata, 39, 201
Kantor, J. Robert, 75
*Keep Your Eye . . . (10/1/72), 95
Keller, Fred, 348

Kennedy, John F., 228, 229, 300
Kennedy, Robert F., 228
*Key to Cognition (11/24/77), 341
Keynes, J. M., 42
Keywords, 263
*Killing the Bearer of Bad News (undated), 166
Kipling, R., 196
kiss, healing, 155
*Knock on Wood (7/10/71, r), 261
knowing about behavior, 212
*Knowing and Understanding People (4/26/75, r), 93
*"Knowing They Know" (9/13/60), 115
*"Knowing What to Do" (8/28/77, r), 231
knowledge, 197, 215, 258, 274–275, 312–313, 339, 352
Knowledge by Acquaintance, 313
*Knowledge by Acquaintance and Knowledge by Description (1/7/77), 184
Knowledge by Description, 313
*Knowledge, Information, the Facts (12/10/76), 213
*Knowledge of What Is Stored (2/21/67), 313
Koestler, Arthur, 99
Köhler, W., 259
Kris—see Lisa
*The Krutch-Barzun Entente (4/3/67), 69
Krutch, J. W., 69

L

labor, 266–267, 299–300
*Labor (1/10/77), 98
labor saving, 33–34, 124, 224, 287–288, 334
La Chamade, 123
La Dame aux Camélias, 74
lady vs. diplomat, 11–12
Lamiel, 35
Lamson, Peggy, 5
Lane, Harlan, 217
language, 304
language—also see verbal behavior
language acquisition, 29–30, 130, 131, 294
*The Language of Music (1/18/59), 131
La Rochefoucauld, 103
Lashley, Karl, 294

115, 189–190, 208–209, 211, 226, 282–283, 306, 314, 330— also see rule-governed vs. contingency-shaped behavior
*Rumor (4/23/69), 149
*Rumpelstiltskin (10/6/68), 2
Runciman, W. G., 329
Russell, Bertrand 49, 66–67, 145, 184–185, 297, 312–313
*Russell on Knowledge (3/12/76), 312
*Russell on Storage (1/29/76), 145
Russia, 36–37, 88, 178
Ryle, Gilbert, 132, 185, 212, 321

S

*The Sabbath as a Cultural Practice (9/23/61), 107
Sacco and Vanzetti case, 207
Sachs, Hanns, 254
*Sacrifice (11/25/61), 55
*Sacrificial Pleasures (12/15/62), 67
sad, to be, 73
sadism, 15–16
Sagan, Françoise, 123
*Salestalk (2/3/62), 128
salvation, 105
Sandburg, C., 10
The Sand Pebble, 57
Santayana, G., 78
satellite, 19–20, 294–295
*Satiation (9/9/68), 152
Saunders, Percy, 66
Savage Messiah, 229
saving, 95, 300
*Saving Labor (3/16/72), 287
*Saving the World (3/27/76), 97
saxophone, 313
*Saying Something While Not Saying It (8/17/66), 271
schedule, stretching a, 123, 150–151, 179–180, 255
schedules, 195—also see ratio schedules, variable-ratio schedules
schedules, stretched, 181, 300
Schedules of Reinforcement, 245
scheduling silence, 123
Schenkman, A., 320
Schopenhauer's Will, 75
science, behavorial, 109
Science and Human Behavior, 108, 115, 262
*Science and the Human Condition (1/27/65), 154

*Science Fiction (12/28/69), 94
scientific discovery, 215–216
scientific methods, 290
*Sciurine Matador (10/16/59), 125
scorn, to, 73
Scott, J. P., 205
screening students, 245
scriptural device, 337
seamen, 316
*Search? (undated), 24
*"Searching One's Memory" (5/28/78), 208
secondary process, 204
*Second Nature (3/3/66), 167
second sight, 37
secret language, 278
*Secret Language, (10/2/59), 294
seeing, 141–142, 227, 239, 309–310, 341
*Seeing "Guilt" (before 1960), 200
seeing something as something else, 117, 239, 337
Seldes, Gilbert, 219
selection, 76
*Selection (10/28/76), 188
*The Selection of Synonyms I (4/28/66 to 7/3/72), 78
*The Selection of Synonyms II (dates unknown), 291
self, 148–149, 156
self, sense of, 148
self-analyses, 69–70, 70–71, 75, 107–108, 147–148, 257, 282–283, 310–311, 349–350, 355
The Self and Its Brain, 92
self-control, 59, 144–145, 202–203, 250, 318, 341
*Self-Control (8/6/57), 357
self-denial, 67
self-knowledge, 318
self-management, 75, 120, 228, 311, 333
*Self-Management and the Will (2/18/74), 96
self-pity, 295
*Self-Programming (5/8/68), 183
self-prompting, 284
self-reliance, 69
self-stimulation, 291
*Self-Understanding (8/19/64), 341
*Sense and Nonsense (10/20/70), 99
*Sensory Invention (9/18/60), 332
sentences, 133